ENTREPRENEUR MAGAZINE'S ULTIMATE BOOK OF BUSINESS FORMS

MICHAEL SPADACCINI

Editorial Director: Jere Calmes
Cover Design: Beth Hanson-Winter
Composition: CWL Publishing Enterprises, Inc., Madison, Wisconsin, www.cwlpub.com

ISBN 1-932156-67-4

Library of Congress Cataloging-in-Publication Data

Spadaccini, Michael, 1964-
Entrepreneur magazine's ultimate book of business forms: over 175 forms to help you start and grow your business / by Michael Spadaccini.
p. cm.
ISBN 1-932156-67-4
1. Business—Forms. I. Title: Ultimate book of business forms. II. Entrepreneur (Santa Monica, Calif.) III. Title.

HF5371.S63 2004
651'.29—dc22

2004043887

Printed in Canada

09 08 07 06 05 10 9 8 7 6 5 4 3 2

Contents

About the Author

Michael Spadaccini is a San Diego-based business attorney. Mr. Spadaccini has practiced business, trademark, securities, and Internet law in California from 1993 to the present. He is admitted to the California Bar, as well as the Bars of the U.S. District Court for Northern California, the U.S. Court of Appeals for the 9th Circuit, and the U.S. Court of Appeals for the U.S. Federal Circuit Appellate Court. He received his bachelor's degree from the University of Rhode Island in 1987 and his law degree from Quinnipiac University in 1992. He is the author of *The Complete Corporate Guide: Incorporate in Any State* and a periodic securities law newsletter entitled *The Securities Law Report*, available at www.learn-aboutlaw.com.

Acknowledgments

I'd like to thank Jere Calmes, editorial director of Entrepreneur Press, for giving me the opportunity to write this first edition of *Entrepreneur Magazine's Ultimate Book of Business Forms.*

I am also grateful to:

- Attorney, friend, and fellow golfer Dan Sweeney, who contributed to this volume by providing invaluable legal research.
- My law professors at Quinnipiac University School of Law, who taught me the foundations of corporate and business law that I now offer to you.
- My family and friends, who offered their support throughout the drafting of this volume.
- John Woods, Bob Magnan, and CWL Publishing Enterprises for turning out the book in its final form.

Note: You will need a copy of Excel® spreadsheet software to work with the spreadsheet files included on the CD packaged with this book. You will also need Adobe Acrobat Reader to open other pdf forms included on the CD. This is available free at www.adobe.com. All other forms in this book are available as Word documents on the CD, ready for you to reformat according to your needs.

CHAPTER 1

Human Resource Recruitment Tools

Attracting and hiring the right employee for your firm is essential to your business success. In this section, you will find forms and worksheets that will help you attract and evaluate suitable candidates. These forms are applicable to nearly any industry. You will find two employment applications, the *Application for Employment—Short Form* and the *Application for Employment—Long Form.* The short form will likely be sufficient for most hires, while the long form is more appropriate for longer-term and executive positions.

As part of the employment application process, insist that your applicants execute the *Authorization to Release Employment Applicant Information.* This important form authorizes the applicant's former employer to release information about the applicant's work history and personal characteristics. Most former employers will insist on receiving such an authorization before divulging any information.

You will also find two versions of a *Pre-Employment Reference Check via Phone.* These two forms are scripts that you should use when making telephone contact with an applicant's former employer. If you wish to contact your applicant's former employer by letter, use the *Pre-Employment Reference Check via Letter* form.

Once you have narrowed your employee search to a handful of candidates, summarize their critical strengths and weaknesses with the *Applicant Comparison Summary Form*; rate each candidate's qualifications for critical job requirements, such as computer skills, foreign languages, and the like. You can rate each applicant's individual skills with *Applicant Rating Form, Part One* and *Applicant Rating Form, Part Two.*

Once you have found your ideal candidate, you can use the *Offer of Employment and Employment Contract.* This form formally announces the offer of employment and documents the terms of the employment agreement. Save a copy in the employee's file. Finally, once you have secured your new employee, use the *New Employee Announcement* to announce your new employee to your other employees.

1. Application for Employment–Short Form

Our policy is to provide equal employment opportunity to all qualified persons without regard to race, creed, color, religious belief, sex, age, national origin, ancestry, physical or mental disability, or veteran status.

Name

Last ______________________ First ____________________ Middle________

Date ____________

Street Address ____

City ________________ State ______ ZIP ______

Telephone ________________

Social Security # ________________

Position applied for ______________________________

How did you hear of this opening? ______________________________

When can you start? ________________ Desired Wage $____________

Are you a U.S. citizen or otherwise authorized to work in the U.S. on an unrestricted basis? (You may be required to provide documentation.) ❑ Yes ❑ No

Are you looking for full-time employment? ❑ Yes ❑ No

If no, what hours are you available? ____________

Are you willing to work swing shift? ❑ Yes ❑ No

Are you willing to work graveyard? ❑ Yes ❑ No

Have you ever been convicted of a felony? (This will not necessarily affect your application.) ❑ Yes ❑ No

If yes, please describe conditions. ____

____

____

____

____

Education	School Name and Location	Year	Major	Degree
High School	______________________________	_____	_____	_____
College	______________________________	_____	_____	_____
College	______________________________	_____	_____	_____
Post-College	______________________________	_____	_____	_____
Other Training	______________________________	_____	_____	_____

In addition to your work history, are there other skills, qualifications, or experience that we should consider?

____

____

____

____

____

____

Employment History (Start with most recent employer)

Company Name ____

Address ______________________________ Telephone ________________

Date Started __________ Starting Wage __________ Starting Position ______________

Date Ended __________ Ending Wage __________ Ending Position ______________

Name of Supervisor ____________________________

May we contact? ❑ Yes ❑ No

Responsibilities ____
____
Reason for leaving ____

Company Name ____
Address ______________________________ Telephone ________________
Date Started ____________ Starting Wage ____________ Starting Position ____________
Date Ended ____________ Ending Wage ____________ Ending Position ____________
Name of Supervisor ______________________________
May we contact? ❑ Yes ❑ No
Responsibilities ____
____
Reason for leaving ____

Company Name ____
Address ______________________________ Telephone ________________
Date Started ____________ Starting Wage ____________ Starting Position ____________
Date Ended ____________ Ending Wage ____________ Ending Position ____________
Name of Supervisor ______________________________
May we contact? ❑ Yes ❑ No
Responsibilities ____
____
Reason for leaving ____

Company Name ____
Address ______________________________ Telephone ________________
Date Started ____________ Starting Wage ____________ Starting Position ____________
Date Ended ____________ Ending Wage ____________ Ending Position ____________
Name of Supervisor ______________________________
May we contact? ❑ Yes ❑ No
Responsibilities ____
____
Reason for leaving ____

Attach additional information if necessary.

I certify that the facts set forth in this application for employment are true and complete to the best of my knowledge. I understand that if I am employed, false statements on this application shall be considered sufficient cause for dismissal. This company is hereby authorized to make any investigations of my prior educational and employment history.

I understand that employment at this company is "at will," which means that either I or this company can terminate the employment relationship at any time, with or without prior notice, and for any reason not prohibited by statute. All employment is continued on that basis. I understand that no supervisor, manager, or executive of this company, other than the president, has any authority to alter the foregoing.

Signature______________________ Date ______________

2. Application for Employment–Long Form

Our policy is to provide equal employment opportunity to all qualified persons without regard to race, creed, color, religious belief, sex, age, national origin, ancestry, physical or mental disability, or veteran status.

Name

Last ______________________ First ______________________ Middle ________

Date ____________

Street Address ____

City ________________ State ______ ZIP ______

Telephone __________________

Social Security # __________________

Position applied for ____________________________

How did you hear of this opening? ____________________________

When can you start? ______________ Desired Wage $____________

Are you a U.S. citizen or otherwise authorized to work in the U.S. on an unrestricted basis? (You may be required to provide documentation.) ❑ Yes ❑ No

Are you looking for full-time employment? ❑ Yes ❑ No

If no, what hours are you available? ____________

Are you willing to work swing shift? ❑ Yes ❑ No

Are you willing to work graveyard? ❑ Yes ❑ No

Have you ever been convicted of a felony? (This will not necessarily affect your application.) ❑ Yes ❑ No

If yes, please describe conditions. ____

____

____

____

____

Employment Desired

Have you ever applied for employment here? ❑ Yes ❑ No

When? ______________________ Where? ______________________

Have you ever been employed by this company? ❑ Yes ❑ No

When? ______________________ Where? ______________________

Are you presently employed? ❑ Yes ❑ No

May we contact your present employer? ❑ Yes ❑ No

Are you available for full-time work? ❑ Yes ❑ No

Are you available for part-time work? ❑ Yes ❑ No

Will you relocate? ❑ Yes ❑ No

Are you willing to travel? ❑ Yes ❑ No If yes, what percent? ______________

Date you can start ____

Desired position ____

Desired starting salary ____

Please list applicable skills ____

____

____

Education: School Name and Location Year Major Degree

High School ______________________ ______ ______ ______

College ______________________ ______ ______ ______

College ______________________ ______ ______ ______

Post-College ______________________ ______ ______ ______

Other Training ______________________ ______ ______ ______

In addition to your work history, are there other skills, qualifications, or experience that we should consider?

____

____

____

____

____

Please list any scholastic honors received and offices held in school.

____

____

Are you planning to continue your studies? ❑ Yes ❑ No

If yes, where and what courses of study?

____

____

Company Name ______________________

Address ______________________ Telephone ______________

Date Started ____________ Starting Wage ____________ Starting Position ____________

Date Ended ____________ Ending Wage ____________ Ending Position ____________

Name of Supervisor ______________________

May we contact? ❑ Yes ❑ No

Responsibilities ______________________

____

Reason for leaving ______________________

Company Name ______________________

Address ______________________ Telephone ______________

Date Started ____________ Starting Wage ____________ Starting Position ____________

Date Ended ____________ Ending Wage ____________ Ending Position ____________

Name of Supervisor ______________________

May we contact? ❑ Yes ❑ No

Responsibilities ______________________

____

Reason for leaving ______________________

Company Name ______________________

Address ______________________ Telephone ______________

Date Started ____________ Starting Wage ____________ Starting Position ____________

Date Ended ____________ Ending Wage ____________ Ending Position ____________

Name of Supervisor ______________________

May we contact? ❑ Yes ❑ No

Responsibilities ______________________

____

Reason for leaving ______________________

Company Name ______________________________
Address ______________________________ Telephone ______________
Date Started __________ Starting Wage __________ Starting Position __________
Date Ended __________ Ending Wage __________ Ending Position __________
Name of Supervisor ______________________________
May we contact? ❑ Yes ❑ No
Responsibilities ______________________________
____
Reason for leaving ______________________________

Company Name ______________________________
Address ______________________________ Telephone ______________
Date Started __________ Starting Wage __________ Starting Position __________
Date Ended __________ Ending Wage __________ Ending Position __________
Name of Supervisor ______________________________
May we contact? ❑ Yes ❑ No
Responsibilities ______________________________
____
Reason for leaving ______________________________

Company Name ______________________________
Address ______________________________ Telephone ______________
Date Started __________ Starting Wage __________ Starting Position __________
Date Ended __________ Ending Wage __________ Ending Position __________
Name of Supervisor ______________________________
May we contact? ❑ Yes ❑ No
Responsibilities ______________________________
____
Reason for leaving ______________________________

References

List three personal references, not related to you, who have known you for more than one year.

Name ______________ Phone ______________ Years Known ________
Address ______________________________

Name ______________ Phone ______________ Years Known ________
Address ______________________________

Name ______________ Phone ______________ Years Known ________
Address ______________________________

Emergency Contact

In case of emergency, please notify: ______________________________

Name ______________ Phone ______________
Address ______________________________

Name ______________ Phone ______________
Address ______________________________

Please Read Before Signing:

I certify that all information provided by me on this application is true and complete to the best of my knowledge and that I have withheld nothing that, if disclosed, would alter the integrity of this application.

I authorize my previous employers, schools, or persons listed as references to give any information regarding employment or educational record. I agree that this company and my previous employers will not be held liable in any respect if a job offer is not extended, or is withdrawn, or employment is terminated because of false statements, omissions, or answers made by myself on this application. In the event of any employment with this company, I will comply with all rules and regulations as set by the company in any communication distributed to the employees.

In compliance with the Immigration Reform and Control Act of 1986, I understand that I am required to provide approved documentation to the company that verifies my right to work in the United States on the first day of employment. I have received from the company a list of the approved documents that are required.

I understand that employment at this company is "at will," which means that either I or this company can terminate the employment relationship at any time, with or without prior notice, and for any reason not prohibited by statute. All employment is continued on that basis. I hereby acknowledge that I have read and understand the above statements.

Signature ______________________________ Date __________________

Immigration Reform and Control Act Requirement

In compliance with the Immigration Reform and Control Act of 1986, you are required to provide approved documentation that verifies your right to work in the United States prior to your employment with this company. Please be prepared to provide us with the following documentation in the event you are offered and accept employment with our company:

Any one of the following: (These establish both identity and employment authorization.)

1. U.S. Passport.
2. Certificate of U.S. Citizenship (issued by USCIS).
3. Certificate of Naturalization (issued by USCIS).
4. Resident alien card or other alien unexpired endorsement card, with photo or other approved identifying information which evidences employment authorization.
5. Unexpired foreign passport with unexpired endorsement authorizing employment.

Or one from List A and List B:

List A (These establish employment authorization.)

1. Social Security card.
2. Birth Certificate or other documentation that establishes U.S. nationality or birth.
3. Other approved documentation.

List B

1. Driver's license or similar government identification card with photo or other approved identifying information.
2. Other approved documentation of identity for applicants under age 16 or in a state that does not issue an I.D. card (other than a driver's license).

3. Authorization to Release Employment Applicant Information

Employment Applicant:

____

____

____

____

To:

____

____

____

____

I have applied for a position with ______________________________.

I have been requested to provide information for their use in reviewing my background and qualifications. Therefore, I authorize the investigation of my past and present work, character, education, military, and employment qualifications.

The release in any manner of all information by you is authorized, whether such information is of record or not, and I do hereby release all persons, agencies, firms, companies, etc., from any damages resulting from providing such information.

This authorization is valid for 90 days from the date of my signature below. Please keep this copy of my release request for your files. Thank you for your cooperation.

Signature______________________________ Date__________________

Note: Medical information is often protected by state laws and civil codes. Consult your attorney if you wish to seek this information.

Note: Many employers are reluctant to provide information on previous employees. If you ask each applicant to distribute this form to his or her references before you contact them, the prior employers may be more willing to release information.

4. Pre-Employment Reference Check via Phone

Applicant's Name______________________ Applying for____________________

"My name is ______________________ from ______________________Company.
______________________ has applied for a position with our company.
I would like to verify the information provided us by ______________________ and
______________________ has given us permission to contact you."

Person Contacted______________________ Company____________________

Phone______________________ ❑ Personnel Department ❑ Ex-Supervisor ❑ Other____________

Comments: ____

____

Job Title ______________________

Employment Date ______________________

Job Responsibilities ____

____

Attendance ______________________

Rehire ______________________

Person Contacted______________________ Company____________________

Phone______________________ ❑ Personnel Department ❑ Ex-Supervisor ❑ Other ____________

Comments: ____

____

Job Title ______________________

Employment Date ______________________

Job Responsibilities ____

____

Attendance ______________________

Rehire ______________________

Person Contacted______________________ Company____________________

Phone______________________ ❑ Personnel Department ❑ Ex-Supervisor ❑ Other ____________

Comments: ____

____

Job Title ______________________

Employment Date ______________________

Job Responsibilities ____

____

Attendance ______________________

Rehire ______________________

References Checked by ______________________ Date ____________

Checker's Comments ____

____

____

5. Pre-Employment Reference Check via Phone (Version Two)

Applicant____________________ Position__________

Company Contacted____________________ Phone__________

Name of Company Representative ____________________

Title of Company Representative ____________________

Dates of Employment: From____________________ To__________

Salary Information:

Regular Pay____________________ Overtime Pay__________

Bonus ____________________ Shift __________

Differential____________________

Date of last wage increase ____________________

What was your relationship with the applicant? ____________________

What were the applicant's job title and duties? ____________________

How long did you supervise this employee? ____________________

How would you compare this employee to others doing similar work and responsibilities? __________

Strong Points

Areas for Improvement

How would you rate this applicant's ability on a scale of 1 to 5 (1 being the lowest) regarding the following?

Attention to Detail ______ Comment ____________________

Learn ______ Comment ____________________

Follow Directions ______ Comment ____________________

Accept Responsibility ______ Comment ____________________

Follow Through ______ Comment ____________________

Initiate ______ Comment ____________________

Supervisory Duties ____________________

Supervisory Ability ____
____

Leadership Potential ____
____

Attendance/Punctuality ____
____

Ability to Work with Others ______________________________________
____

Reason for Leaving ____
____

Would You Rehire? ____
____

Other Comments ____
____

References Checked by ______________________________ Date ________________

6. Pre-Employment Reference Check via Letter

From:

____

____

____

____

To:

____

____

____

____

We would appreciate your assistance in verifying the information listed below regarding an employment application. It is to be understood that all information is confidential and will be treated as such in our company personnel files. Attached, please find an authorization to release information signed by the applicant. A self-addressed, stamped envelope is enclosed for your convenience in replying. We appreciate your assistance in this matter. Thank you.

Yours truly,

Personnel Manager

The following information was provided to us by the applicant. Please make any appropriate corrections:
Name ______________________________________ SS # ___________________________
Job Title ___________________________ Final Salary $___________________________
Date of Employment ___________________________
Reason for Termination ____

Please complete the following requested information:
Would you rehire this applicant? ❑ Yes ❑ No
If no, why not? ____
____

Please review and rate the applicant in these areas:

	Unsatisfactory		Average		Outstanding
Attendance	1	2	3	4	5
Quality of work	1	2	3	4	5
Quantity of work	1	2	3	4	5
Cooperation	1	2	3	4	5
Responsibility	1	2	3	4	5

Signed ________________________________ Title ____________________

Date _______________________

7. Applicant Comparison Summary Form

Position________________________ Date Interviewed ____________________

Interviewed by____

Candidate 1____

Candidate 2____

Candidate 3____

Candidate 4____

Critical Job Requirements	Candidate #1	#2	#3	#4	Comments

Legend:
✓ Meets critical job requirements
+ Exceeds critical job requirements
– Does not meet critical job requirements

8. Applicant Rating Form, Part One

Applicant's Name ______________________________

Position and Department ______________________________

Interviewed by ______________________________ Date ______________

Critical Job Requirements	Below Average			Average			Above Average			Excellent
______________	1	2	3	4	5	6	7	8	9	10
______________	1	2	3	4	5	6	7	8	9	10
______________	1	2	3	4	5	6	7	8	9	10
______________	1	2	3	4	5	6	7	8	9	10
______________	1	2	3	4	5	6	7	8	9	10
______________	1	2	3	4	5	6	7	8	9	10
______________	1	2	3	4	5	6	7	8	9	10
______________	1	2	3	4	5	6	7	8	9	10
______________	1	2	3	4	5	6	7	8	9	10
______________	1	2	3	4	5	6	7	8	9	10
______________	1	2	3	4	5	6	7	8	9	10
______________	1	2	3	4	5	6	7	8	9	10
______________	1	2	3	4	5	6	7	8	9	10
______________	1	2	3	4	5	6	7	8	9	10
______________	1	2	3	4	5	6	7	8	9	10
______________	1	2	3	4	5	6	7	8	9	10

Comments:

Strong Points ______________________________

____

____

Weak Areas ______________________________

____

____

Other ______________________________

____

____

9. Applicant Rating Form, Part Two

Applicant's Name ______________________________

Position and Department ______________________________

Interviewed by ______________________________ Date ______________

Job Experience:	**Poor**				**Outstanding**
Relevance to Position	1	2	3	4	5
Accomplishments	1	2	3	4	5
Analytical/Problem Solving	1	2	3	4	5
Leadership	1	2	3	4	5
Career Goals	1	2	3	4	5
Academics:					
Relevance of Studies to Job	1	2	3	4	5
Extent, Variety in Activities	1	2	3	4	5
Abilities as a Student	1	2	3	4	5
Characteristics:					
Grooming	1	2	3	4	5
Bearing	1	2	3	4	5
Initiative	1	2	3	4	5
Grasp of Ideas	1	2	3	4	5
Stability	1	2	3	4	5
Personality	1	2	3	4	5
Preparation for Interview:					
Knowledge of Company	1	2	3	4	5
Relevance of Questions	1	2	3	4	5

Summary of Strength and Shortcomings:

Talent, Skills, Knowledge, Energy

____

____

Motivation, Interests

____

____

Personal Qualities, Effectiveness

____

____

Other Comments

____

____

10. Offer of Employment and Employment Contract

Date
Employee Name ________________________
Address ______________________________
____

Dear ______________________:

We are pleased to offer you a position with ______________________________ ("Company"). Your start date, manager, compensation, benefits, and other terms of employment will be as set forth below and on EXHIBIT A.

TERMS OF EMPLOYMENT

1. **Position and Duties.** Company shall employ you, and you agree to competently and professionally perform such duties as are customarily the responsibility of the position as set forth in the job description attached as EXHIBIT A and as reasonably assigned to you from time to time by your Manager as set forth in EXHIBIT A.
2. **Outside Business Activities.** During your employment with Company, you shall devote competent energies, interests, and abilities to the performance of your duties under this Agreement. During the term of this Agreement, you shall not, without Company's prior written consent, render any services to others for compensation or engage or participate, actively or passively, in any other business activities that would interfere with the performance of your duties hereunder or compete with Company's business.
3. **Employment Classification.** You shall be a Full-Time Employee and shall not be entitled to benefits except as specifically outlined herein.
4. **Compensation/Benefits.**
   4.1 Wage. Company shall pay you the wage as set forth in the job description attached as EXHIBIT A.
   4.2 Reimbursement of Expenses. You shall be reimbursed for all reasonable and necessary expenses paid or incurred by you in the performance of your duties. You shall provide Company with original receipts for such expenses.
   4.3 Withholdings. All compensation paid to you under this Agreement, including payment of salary and taxable benefits, shall be subject to such withholdings as may be required by law or Company's general practices.
   4.4 Benefits. You will also receive Company's standard employee benefits package (including health insurance), and will be subject to Company's vacation policy as such package and policy are in effect from time to time.
5. **At-Will Employment.** Either party may terminate this Agreement by written notice at any time for any reason or for no reason. This Agreement is intended to be and shall be deemed to be an at-will employment Agreement and does not constitute a guarantee of continuing employment for any term.
6. **Nondisclosure Agreement.** You agree to sign Company's standard Employee Nondisclosure Agreement and Proprietary Rights Assignment as a condition of your employment. We wish to impress upon you that we do not wish you to bring with you any confidential or proprietary material of any former employer or to violate any other obligation to your former employers.
7. **Authorization to Work.** Because of federal regulations adopted in the Immigration Reform and Control Act of 1986, you will need to present documentation demonstrating that you have authorization to work in the United States.
8. **Further Assurances.** Each party shall perform any and all further acts and execute and deliver any documents that are reasonably necessary to carry out the intent of this Agreement.
9. **Notices.** All notices or other communications required or permitted by this Agreement or by law shall be in writing and shall be deemed duly served and given when delivered personally or by facsimile, air courier, certified

mail (return receipt requested), postage and fees prepaid, to the party at the address indicated in the signature block or at such other address as a party may request in writing.

10. **Governing Law.** This Agreement shall be governed and interpreted in accordance with the laws of the State of California, as such laws are applied to agreements between residents of California to be performed entirely within the State of California.

11. **Entire Agreement.** This Agreement sets forth the entire Agreement between the parties pertaining to the subject matter hereof and supersedes all prior written agreements and all prior or contemporaneous oral Agreements and understandings, expressed or implied.

12. **Written Modification and Waiver.** No modification to this Agreement, nor any waiver of any rights, shall be effective unless assented to in writing by the party to be charged, and the waiver of any breach or default shall not constitute a waiver of any other right or any subsequent breach or default.

13. **Assignment.** This Agreement is personal in nature, and neither of the parties shall, without the consent of the other, assign or transfer this Agreement or any rights or obligations under this Agreement, except that Company may assign or transfer this Agreement to a successor of Company's business, in the event of the transfer or sale of all or substantially all of the assets of Company's business, or to a subsidiary, provided that in the case of any assignment or transfer under the terms of this Section, this Agreement shall be binding on and inure to the benefit of the successor of Company's business, and the successor of Company's business shall discharge and perform all of the obligations of Company under this Agreement.

14. **Severability.** If any of the provisions of this Agreement are determined to be invalid, illegal, or unenforceable, such provisions shall be modified to the minimum extent necessary to make such provisions enforceable, and the remaining provisions shall continue in full force and effect to the extent the economic benefits conferred upon the parties by this Agreement remain substantially unimpaired.

15. **Arbitration of Disputes.** Any controversy or claim arising out of or relating to this contract, or the breach thereof, shall be settled by arbitration administered by the American Arbitration Association under its National Rules for the Resolution of Employment Disputes, and judgment upon the award rendered by the arbitrator(s) may be entered by any court having jurisdiction thereof.

We look forward to your arrival and what we hope will be the start of a mutually satisfying work relationship.

Sincerely,
Company

By: ____________________________

Acknowledged, Accepted, and Agreed

Date: ________________________________

____

Employee Signature

11. New Employee Announcement

Date ____________________

To: All Employees

From: ____________________________________

Subject: New Employee

I am pleased to announce that ______________________________ (new employee name) has joined our staff as a ____________________________________ (job title).

In his/her new position, ______________________________ will report to____________________.

Our new employee comes to us from ______________________________ (last employer), where he/she was ______________________________________ (job title and major responsibilities) and prior to that was __________________________ (job title and major responsibilities).

Please join me in welcoming our new employee to our staff and in wishing him/her much success!

CHAPTER 2

Employee Records and Human Resource Management

Now that you've got the best candidate in the door, it's very important to keep him or her there and to maintain adequate records. You should always maintain a master database of your employees with the *Employee Master Database*. With this form you can maintain an accurate and convenient master list of the name, Social Security number, date of birth, address, and hire date of each current or former employee. (Always maintain records for five years after an employee leaves his or her position.) You can also maintain records of whether the employee is current or former and full or part time. The *Employee Master Database* also contains columns for whether your employees have executed an employment agreement, stock option agreement, employee handbook acknowledgment, non-disclosure agreement, and W-4 form. Once you have these documents on file, indicate so by writing "OF" in each appropriate cell.

The *Company Employee Handbook* is a full-featured handbook that outlines a company's employment-related policies. You should carefully customize this document to suit your individual needs. When you present the *Company Employee Handbook* to your employees, also present them with an *Acknowledgment of Receipt of Employee Handbook* and ensure that they return the *Acknowledgment* to you; this *Acknowledgment* is your proof that the employee has read the *Handbook* and agreed to its terms.

In each employee's file, you should insert a completed *Employee Personal Information* form. You should have the employee fill out the form immediately after he or she is hired.

The *Employee Vacation Request* is filled out by an employee desiring vacation time and presented to the human resources department.

If your human resources department deducts money from an employee's pay for any reason other than ordinary tax withholding, such as 401(k) plans, savings plans, union dues, etc., be sure to have the employee consent to such deduction by executing the *Payroll Deduction Authorization*. If your human resources department makes a direct deposit of an employee's pay, have the employee authorize direct deposit by executing the *Direct Deposit Authorization*. As with any employment record, maintain a copy of either *Authorization* in the employee's file.

If your employee's position prevents him or her from being fully relieved from all responsibilities during a meal period, you should pay the employee for the meal period and have him or her agree to the arrangement by submitting to you a *Pay for Meal Period* form.

If a department head wants to hire, he or she would submit either the *Personnel Requisition*

(Non-Management) or the *Personnel Requisition (Management)* to the human resources department. The *Salary Recommendation Form* is a valuable internal document that enables staff to determine the appropriate salary in the case of a new hire or a promotion.

The *Job Announcement: Open Position* form announces to existing staff the availability of a new position. Remember: your current employees are a great resource both for filling new positions and for getting recommendations for new employees. The *Job Posting: Open Position* announces a new position to the general public. The *Job Position Description* presents a detailed description of a new position. Use the *Description* to alert staff of the details of the position.

Employees whose contact information changes should submit a *Personnel Data Change Form* to the human resources department. When employees are promoted, are terminated, resign, go on sick leave, etc, fill out an *Employee Status Change* form to keep track. Both the *Career Development Worksheet for Management Employee Career Interests* and the *Career Development Worksheet for Non-Management Employee Career Interests* enable your employees to clarify and communicate their career development goals. You should always aspire to have your employees grow as your company grows. The *Employee Career Development Worksheet Objectives and Results* form tracks the employee's goals and progress.

Unfortunately, you may find it necessary to discipline your employees. Be careful to document each incident and the recommended discipline and to treat employees evenhandedly. The employer-employee relationship is a contractual relationship and an employer owes tremendous duties of fairness to its employees. Many employer-employee disputes ripen into expensive litigation. You can minimize this undesirable result by maintaining meticulous employee discipline records. When one or more of your employees commits misconduct worthy of disciplinary action, fill out an *Employee Incident and Discipline Documentation Form*. Once an appropriate course of employee discipline has been decided, commit the recommended course in a *Disciplinary Notice*. The *Notice* serves as a formal written warning to errant employees. The *Notice* can also serve to refute any arguments offered by the employee suggesting that he or she did not receive warnings or discipline.

To evaluate and record an employee's performance, you can use the *Employee Performance Review.*

The *Time Sheet—Hourly Employees* records the hours worked by each employee and can help calculate overtime. Note that state law differs widely on the amount and rate of overtime that must be paid. The *Annual Attendance Record* allows you to compile and analyze an employee's attendance, sick days, tardiness, vacation days, and much more for a full year. An employee who seeks a leave of absence should complete a *Request for Leave of Absence Without Pay* and deliver it to the person with human resource responsibilities.

An employee who wishes to see his or her personnel file should complete a *Request to Inspect Personnel File* and deliver it to the person with human resource responsibilities. If an employee has a serious grievance, insist that he or she complete an *Employee Grievance Form*, to accurately and fully document the grievance.

12. Employee Master Database

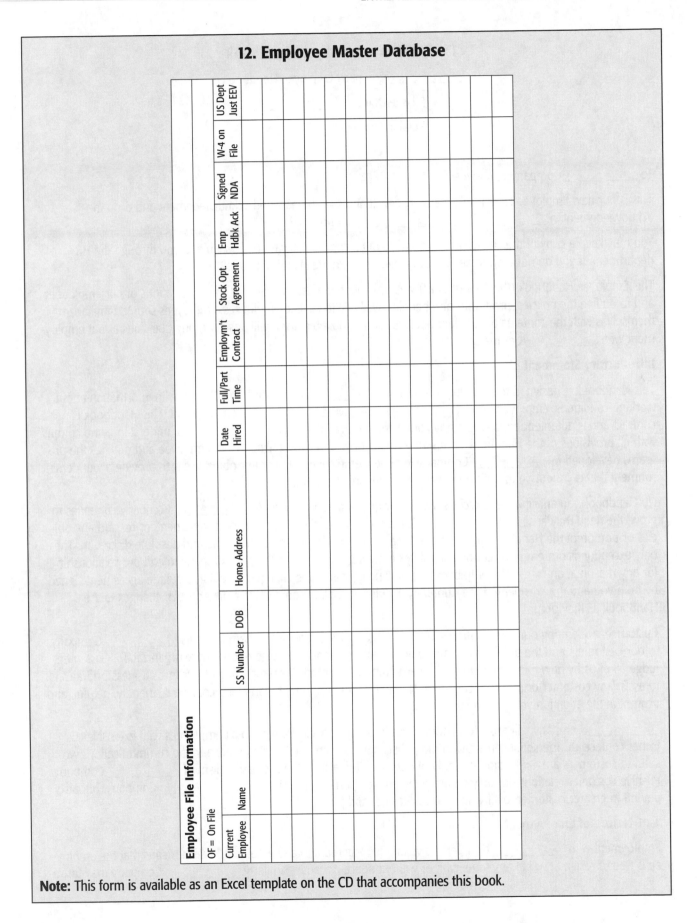

Employee File Information

OF = On File

Current Employee	Name	SS Number	DOB	Home Address	Date Hired	Full/Part Time	Employm't Contract	Stock Opt. Agreement	Emp Hdbk Ack	Signed NDA	W-4 on File	US Dept Just EEV

Note: This form is available as an Excel template on the CD that accompanies this book.

13. Company Employee Handbook

__________ Company Employee Handbook

Issue Date: ____________

Version Number: __________

To __________ Company Employees:

This is our new Employee Handbook. Please review it and sign the attached acknowledgment and drop the acknowledgment in __________________________'s in box.

You may keep a copy of the Handbook if you wish, but a copy will always be available to you through the HR department. If you do not wish to keep a copy, please return the Handbook to HR.

This Employee Handbook (the "Handbook") was developed to describe some of the expectations of our employees and to outline the policies, programs, and benefits available to eligible employees. Employees should familiarize themselves with the contents of the Handbook as soon as possible, for it will answer many questions about employment with __________ Company.

Introductory Statement

This Handbook is designed to acquaint you with __________ Company and provide you with information about working conditions, employee benefits, and some of the policies affecting your employment. This Handbook is not a contract and is not intended to create any contractual or legal obligations. You should read, understand, and comply with all provisions of the Handbook. It describes many of your responsibilities as an employee and outlines the programs developed by __________ Company to benefit employees. One of our objectives is to provide a work environment that is conducive to both personal and professional growth.

No Handbook can anticipate every circumstance or question about policy. As __________ Company continues to grow, the need may arise and __________ Company reserves the right to revise, supplement, or rescind any policies or portion of the Handbook from time to time as it deems appropriate, in its sole and absolute discretion. The only exception is our employment-at-will policy permitting you or __________ Company to end our relationship for any reason at any time. The employment-at-will policy cannot be changed except in a written agreement signed by both you and the President of the Company. Employees will, of course, be notified of such changes to the Handbook as they occur.

Customers are among our organization's most valuable assets. Every employee represents __________ Company to our customers and the public. The way we do our jobs presents an image of our entire organization. Customers judge all of us by how they are treated with each employee contact. Therefore, one of our first business priorities is to assist any customer or potential customer. Nothing is more important than being courteous, friendly, helpful, and prompt in the attention you give to customers.

__________ Company will provide customer relations and services training to all employees with extensive customer contact. Our personal contact with the public, our manners on the telephone, and the communications we send to customers are a reflection not only of ourselves, but also of the professionalism of __________ Company. Positive customer relations not only enhance the public's perception or image of __________ Company, but also pay off in greater customer loyalty and increased sales and profit.

1-01 Nature of Employment

Employment with __________ Company is voluntarily entered into and is "at-will," which means that the employee is free to resign at will at any time, with or without notice or cause. Similarly, __________ Company may terminate the employment relationship at any time, with or without notice or cause, so long as there is no violation of applicable federal or state law. No one has the authority to make verbal statements that change the at-will nature of employment, and the at-will relationship cannot be changed or modified for any employee except in a written agreement signed by that employee and the President of __________ Company.

Policies set forth in this Handbook are not intended to create a contract, nor are they to be construed to constitute contractual obligations of any kind or a contract of employment between __________ Company and any of its employees. The provisions of the Handbook have been developed at the discretion of management and, except for its policy of employment-at-will, may be amended or cancelled at any time, at __________ Company's sole discretion.

These provisions supersede all existing policies and practices and may not be amended or added to without the express written approval of the CEO or person designated by the CEO of __________ Company.

1-02 Employee Relations

__________ Company believes that the work conditions, wages, and benefits it offers to its employees are competitive with those offered by other employers in this area and in this industry. If employees have concerns about work conditions or compensation, they are strongly encouraged to voice these concerns openly and directly to their supervisors.

Our experience has shown that when employees deal openly and directly with supervisors, the work environment can be excellent, communications can be clear, and attitudes can be positive. We believe that __________ Company amply demonstrates its commitment to employees by responding effectively to employee concerns.

1-03 Equal Employment Opportunity

In order to provide equal employment and advancement opportunities to all individuals, employment decisions at __________ Company will be based on merit, qualifications, and the needs of the company. __________ Company does not unlawfully discriminate in employment opportunities or practices on the basis of race, color, religion, sex, national origin, age, disability, ancestry, medical conditions, family care status, sexual orientation, or any other basis prohibited by law.

__________ Company will make reasonable accommodations for qualified individuals with known disabilities unless doing so would result in an undue hardship to the extent required by law. This policy governs all aspects of employment, including selection, job assignment, compensation, discipline, termination, and access to benefits and training.

Any employees with questions or concerns about any type of discrimination in the workplace are encouraged to bring these issues to the attention of their immediate supervisor or the Human Resources Department. Employees can raise concerns and make reports without fear of reprisal. Anyone found to be engaging in any type of unlawful discrimination will be subject to disciplinary action, up to and including termination of employment.

1-04 Business Ethics and Conduct

The successful business operation and reputation of __________ Company are built upon the principles of fair dealing and ethical conduct of our employees. Our reputation for integrity and excellence requires careful observance of the spirit and the letter of all applicable laws and regulations, as well as a scrupulous regard for the highest standards of conduct and personal integrity.

The continued success of __________ Company is dependent upon our customers' trust and we are dedicated to preserving that trust. Employees owe a duty to __________ Company, its customers, and its shareholders to act in a way that will merit the continued trust and confidence of the public.

__________ Company will comply with all applicable laws and regulations and expects its directors, officers, and employees to conduct business in accordance with the letter, spirit, and intent of all relevant laws and to refrain from any illegal, dishonest, or unethical conduct.

In general, the use of good judgment, based on high ethical principles, will guide you with respect to lines of acceptable conduct. If a situation arises where it is difficult to determine the proper course of action, the matter should be discussed openly with your immediate supervisor and, if necessary, with the Human Resources Department for advice and consultation.

Compliance with this policy of business ethics and conduct is the responsibility of every __________ Company employee. Disregarding or failing to comply with this standard of business ethics and conduct could lead to disciplinary action, up to and including possible termination of employment.

1-05 Personal Relationships in the Workplace

The employment of relatives or individuals involved in a dating relationship in the same area of an organization may cause serious conflicts and problems with favoritism and employee morale. In addition to claims of partiality in treatment at work, personal conflicts from outside the work environment can be carried over into day-to-day working relationships.

For purposes of this policy, relatives are any persons who are related to each other by blood or marriage or whose relationship is similar to that of persons who are related by blood or marriage. A dating relationship is defined as a relationship that may be reasonably expected to lead to the formation of a consensual "romantic" or sexual relationship. This policy applies to all employees without regard to the gender or sexual orientation of the individuals involved.

Relatives of current employees may not occupy a position that will be working directly for or supervising their relative except as required by law. Individuals involved in a dating relationship with a current employee may also not occupy a position that will be working directly for or supervising the employee with whom they are involved in a dating relationship. __________ Company also reserves the right to take prompt action if an actual or potential conflict of interest arises involving relatives or individuals involved in a dating relationship who occupy positions at any level (higher or lower) in the same line of authority that may affect the review of employment decisions.

If a relative relationship or dating relationship is established after employment between employees who are in a reporting situation described above, it is the responsibility and obligation of the supervisor involved in the relationship to disclose the existence of the relationship to management.

In other cases where a conflict or the potential for conflict arises because of the relationship between employees, even if there is no line of authority or reporting involved, the employees may be separated by reassignment or terminated from employment. Employees in a close personal relationship should refrain from public workplace displays of affection or excessive personal conversation.

1-07 Immigration Law Compliance

__________ Company is committed to employing only United States citizens and aliens who are authorized to work in the United States and does not unlawfully discriminate on the basis of citizenship or national origin.

In compliance with the Immigration Reform and Control Act of 1986, each new employee, as a condition of employment, must complete the Employment Eligibility Verification Form I-9 and present documentation establishing identity and employment eligibility. Former employees who are rehired must also complete the form if they have not completed an I-9 with __________ Company within the past three years or if their previous I-9 is no longer retained or valid.

Employees with questions or seeking more information on immigration law issues are encouraged to contact the Human Resources Department. Employees may raise questions or complaints about immigration law compliance without fear of reprisal.

1-08 Conflicts of Interest

Employees have an obligation to conduct business within guidelines that prohibit actual or potential conflicts of interest. This policy establishes only the framework within which __________ Company wishes the business to operate. The purpose of these guidelines is to provide general direction so that employees can seek further clarification on issues related to the subject of acceptable standards of operation. Contact the Human Resources Department for more information or questions about conflicts of interest.

An actual or potential conflict of interest occurs when an employee is in a position to influence a decision that may result in a personal gain for that employee or for a relative as a result of __________ Company's business dealings. For the purposes of this policy, a relative is any person who is related by blood or marriage or whose relationship with the employee is similar to that of persons who are related by blood or marriage.

No "presumption of guilt" is created by the mere existence of a relationship with outside firms. However, if employees have any influence on transactions involving purchases, contracts, or leases, it is imperative that they disclose to an officer of __________ Company as soon as possible the existence of any actual or potential conflict of interest so that safeguards can be established to protect all parties.

Personal gain may result not only in cases where an employee or relative has a significant ownership in a firm with which __________ Company does business, but also when an employee or relative receives any kickback, bribe, substantial gift, or special consideration as a result of any transaction or business dealings involving __________ Company.

1-12 Non-Disclosure

The protection of confidential business information and trade secrets is vital to the interests and the success of __________ Company. Such confidential information includes, but is not limited to, the following examples:

- acquisitions
- compensation data
- computer processes
- computer programs and codes
- customer lists
- customer preferences
- financial information
- investments
- labor relations strategies
- marketing strategies
- new materials research
- partnerships
- pending projects and proposals
- proprietary production processes
- research and development strategies
- scientific data
- scientific formulae
- scientific prototypes
- technological data
- technological prototypes

All employees may be required to sign a non-disclosure agreement as a condition of employment. Employees who improperly use or disclose trade secrets or confidential business information will be subject to disciplinary action, up to and including termination of employment and legal action, even if they do not actually benefit from the disclosed information.

1-14 Disability Accommodation

__________ Company is committed to complying fully with applicable disability laws and ensuring equal opportunity in employment for qualified persons with disabilities.

Hiring procedures have been reviewed and provide persons with disabilities meaningful employment opportunities. Pre-employment inquiries are made regarding only an applicant's ability to perform the duties of the position.

Reasonable accommodation is available to all disabled employees, where their disability affects the performance of job functions to the extent required by law. All employment decisions are based on the merits of the situation and the needs of the company, not the disability of the individual.

__________ Company is also committed to not unlawfully discriminating against any qualified employees or applicants because they are related to or associated with a person with a disability.

This policy is neither exhaustive nor exclusive. __________ Company is committed to taking all other actions necessary to ensure equal employment opportunity for persons with disabilities in accordance with the ADA and all other applicable federal, state, and local laws.

2-01 Employment Categories

It is the intent of __________ Company to clarify the definitions of employment classifications so that employees understand their employment status and benefit eligibility. These classifications do not guarantee employment for any specified period of time. Accordingly, the right to terminate the employment relationship at will at any time is retained by both the employee and __________ Company.

Each employee is designated as either NONEXEMPT or EXEMPT from federal and state wage and hour laws. NONEXEMPT employees are entitled to overtime pay under the specific provisions of federal and state laws. EXEMPT employees are excluded from specific provisions of federal and state wage and hour laws. An employee's EXEMPT or NONEXEMPT classification may be changed only upon written notification by __________ Company management.

In addition to the above categories, each employee will belong to one other employment category:

REGULAR FULL-TIME employees are those who are not in a temporary or introductory status and who are regularly scheduled to work __________ Company's full-time schedule. Generally, they are eligible for __________ Company's benefit package, subject to the terms, conditions, and limitations of each benefit program.

INTRODUCTORY employees are those whose performance is being evaluated to determine whether further employment in a specific position or with __________ Company is appropriate. Employees who satisfactorily complete the introductory period will be notified of their new employment classification.

TEMPORARY employees are those who are hired as interim replacements, to temporarily supplement the work force, or to assist in the completion of a specific project. Employment assignments in this category are of a limited duration. Employment beyond any initially stated period does not in any way imply a change in employment status. Temporary employees retain that status unless and until notified of a change. While temporary employees receive all legally mandated benefits (such as workers' compensation insurance and Social Security), they are ineligible for all of __________ Company's other benefit programs.

2-02 Access to Personnel Files

__________ Company maintains a personnel file on each employee. The personnel file includes such information as the employee's job application, résumé, records of training, documentation of performance appraisals and salary increases, and other employment records.

Personnel files are the property of __________ Company and access to the information they contain is restricted. Generally, only supervisors and management personnel of __________ Company who have a legitimate reason to review information in a file are allowed to do so.

Employees who wish to review their own file should contact the Human Resources Department. With reasonable advance notice, employees may review their own personnel files in __________ Company's offices and in the presence of an individual appointed by __________ Company to maintain the files.

2-04 Personal Data Changes

It is the responsibility of each employee to promptly notify __________ Company of any changes in personal data. Personal mailing addresses, telephone numbers, number and names of dependents, individuals to be contacted in the event of an emergency, educational accomplishments, and other such status reports should be accurate and current at all times. If any personal data has changed, notify the Human Resources Department.

2-05 Introductory Period

The introductory period is intended to give new employees the opportunity to demonstrate their ability to achieve a satisfactory level of performance and to determine whether the new position meets their expectations. __________ Company uses this period to evaluate employee capabilities, work habits, and overall performance. Either the employee or __________ Company may end the employment relationship at will at any time during or after the introductory period, with or without cause or advance notice.

All new and rehired employees work on an introductory basis for the first 90 calendar days after their date of hire. Any significant absence will automatically extend an introductory period by the length of the absence. If __________ Company determines that the designated introductory period does not allow sufficient time to thoroughly evaluate the employee's performance, the introductory period may be extended for a specified period.

2-08 Employment Applications

__________ Company relies upon the accuracy of information contained in the employment application, as well as the accuracy of other data presented throughout the hiring process and employment. Any misrepresentations, falsifications, or material omissions in any of this information or data may result in the exclusion of the individual from further consideration for employment or, if the person has been hired, termination of employment.

In processing employment applications, __________ Company may obtain a consumer credit report or background check for employment. If __________ Company takes an adverse employment action based in whole or in part on any report caused by the Fair Credit Reporting Act, a copy of the report and a summary of your rights under the Fair Credit Reporting Act will be provided as well as any other documents required by law.

2-09 Performance Evaluation

Supervisors and employees are strongly encouraged to discuss job performance and goals on an informal, day-to-day basis. A formal written performance evaluation will be conducted following an employee's introductory period. Additional formal performance evaluations are conducted to provide both supervisors and employees the opportunity to discuss job tasks, identify and correct weaknesses, encourage and recognize strengths, and discuss positive, purposeful approaches for meeting goals.

2-10 Job Descriptions

__________ Company maintains job descriptions to aid in orienting new employees to their jobs, identifying the requirements of each position, establishing hiring criteria, setting standards for employee performance evaluations, and establishing a basis for making reasonable accommodations for individuals with disabilities.

The Human Resources Department and the hiring manager prepare job descriptions when new positions are created. Existing job descriptions are also reviewed and revised in order to ensure that they are up to date. Job descriptions may also be rewritten periodically to reflect any changes in position duties and responsibilities. All employees will be expected to help ensure that their job descriptions are accurate and current, reflecting the work being done.

Employees should remember that job descriptions do not necessarily cover every task or duty that might be assigned, and that additional responsibilities may be assigned as necessary. Contact the Human Resources Department if you have any questions or concerns about your job description.

3-01 Employee Benefits

Eligible employees at __________ Company are provided a wide range of benefits. A number of the programs (such as Social Security, workers' compensation, state disability, and unemployment insurance) cover all employees in the manner prescribed by law.

Benefits eligibility is dependent upon a variety of factors, including employee classification. Your supervisor can identify the programs for which you are eligible. Details of many of these programs can be found elsewhere in the Handbook.

The following benefit programs are available to eligible employees:

- auto mileage
- bereavement leave
- dental insurance
- holidays
- medical insurance
- stock options
- vacation benefits

Some benefit programs require contributions from the employee, but most are fully paid by __________ Company. Many benefits are described in separate Summary Plan Descriptions, or Plans, which may change from time to time. The Summary Plan Description will have control over any policy in this Handbook. You will receive a copy of each Summary Plan Description applicable to you. Contact the Human Resources Department if you need a Summary Plan Description or have any questions.

3-03 Vacation Benefits

Vacation time off with pay is available to eligible employees to provide opportunities for rest, relaxation, and personal pursuits. Employees in the following employment classification(s) are eligible to earn and use vacation time as described in this policy:

Regular full-time employees

The amount of paid vacation time employees receive each year increases with the length of their employment, as shown in the following schedule:

- Upon initial eligibility, the employee is entitled to 10 vacation days each year, accrued monthly at the rate of 0.833 days.
- After four years of eligible service, the employee is entitled to 15 vacation days each year, accrued monthly at the rate of 1.250 days.

The length of eligible service is calculated on the basis of a "benefit year." This is the 12-month period that begins when the employee starts to earn vacation time. An employee's benefit year may be extended for any significant leave of absence except military leave of absence. Military leave has no effect on this calculation. (See individual leave of absence policies for more information.)

Once employees enter an eligible employment classification, they begin to earn paid vacation time according to the schedule. They can request use of vacation time after it is earned.

Paid vacation time can be used in minimum increments of one day. To take vacation, employees should request advance approval from their supervisors. Requests will be reviewed based on a number of factors, including business needs and staffing requirements.

Vacation time off is paid at the employee's base pay rate at the time of vacation. It does not include overtime or any special forms of compensation such as incentives, commissions, bonuses, or shift differentials.

As stated above, employees are encouraged to use available paid vacation time for rest, relaxation, and personal pursuits. In the event that available vacation is not used by the end of the benefit year, employees may carry unused time forward to the next benefit year. If the total amount of unused vacation time reaches a "cap" equal to two times the annual vacation amount, further vacation accrual will stop. When the employee uses paid vacation time and brings the available amount below the cap, vacation accrual will begin again.

Upon termination of employment, employees will be paid for unused vacation time that has been earned through the last day of work.

3-05 Holidays

__________ Company will grant holiday time off to all employees on the holidays listed below:

- New Year's Day (January 1)
- Martin Luther King, Jr. Day (third Monday in January)
- Presidents' Day (third Monday in February)
- Memorial Day (last Monday in May)
- Independence Day (July 4)
- Labor Day (first Monday in September)
- Thanksgiving (fourth Thursday in November)
- Christmas (December 25)
- New Year's Eve (December 31)

__________ Company will grant paid holiday time off to all eligible employees immediately upon assignment to an eligible employment classification. Holiday pay will be calculated based on the employee's straight-time pay rate (as of the date of the holiday) times the number of hours the employee would otherwise have worked on that day. Eligible employee classification(s):

Regular full-time employees

If a recognized holiday falls during an eligible employee's paid absence (e.g., vacation, sick leave), the employee will be ineligible for holiday pay. If eligible nonexempt employees work on a recognized holiday, they will receive holiday pay plus wages at their straight-time rate for the hours worked on the holiday. In addition to the recognized holidays previously listed, eligible employees will receive two floating holidays in each anniversary year. To be eligible, employees must complete three calendar days of service in an eligible employment classification. These holidays must be scheduled with the prior approval of the employee's supervisor.

Paid time off for holidays will be counted as hours worked for the purposes of determining whether overtime pay is owed.

3-06 Workers' Compensation Insurance

__________ Company provides a comprehensive workers' compensation insurance program at no cost to employees, pursuant to law. This program covers any injury or illness sustained in the course of employment that requires medical, surgical, or hospital treatment. Subject to applicable legal requirements, workers' compensation insurance provides benefits after a short waiting period or, if the employee is hospitalized, immediately.

Employees who sustain work-related injuries or illnesses should inform their supervisor immediately. No matter how minor an on-the-job injury may appear, it is important that it be reported immediately. This will enable an eligible employee to qualify for coverage as quickly as possible.

3-07 Sick Leave Benefits

__________ Company provides paid sick leave benefits to all eligible employees for periods of temporary absence due to illnesses or injuries. Eligible employee classification(s):

Regular full-time employees

Eligible employees will accrue sick leave benefits at the rate of 10 days per year (.83 of a day for every full month of service). Sick leave benefits are calculated on the basis of a "benefit year," the 12-month period that begins when the employee starts to earn sick leave benefits.

Paid sick leave can be used in minimum increments of one day. An eligible employee may use sick leave benefits for an absence due to his or her own illness or injury, or that of a child, parent, or spouse of the employee.

Employees who are unable to report to work due to illness or injury should notify their direct supervisor before the scheduled start of their workday if possible. The direct supervisor must also be contacted on each additional day of absence. If an employee is absent for three or more consecutive days due to illness or injury, the company may require a physician's statement verifying the illness or injury and its beginning and expected ending dates. Such verification may be requested for other sick leave absences as well and may be required as a condition to receiving sick leave benefits.

Sick leave benefits will be calculated based on the employee's base pay rate at the time of absence and will not include any special forms of compensation, such as incentives, commissions, bonuses, or shift differentials.

Sick leave benefits are intended solely to provide income protection in the event of illness or injury, and may not be used for any other absence. Unused sick leave benefits will not be paid to employees while they are employed or upon termination of employment.

3-08 Time Off to Vote

__________ Company encourages employees to fulfill their civic responsibilities by participating in elections. Generally, employees are able to find time to vote either before or after their regular work schedule. If employees are unable to vote in an election during their nonworking hours, __________ Company will grant up to two hours of paid time off to vote.

Employees should request time off to vote from their supervisor at least two working days prior to the Election Day. Advance notice is required so that the necessary time off can be scheduled at the beginning or end of the work shift, whichever causes less disruption to the normal work schedule.

Employees must submit a voter's receipt on the first working day following the election to qualify for paid time off.

3-09 Bereavement Leave

Employees who wish to take time off due to the death of an immediate family member should notify their supervisor immediately.

Up to three days of paid bereavement leave will be provided to eligible employees in the following classification(s):

Regular full-time employees

Bereavement pay is calculated based on the base pay rate at the time of absence and will not include any special forms of compensation, such as incentives, commissions, bonuses, or shift differentials.

Bereavement leave will normally be granted unless there are unusual business needs or staffing requirements. Employees may, with their supervisors' approval, use any available paid leave for additional time off as necessary.

__________ Company defines "immediate family" as the employee's spouse, parent, child, or sibling.

3-11 Jury Duty

__________ Company encourages employees to fulfill their civic responsibilities by serving jury duty when required. Employees may request unpaid jury duty leave for the length of absence. If desired, employees may use any available paid time off (for example, vacation benefits).

Employees must show the jury duty summons to their supervisor as soon as possible so that the supervisor may make arrangements to accommodate their absence. Of course, employees are expected to report for work whenever the court schedule permits.

Either __________ Company or the employee may request an excuse from jury duty if, in __________ Company's judgment, the employee's absence would create serious operational difficulties.

__________ Company will continue to provide health insurance benefits for the full term of the jury duty absence.

Vacation, sick leave, and holiday benefits will continue to accrue during unpaid jury duty leave.

3-13 Benefits Continuation (COBRA)

The federal Consolidated Omnibus Budget Reconciliation Act (COBRA) gives employees and their qualified beneficiaries the opportunity to continue health insurance coverage under __________ Company's health plan when a "qualifying event" would normally result in the loss of eligibility. Some common qualifying events are resignation, termination of employment, or death of an employee; a reduction in an employee's hours or a leave of absence; an employee's divorce or legal separation; and a dependent child no longer meeting eligibility requirements.

Under COBRA, the employee or beneficiary pays the full cost of coverage at __________ Company's group rates plus an administration fee. __________ Company provides each eligible employee with a written notice describing rights granted under COBRA when the employee becomes eligible for coverage under __________ Company's health insurance plan. The notice contains important information about the employee's rights and obligations. Contact the Human Resources Department for more information about COBRA.

3-16 Health Insurance

__________ Company's health insurance plan provides employees access to medical and dental insurance benefits. Employees in the following employment classification(s) are eligible to participate in the health insurance plan:

Regular full-time employees

Eligible employees may participate in the health insurance plan subject to all terms and conditions of the agreement between __________ Company and the insurance carrier.

A change in employment classification that would result in loss of eligibility to participate in the health insurance plan may qualify an employee for benefits continuation under the Consolidated Omnibus Budget Reconciliation Act (COBRA). Refer to the "Benefits Continuation (COBRA)" policy section 3-13 for more information.

Details of the health insurance plan are described in the Summary Plan Description (SPD). An SPD and information on cost of coverage will be provided in advance of enrollment to eligible employees. Contact the Human Resources Department for more information about health insurance benefits.

4-03 Paydays

All employees are paid monthly on the first day of the month. Each paycheck will include earnings for all work performed through the end of the previous payroll period.

In the event that a regularly scheduled payday falls on a day off, such as a weekend or holiday, employees will receive pay on the last day of work before the regularly scheduled payday.

If a regular payday falls during an employee's vacation, the employee may receive his or her earned wages before departing for vacation if a written request is submitted at least one week prior to departing for vacation.

4-05 Employment Termination

Termination of employment is an inevitable part of personnel activity within any organization and many of the reasons for termination are routine. Below are examples of some of the most common circumstances under which employment is terminated:

- Resignation–voluntary employment termination initiated by an employee.
- Discharge–involuntary employment termination initiated by the organization.
- Layoff–involuntary employment termination initiated by the organization because of an organizational change.
- Retirement–voluntary employment termination initiated by the employee meeting age, length of service, and any other criteria for retirement from the organization.

__________ Company will generally schedule exit interviews at the time of employment termination. The exit interview will afford an opportunity to discuss such issues as employee benefits, conversion privileges, repayment of outstanding debts to __________ Company, or return of __________ Company-owned property. Suggestions, complaints, and questions can also be voiced.

Nothing in this policy is intended to change the company's at-will employment policy. Since employment with __________ Company is based on mutual consent, both the employee and __________ Company have the right to terminate employment at will, with or without cause, at any time. Employees will receive their final pay in accordance with applicable state law.

Employee benefits will be affected by employment termination in the following manner. All accrued, vested benefits that are due and payable at termination will be paid. Some benefits may be continued at the employee's expense if the employee so chooses. The employee will be notified in writing of the benefits that may be continued and of the terms, conditions, and limitations of such continuance. See the "Benefits Continuation (COBRA)" policy section 3-13.

4-09 Administrative Pay Corrections

__________ Company takes all reasonable steps to ensure that employees receive the correct amount of pay in each paycheck and that employees are paid promptly on the scheduled payday.

In the unlikely event that there is an error in the amount of pay, the employee should promptly bring the discrepancy to the attention of the Human Resources Department so that corrections can be made as quickly as possible.

4-10 Pay Deductions and Setoffs

The law requires that __________ Company make certain deductions from every employee's compensation. Among these are applicable federal, state, and local income taxes. __________ Company also must deduct Social Security taxes on each employee's earnings up to a specified limit that is called the Social Security "wage base." __________ Company matches the amount of Social Security taxes paid by each employee.

__________ Company offers programs and benefits beyond those required by law. Eligible employees may voluntarily authorize deductions from their paychecks to cover the costs of participation in these programs. Pay setoffs are pay deductions taken by __________ Company, usually to help pay off a debt or obligation to __________ Company or others. If you have questions concerning why deductions were made from your paycheck or how they were calculated, the Human Resources Department can assist in having your questions answered.

5-01 Safety

To assist in providing a safe and healthful work environment for employees, customers, and visitors, __________ Company has established a workplace safety program. This program is a top priority for __________ Company. The Human Resources Department has responsibility for implementing, administering, monitoring, and evaluating the safety program. Its success depends on the alertness and personal commitment of all.

__________ Company provides information to employees about workplace safety and health issues through regular internal communication channels such as supervisor-employee meetings, bulletin board postings, e-mail, memos, or other written communications.

Some of the best safety improvement ideas come from employees. Those with ideas, concerns, or suggestions for improved safety in the workplace are encouraged to raise them with their supervisor, or with another supervisor or manager, or bring them to the attention of the Human Resources Department. Reports and concerns about workplace safety issues may be made anonymously if the employee wishes. All reports can be made without fear of reprisal.

Each employee is expected to obey safety rules and to exercise caution in all work activities. Employees must immediately report any unsafe condition to the appropriate supervisor. Employees who violate safety standards, who cause hazardous or dangerous situations, or who fail to report or, where appropriate, remedy such situations may be subject to disciplinary action, up to and including termination of employment.

In the case of accidents that result in injury, regardless of how insignificant the injury may appear, employees should immediately notify the Human Resources Department or the appropriate supervisor. Such reports are necessary to comply with laws and initiate insurance and workers' compensation benefits procedures.

5-02 Work Schedules

Work schedules for employees vary throughout our organization. 9:00 a.m.-6:00 p.m. is a standard workday. Supervisors will advise employees of their individual work schedules. Staffing needs and operational demands may necessitate variations in starting and ending times, as well as variations in the total hours that may be scheduled each day and week.

5-04 Use of Phone and Mail Systems

Personal use of the telephone for long-distance and toll calls is not permitted. Employees should practice discretion when making local personal calls and may be required to reimburse __________ Company for any charges resulting from their personal use of the telephone. To ensure effective telephone communications, employees should always use the approved greeting ("Good Morning, __________ Company" or "Good Afternoon, __________ Company," as applicable) and speak in a courteous and professional manner. Please confirm information received from the caller and hang up only after the caller has done so.

The mail system is reserved for business purposes only. Employees should refrain from sending or receiving personal mail at the workplace. The e-mail system is the property of __________ Company. Occasional use of the e-mail system for personal messages is permitted, within reasonable limits. __________ Company will not guarantee the privacy of the e-mail system except to the extent required by law.

5-05 Smoking

Smoking is prohibited throughout the workplace, as required by law. This policy applies equally to all employees, customers, and visitors.

5-06 Rest and Meal Periods

All employees are provided with one one-hour meal period each workday. Supervisors will schedule meal periods to accommodate operating requirements. Employees will be relieved of all active responsibilities and restrictions during meal periods and will not be compensated for that time. Brief rest periods will be allowed, as required by California law.

5-10 Emergency Closings

At times, emergencies such as severe weather, fires, power failures, or earthquakes can disrupt company operations. In extreme cases, these circumstances may require the closing of a work facility.

In cases where an emergency closing is not authorized, employees who fail to report for work will not be paid for the time off. Employees may request available paid leave time such as unused vacation benefits.

5-12 Business Travel Expenses

__________ Company will reimburse employees for reasonable business travel expenses incurred while on assignments away from the normal work location. All business travel must be approved in advance by the President. Employees whose travel plans have been approved should make all travel arrangements through __________ Company's designated travel agency.

When approved, the actual costs of travel, meals, lodging, and other expenses directly related to accomplishing business travel objectives will be reimbursed by __________ Company. Employees are expected to limit expenses to reasonable amounts.

Expenses that generally will be reimbursed include the following:

- airfare or train fare for travel in coach or economy class or the lowest available fare
- car rental fees, only for compact or mid-sized cars
- fares for shuttle or airport bus service, where available; costs of public transportation for other ground travel
- taxi fares, only when there is no less expensive alternative
- mileage costs for use of personal cars, only when less expensive transportation is not available
- cost of standard accommodations in low- to mid-priced hotels, motels, or similar lodgings
- cost of meals, no more than $30.00 a day
- tips not exceeding 15% of the total cost of a meal or 10% of a taxi fare
- charges for telephone calls, fax, and similar services required for business purposes

Employees who are involved in an accident while traveling on business must promptly report the incident to their immediate supervisor. Vehicles owned, leased, or rented by __________ Company may not be used for personal use without prior approval. When travel is completed, employees should submit completed travel expense reports within 30 days. Reports should be accompanied by receipts for all individual expenses. Employees should contact their supervisor for guidance and assistance on procedures related to travel arrangements, expense reports, reimbursement for specific expenses, or any other business travel issues. Abuse of this business travel expenses policy, including falsifying expense reports to reflect costs not incurred by the employee, can be grounds for disciplinary action, up to and including termination of employment.

5-14 Visitors in the Workplace

To provide for the safety and security of employees and the facilities at __________ Company, only authorized visitors are allowed in the workplace. Restricting unauthorized visitors helps maintain safety standards, protects against theft, ensures security of equipment, protects confidential information, safeguards employee welfare, and avoids potential distractions and disturbances. All visitors should enter __________ Company at the main entrance. Authorized visitors will receive directions or be escorted to their destination. Employees are responsible for the conduct and safety of their visitors. If an unauthorized individual is observed on __________ Company's premises, employees should immediately notify their supervisor or, if necessary, direct the individual to the main entrance.

5-16 Computer and E-mail Usage

Computers, computer files, the e-mail system, and software furnished to employees are __________ Company property intended for business use. Employees should not use a password, access a file, or retrieve any stored communication without authorization.

__________ Company strives to maintain a workplace free of harassment and is sensitive to the diversity of its employees. Therefore, __________ Company prohibits the use of computers and the e-mail system in ways that are disruptive, offensive to others, or harmful to morale.

For example, the display or transmission of sexually explicit images, messages, and cartoons is not allowed. Other such misuse includes, but is not limited to, ethnic slurs, racial comments, off-color jokes, or anything that may be construed as harassment or showing disrespect for others. Employees should notify their immediate supervisor, the Human Resources Department, or any member of management upon learning of violations of this policy. Employees who violate this policy will be subject to disciplinary action, up to and including termination of employment.

5-17 Internet Usage

Internet access to global electronic information resources on the World Wide Web is provided by __________ Company to assist employees in obtaining work-related data and technology. The following guidelines have been established to help ensure responsible and productive Internet usage. While Internet usage is intended for job-related activities, incidental and occasional brief personal use of e-mail and the Internet is permitted within reasonable limits.

All Internet data that is composed, transmitted, or received via our computer communications systems is considered to be part of the official records of __________ Company and, as such, is subject to disclosure to law enforcement or other third parties. Employees should expect only the level of privacy that is warranted by existing law and no more. Consequently, employees should always ensure that the business information contained in Internet e-mail messages and other transmissions is accurate, appropriate, ethical, and lawful. Any questions regarding the legal effect of a message or transmission should be brought to our General Counsel.

Data that is composed, transmitted, accessed, or received via the Internet must not contain content that could be considered discriminatory, offensive, obscene, threatening, harassing, intimidating, or disruptive to any employee or other person. Examples of unacceptable content may include, but are not limited to, sexual comments or images, racial slurs, gender-specific comments, or any other comments or images that could reasonably offend someone on the basis of race, age, sex, religious or political beliefs, national origin, disability, sexual orientation, or any other characteristic protected by law.

The unauthorized use, installation, copying, or distribution of copyrighted, trademarked, or patented material on the Internet is expressly prohibited. As a general rule, if an employee did not create material, does not own the rights to it, or has not gotten authorization for its use, it should not be put on the Internet. Employees are also responsible for ensuring that the person sending any material over the Internet has the appropriate distribution rights. Any questions regarding the use of such information should be brought to our General Counsel.

Internet users should take the necessary anti-virus precautions before downloading or copying any file from the Internet. All downloaded files are to be checked for viruses; all compressed files are to be checked before and after decompression.

Abuse of the Internet access provided by __________ Company in violation of the law or __________ Company policies will result in disciplinary action, up to and including termination of employment. Employees may also be held personally liable for any violations of this policy. The following behaviors are examples of previously stated or additional actions and activities that are prohibited and can result in disciplinary action:

- Sending or posting discriminatory, harassing, or threatening messages or images
- Using the organization's time and resources for personal gain
- Stealing, using, or disclosing someone else's code or password without authorization
- Copying, pirating, or downloading software and electronic files without permission
- Sending or posting confidential material, trade secrets, or proprietary information outside of the organization
- Violating copyright law
- Failing to observe licensing agreements
- Engaging in unauthorized transactions that may incur a cost to the organization or initiate unwanted Internet services and transmissions
- Sending or posting messages or material that could damage the organization's image or reputation
- Participating in the viewing or exchange of pornography or obscene materials
- Sending or posting messages that defame or slander other individuals

- Attempting to break into the computer system of another organization or person
- Refusing to cooperate with a security investigation
- Sending or posting chain letters, solicitations, or advertisements not related to business purposes or activities
- Using the Internet for political causes or activities, religious activities, or any sort of gambling
- Jeopardizing the security of the organization's electronic communications systems
- Sending or posting messages that disparage another organization's products or services
- Passing off personal views as representing those of the organization
- Sending anonymous e-mail messages
- Engaging in any other illegal activities

5-22 Workplace Violence Prevention

__________ Company is committed to preventing workplace violence and to maintaining a safe work environment. Given the increasing violence in society in general, __________ Company has adopted the following guidelines to deal with intimidation, harassment, or other threats of (or actual) violence that may occur during business hours or on its premises.

All employees, including supervisors and temporary employees, should be treated with courtesy and respect at all times. Employees are expected to refrain from fighting, "horseplay," or other conduct that may be dangerous to others. Firearms, weapons, and other dangerous or hazardous devices or substances are prohibited from the premises of __________ Company without proper authorization.

Conduct that threatens, intimidates, or coerces another employee, a customer, or a member of the public at any time, including off-duty periods, will not be tolerated. This prohibition includes all acts of harassment, including harassment that is based on an individual's sex, race, age, or any characteristic protected by federal, state, or local law.

All threats of (or actual) violence, both direct and indirect, should be reported as soon as possible to your immediate supervisor or any other member of management. This includes threats by employees, as well as threats by customers, vendors, solicitors, or other members of the public. When reporting a threat of violence, you should be as specific and detailed as possible.

All suspicious individuals or activities should also be reported as soon as possible to a supervisor. Do not place yourself in peril. If you see or hear a commotion or disturbance near your workstation, do not try to intercede or see what is happening. __________ Company will promptly and thoroughly investigate all reports of threats of (or actual) violence and of suspicious individuals or activities. The identity of the individual making a report will be protected as much as is practical.

Anyone determined to be responsible for threats of (or actual) violence or other conduct that is in violation of these guidelines will be subject to prompt disciplinary action, up to and including termination of employment.

__________ Company encourages employees to bring their disputes or differences with other employees to the attention of their supervisors or the Human Resources Department before the situation escalates into potential violence. __________ Company is eager to assist in the resolution of employee disputes and will not discipline employees for raising such concerns.

6-01 Medical Leave

__________ Company provides medical leaves of absence without pay to eligible employees who are temporarily unable to work due to a serious health condition or disability. For purposes of this policy, serious health conditions or disabilities include inpatient care in a hospital, hospice, or residential medical care facility and continuing treatment by a health care provider.

Employees in the following employment classifications are eligible to request medical leave as described in this policy:

Regular full-time employees

Eligible employees should make requests for medical leave to their supervisors at least 30 days in advance of foreseeable events and as soon as possible for unforeseeable events.

A health care provider's statement must be submitted verifying the need for medical leave and its beginning and expected ending dates. Any changes in this information should be promptly reported to __________ Company. Employees returning from medical leave must submit a health care provider's verification of their fitness to return to work.

Eligible employees are normally granted leave for the period of the disability, up to a maximum of 12 weeks within any 12-month period. Any combination of medical leave and family leave may not exceed this maximum limit. If the initial period of approved absence proves insufficient, consideration will be given to a request for an extension.

Employees who sustain work-related injuries are eligible for a medical leave of absence for the period of the disability, in accordance with all applicable laws covering occupational disabilities.

Subject to the terms, conditions, and limitations of the applicable plans, __________ Company will continue to provide health insurance benefits for the full period of the approved medical leave.

Benefit accruals, such as vacation, sick leave, and holiday benefits, will continue during the approved medical leave period.

So that an employee's return to work can be properly scheduled, an employee on medical leave is requested to provide __________ Company with at least two weeks' advance notice of the date the employee intends to return to work. When a medical leave ends, the employee will be reinstated to the same position, if it is available, or to an equivalent position for which the employee is qualified.

If an employee fails to return to work on the agreed-upon return date, __________ Company will assume that the employee has resigned.

6-02 Family Leave

__________ Company provides family leaves of absence without pay to eligible employees who wish to take time off from work duties to fulfill family obligations relating directly to childbirth, adoption, or placement of a foster child or to care for a child, spouse, or parent with a serious health condition. A "serious health condition" means an illness, injury, impairment, or physical or mental condition that involves inpatient care in a hospital, hospice, or residential medical care facility or continuing treatment by a health care provider.

Employees in the following employment classifications are eligible to request family leave as described in this policy:

Regular full-time employees

Eligible employees should make requests for family leave to their supervisors at least 30 days in advance of foreseeable events and as soon as possible for unforeseeable events. Employees requesting family leave related to the serious health condition of a child, spouse, or parent may be required to submit a health care provider's statement verifying the need for family leave to provide care, its beginning and expected ending dates, and the estimated time required.

Eligible employees may request up to a maximum of 12 weeks of family leave within any 12-month period. Any combination of family leave and medical leave may not exceed this maximum. Married employee couples may be restricted to a combined total of 12 weeks leave within any 12-month period for childbirth, adoption, or placement of a foster child or to care for a parent with a serious health condition.

Subject to the terms, conditions, and limitations of the applicable plans, __________ Company will continue to provide health insurance benefits for the full period of the approved family leave. Benefit accruals, such as vacation, sick leave, and holiday benefits, will continue during the approved family leave period.

So that an employee's return to work can be properly scheduled, an employee on family leave is requested to provide __________ Company with at least two weeks' advance notice of the date the employee intends to return to work. When a family leave ends, the employee will be reinstated to the same position, if it is available, or to an equivalent position for which the employee is qualified. If an employee fails to return to work on the agreed-upon return date, __________ Company will assume that the employee has resigned.

6-07 Pregnancy Disability Leave

__________ Company provides pregnancy disability leaves of absence without pay to eligible employees who are temporarily unable to work due to a disability related to pregnancy, childbirth, or related medical conditions. Any employee is eligible to request pregnancy disability leave as described in this policy. Employees should make requests for pregnancy disability leave to their supervisors at least 30 days in advance of foreseeable events and as soon as possible for unforeseeable events. A health care provider's statement must be submitted verifying the need for pregnancy disability leave and its beginning and expected ending dates. Any changes in this information should be promptly reported to __________ Company. Employees returning from pregnancy disability leave must submit a health care provider's verification of their fitness to return to work.

Employees are normally granted unpaid leave for the period of the disability, up to a maximum of four months. Employees may substitute any accrued paid leave time for unpaid leave as part of the pregnancy disability leave period. Subject to the terms, conditions, and limitations of the applicable plans, __________ Company will continue to provide health insurance benefits for the full period of the approved pregnancy disability leave. So that an employee's return to work can be properly scheduled, an employee on pregnancy disability leave is requested to provide __________ Company with at least two weeks' advance notice of the date she intends to return to work.

When a pregnancy disability leave ends, the employee will be reinstated to the same position, unless either the employee would not otherwise have been employed for legitimate business reasons or each means of preserving the job would substantially undermine the ability to operate __________ Company safely and efficiently. If the same position is not available, the employee will be offered a comparable position in terms of such issues as pay, location, job content, and promotional opportunities.

If an employee fails to report to work promptly at the end of the pregnancy disability leave, __________ Company will assume that the employee has resigned.

7-01 Employee Conduct and Work Rules

To ensure orderly operations and provide the best possible work environment, __________ Company expects employees to follow rules of conduct that will protect the interests and safety of all employees and the organization.

It is not possible to list all the forms of behavior that are considered unacceptable in the workplace. The following are examples of infractions of rules of conduct that may result in disciplinary action, up to and including termination of employment:

- Theft or inappropriate removal or possession of property
- Falsification of timekeeping records
- Working under the influence of alcohol or illegal drugs
- Possession, distribution, sale, transfer, or use of alcohol or illegal drugs in the workplace, while on duty or while operating employer-owned vehicles or equipment
- Fighting or threatening violence in the workplace
- Boisterous or disruptive activity in the workplace
- Negligence or improper conduct leading to damage of employer-owned or customer-owned property
- Insubordination or other disrespectful conduct
- Violation of safety or health rules
- Smoking in the workplace

- Sexual or other unlawful or unwelcome harassment
- Possession of dangerous or unauthorized materials, such as explosives or firearms, in the workplace
- Excessive absenteeism or any absence without notice
- Unauthorized disclosure of business "secrets" or confidential information
- Violation of personnel policies
- Unsatisfactory performance or conduct

Nothing is this policy is intended to change the company's at-will employment policy. Employment with __________ Company is at the mutual consent of __________ Company and the employee, and either party may terminate that relationship at any time, with or without cause, and with or without advance notice.

7-02 Drug and Alcohol Use

It is __________ Company's desire to provide a drug-free, healthful, and safe workplace. To promote this goal, employees are required to report to work in appropriate mental and physical condition to perform their jobs in a satisfactory manner.

While on __________ Company premises and while conducting business-related activities off __________ Company premises, no employee may use, possess, distribute, sell, or be under the influence of alcohol or illegal drugs. The legal use of prescribed drugs is permitted on the job only if it does not impair an employee's ability to perform the essential functions of the job effectively and in a safe manner that does not endanger other individuals in the workplace.

Violations of this policy may lead to disciplinary action, up to and including immediate termination of employment, and/or required participation in a substance abuse rehabilitation or treatment program. Such violations may also have legal consequences.

Employees with questions or concerns about substance dependency or abuse are encouraged to discuss these matters with their supervisor or the Human Resources Department to receive assistance or referrals to appropriate resources in the community.

Employees with problems with alcohol and certain drugs that have not resulted in, and are not the immediate subject of, disciplinary action may request approval to take unpaid time off to participate in a rehabilitation or treatment program through __________ Company's health insurance benefit coverage. Leave may be granted if the employee agrees to abstain from use of the problem substance and abides by all __________ Company policies, rules, and prohibitions relating to conduct in the workplace; and if granting the leave will not cause __________ Company any undue hardship.

Employees with questions on this policy or issues related to drug or alcohol use in the workplace should raise their concerns with their supervisor or the Human Resources Department without fear of reprisal.

7-03 Sexual and Other Unlawful Harassment

__________ Company is committed to providing a work environment that is free from all forms of discrimination and conduct that can be considered harassing, coercive, or disruptive, including sexual harassment. Actions, words, jokes, or comments based on an individual's sex, race, color, national origin, age, religion, disability, sexual orientation, or any other legally protected characteristic will not be tolerated.

Sexual harassment is defined as unwanted sexual advances, or visual, verbal, or physical conduct of a sexual nature. This definition includes many forms of offensive behavior and includes gender-based harassment of a person of the same sex as the harasser. The following is a partial list of sexual harassment examples:

- Unwanted sexual advances
- Offering employment benefits in exchange for sexual favors
- Making or threatening reprisals after a negative response to sexual advances

- Visual conduct that includes leering, making sexual gestures, or displaying of sexually suggestive objects or pictures, cartoons, or posters
- Verbal conduct that includes making or using derogatory comments, epithets, slurs, or jokes
- Verbal sexual advances or propositions
- Verbal abuse of a sexual nature, graphic verbal commentaries about an individual's body, sexually degrading words used to describe an individual, or suggestive or obscene letters, notes, or invitations
- Physical conduct that includes touching, assaulting, or impeding or blocking movements

Unwelcome sexual advances (either verbal or physical), requests for sexual favors, and other verbal or physical conduct of a sexual nature constitute sexual harassment when: (1) submission to such conduct is made either explicitly or implicitly a term or condition of employment; (2) submission to or rejection of the conduct is used as a basis for making employment decisions; or (3) the conduct has the purpose or effect of interfering with work performance or creating an intimidating, hostile, or offensive work environment.

If you experience or witness sexual or other unlawful harassment in the workplace, report it immediately to your supervisor. If the supervisor is unavailable or you believe it would be inappropriate to contact that person, you should immediately contact the Human Resources Department or any other member of management. You can raise concerns and make reports without fear of reprisal or retaliation.

All allegations of sexual harassment will be quickly and discreetly investigated. To the extent possible, your confidentiality and that of any witnesses and the alleged harasser will be protected against unnecessary disclosure. When the investigation is completed, you will be informed of the outcome of the investigation.

Any supervisor or manager who becomes aware of possible sexual or other unlawful harassment must immediately advise the Human Resources Department or the President of the company so it can be investigated in a timely and confidential manner. Anyone engaging in sexual or other unlawful behavior will be subject to disciplinary action, up to and including termination of employment.

7-04 Attendance and Punctuality

To maintain a safe and productive work environment, __________ Company expects employees to be reliable and to be punctual in reporting for scheduled work. Absenteeism and tardiness place a burden on other employees and on __________ Company. In the rare instances when employees cannot avoid being late to work or are unable to work as scheduled, they should notify their supervisor or the Human Resources Department as soon as possible in advance of the anticipated tardiness or absence.

Poor attendance and excessive tardiness are disruptive. Either may lead to disciplinary action, up to and including termination of employment.

7-05 Personal Appearance

Dress, grooming, and personal cleanliness standards contribute to the morale of all employees and affect the business image that __________ Company presents to the community.

During business hours or when representing __________ Company, you are expected to present a clean, neat, and tasteful appearance. You should dress and groom yourself according to the requirements of your position and accepted social standards.

Your supervisor or department head is responsible for establishing a reasonable dress code appropriate to the job you perform. If your supervisor feels that your personal appearance is inappropriate, you may be asked to leave the workplace until you are properly dressed or groomed. Under such circumstances, you will not be compensated for the time away from work. Consult your supervisor if you have questions as to what constitutes appropriate appearance. Where necessary, reasonable accommodation may be made to a person with a disability.

7-06 Return of Property

Employees are responsible for all __________ Company property, materials, or written information issued to them or in their possession or control. Employees must return all __________ Company property immediately upon request or upon termination of employment. Where permitted by applicable laws, __________ Company may withhold from the employee's check or final paycheck the cost of any items that are not returned when required. __________ Company may also take all action deemed appropriate to recover or protect its property.

7-08 Resignation

Resignation is a voluntary act initiated by the employee to terminate employment with __________ Company. Although advance notice is not required, __________ Company requests at least two weeks' written notice of resignation from nonexempt employees and two weeks' written notice of resignation from exempt employees.

Prior to an employee's departure, an exit interview will be scheduled to discuss the reasons for resignation and the effect of the resignation on benefits.

7-10 Security Inspections

__________ Company wishes to maintain a work environment that is free of illegal drugs, alcohol, firearms, explosives, or other improper materials. To this end, __________ Company prohibits the possession, transfer, sale, or use of such materials on its premises. __________ Company requires the cooperation of all employees in administering this policy.

Desks, lockers, and other storage devices may be provided for the convenience of employees but remain the sole property of __________ Company. Accordingly, they, as well as any articles found within them, can be inspected by any agent or representative of __________ Company at any time, either with or without prior notice.

7-12 Solicitation

In an effort to ensure a productive and harmonious work environment, persons not employed by __________ Company may not solicit or distribute literature in the workplace at any time for any purpose.

__________ Company recognizes that employees may have interests in events and organizations outside the workplace. However, employees may not solicit or distribute literature concerning these activities during working time. (Working time does not include lunch periods, work breaks, or any other periods in which employees are not on duty.)

Examples of impermissible forms of solicitation include:

- The collection of money, goods, or gifts for community groups
- The collection of money, goods, or gifts for religious groups
- The collection of money, goods, or gifts for political groups
- The collection of money, goods, or gifts for charitable groups
- The sale of goods, services, or subscriptions outside the scope of official organization business
- The circulation of petitions
- The distribution of literature in working areas at any time
- The solicitation of memberships, fees, or dues

In addition, the posting of written solicitations on company bulletin boards and solicitations by e-mail are restricted. Company bulletin boards display important information; employees should consult them frequently for:

- Affirmative Action statement
- Employee announcements
- Workers' compensation insurance information
- State disability insurance/unemployment insurance information

If employees have a message of interest to the workplace, they may submit it to the Human Resources Director for approval. All approved messages will be posted by the Human Resources Director.

7-16 Progressive Discipline

The purpose of this policy is to state __________ Company's position on administering equitable and consistent discipline for unsatisfactory conduct in the workplace. The best disciplinary measure is the one that does not have to be enforced and comes from good leadership and fair supervision at all employment levels.

__________ Company's own best interest lies in ensuring fair treatment of all employees and in making certain that disciplinary actions are prompt, uniform, and impartial. The major purpose of any disciplinary action is to correct the problem, prevent recurrence, and prepare the employee for satisfactory service in the future.

Although employment with __________ Company is based on mutual consent and both the employee and __________ Company have the right to terminate employment at will, with or without cause or advance notice, __________ Company may use progressive discipline at its discretion.

Disciplinary action may call for any of four steps–verbal warning, written warning, suspension with or without pay, or termination of employment–depending on the severity of the problem and the number of occurrences.

Progressive discipline means that, with respect to many disciplinary problems, these four steps will normally be followed. However, there may be circumstances when one or more steps are bypassed.

__________ Company recognizes that there are certain types of employee problems that are serious enough to justify either a suspension or, in extreme situations, termination of employment, without going through the usual progressive discipline steps.

While it is impossible to list every type of behavior that may be deemed a serious offense, the Employee Conduct and Work Rules policy includes examples of problems that may result in immediate suspension or termination of employment. However, the problems listed are not all necessarily serious offenses, but may be examples of unsatisfactory conduct that will trigger progressive discipline.

By using progressive discipline, we hope that most employee problems can be corrected at an early stage, benefiting both the employee and __________ Company.

7-18 Problem Resolution

__________ Company is committed to providing the best possible working conditions for its employees. Part of this commitment is encouraging an open and frank atmosphere in which any problem, complaint, suggestion, or question receives a timely response from __________ Company supervisors and management.

__________ Company strives to ensure fair and honest treatment of all employees. Supervisors, managers, and employees are expected to treat each other with respect. Employees are encouraged to offer positive and constructive criticism.

If employees disagree with established rules of conduct, policies, or practices, they can express their concern through the problem resolution procedure. No employee will be penalized, formally or informally, for voicing a complaint with __________ Company in a reasonable, business-like manner, or for using the problem resolution procedure.

If a situation occurs when employees believe that a condition of employment or a decision affecting them is unjust or inequitable, they are encouraged to make use of the following steps. The employee may discontinue the procedure at any step.

1. The employee presents the problem to his or her immediate supervisor after the incident occurs. If the supervisor is unavailable or the employee believes it would be inappropriate to contact that person, the employee may present the problem to the Human Resources Department or the CEO.

2. The supervisor responds to the problem during discussion or after consulting with appropriate management, when necessary. The supervisor documents this discussion.
3. The employee presents the problem to the Human Resources Department if the problem is unresolved.
4. The Human Resources Department counsels and advises the employee, assists in putting the problem in writing, and visits with the employee's manager(s).

Not every problem can be resolved to everyone's total satisfaction, but only through understanding and discussing mutual problems can employees and management develop confidence in each other. This confidence is important to the operation of an efficient and harmonious work environment.

8-00 Life-Threatening Illnesses in the Workplace

Employees with life-threatening illnesses, such as cancer, heart disease, and AIDS, often wish to continue their normal pursuits, including work, to the extent allowed by their condition. __________ Company supports these endeavors as long as the employees are able to meet acceptable performance standards. As in the case of other disabilities, __________ Company will make reasonable accommodations in accordance with all legal requirements, to allow qualified employees with life-threatening illnesses to perform the essential functions of their jobs.

Medical information on individual employees is treated confidentially. __________ Company will take reasonable precautions to protect such information from inappropriate disclosure. Managers and other employees have a responsibility to respect and maintain the confidentiality of employee medical information. Anyone inappropriately disclosing such information is subject to disciplinary action, up to and including termination of employment.

Employees with questions or concerns about life-threatening illnesses are encouraged to contact the Human Resources Department for information and referral to appropriate services and resources.

8-06 Suggestions

As employees of __________ Company, you have the opportunity to contribute to our future success and growth by submitting suggestions for practical work-improvement or cost-savings ideas.

All regular employees are eligible to participate in the suggestion program.

A suggestion is an idea that will benefit __________ Company by solving a problem, reducing costs, improving operations or procedures, enhancing customer service, eliminating waste or spoilage, or making __________ Company a better or safer place to work. All suggestions should contain a description of the problem or condition to be improved, a detailed explanation of the solution or improvement, and the reasons why it should be implemented. Statements of problems without accompanying solutions or recommendations concerning co-workers and management are not appropriate suggestions. If you have questions or need advice about your idea, contact your supervisor for help.

Submit suggestions to the Human Resources Department and, after review, they will be forwarded to the Suggestion Committee. As soon as possible, you will be notified of the adoption or rejection of your suggestion. Special recognition and, optionally, a cash award will be given to employees who submit a suggestion that is implemented.

14. Acknowledgment of Receipt of Employee Handbook

The Employee Handbook describes important information about _______________ Company, and I understand that I should consult the Human Resources Department regarding any questions not answered in the Employee Handbook.

Since the information, policies, and benefits described here are necessarily subject to change, I acknowledge that revisions to the Employee Handbook may occur. All such changes will be communicated through official notices. I understand that revised information may supersede, modify, or eliminate existing policies.

Furthermore, I acknowledge that this Employee Handbook is neither a contract of employment nor a legal document. I have received the Employee Handbook and I understand that it is my responsibility to read and comply with the policies contained in this Employee Handbook and any revisions made to it.

Employee's Name (printed): ____________________________________

Employee's Signature: ____________________________________

Date: ________________

15. Employee Personal Information

You should have your new employee complete this form only after he or she has been hired. This information should be kept with the company's important records and should remain strictly confidential.

Date___________________

Last Name________________________________ First_________________________ Middle ______

Street Address ____

City____ State _____________ ZIP _____________

Home Phone Number ________________________________

Driver's License Number_______________________________________

Social Security Number______________________________________

Marital Status: ❑ Single ❑ Married ❑ Divorced

Date of Birth __________________________

Height: _____________ft. ____________in.

Weight _____________lbs.

Sex: ❑ Male ❑ Female

Name of Spouse ____

Phone _______________________________________

Spouse's Employer ____

Person to notify in case of emergency other than your spouse:

Name____ Relation __________________________

Phone ___________________________ Cell Phone ___________________________

What was your previous address? ____

____

How long have you been at your present address? _____________ Years

Please fill out and return to the Human Resources Department.

16. Employee Vacation Request

Employee Name____ Date______________

Employee has requested vacation from the following date ______________ to the following date ______________.

Total Vacation Days Accrued _______

Total Vacation Days Taken _______

Total Vacation Days Available _______

Number of Days Requested _______

Total Vacation Days Remaining _______

(if request approved)

Approval __________________

Manager Signature __________________________________ Date ______________

17. Payroll Deduction Authorization

I authorize ____

to deduct $ ____

from my gross earnings each payroll period beginning ______________________________

In payment for:	Amount:
❑ Credit Union	$__________
❑ Employee Savings Plan	$__________
❑ 401(k) Plan	$__________
❑ Union Dues	$__________
❑ ____________	$__________
❑ ____________	$__________
❑ ____________	$__________
❑ ____________	$__________
Total	$__________

Signature ____________________________ Date ______________

Print Name ____

Social Security # ___________________________

Please keep a copy of this for your records.

18. Payroll Deduction Authorization

I authorize ______________________________

to deduct $ ______________________________

from my gross earnings each payroll period beginning ______________________________

in payment for ____

These deductions are to continue until the amount of my obligation is paid in full or until my employment with this company is terminated for any reason. If my employment is terminated before this obligation is paid, I agree to pay the balance owed on or before the termination date.

Signature ______________________________ Date ______________

Print Name ______________________________

Social Security # __________________________

Please keep a copy of this for your records.

19. Direct Deposit Authorization

Name ______________________________________

ID # ______________________________________

Social Security # ____________________________

Bank Name and Branch ____

Account Number ____

❑ Yes, Direct Deposit:

I hereby request the deposit of my entire net payroll check into the specified bank account each pay period.

I authorize ______________________________ and ____________________________________
to withdraw any funds deposited in error into my account.

❑ Yes, Direct Payroll Deduction:

I hereby request and authorize the sum of ________________________ dollars ($________________)
be deducted from my paycheck each pay period and deposited directly into the bank account named above.

❑ I would like to cancel my deposit authorization:

I hereby cancel the authorization for direct deposit or payroll deduction deposit previously submitted.

Employee Signature ________________________________Date ________________

Please attach a copy of the deposit slip.

20. Pay for Meal Period

To: ______________________________ (employee)

Since the nature of your job prevents us from relieving you of all duty and responsibilities during your regular meal period, we will pay you for an on-the-job meal period at your regular rate of pay.

If you voluntarily agree to this arrangement, please sign below.

Manager ____ Date ________________

Agreed:

Employee Signature ________________________________ Date ________________

21. Personnel Requisition (Non-Management)

Job Title ______________________________

Department ______________________________

Reports to ______________________________

Pay Grade ______________________________

Date Required ______________________ ❑ Full Time ❑ Part Time

If part time, what is length needed? ______________________

Hours/Days ______________________________

New Position? ❑ Yes ❑ No If yes, approved? ______________________

Replacement? ❑ Yes ❑ No Name ______________________

Position budgeted for? ❑ Yes ❑ No Amount $ ______________

Outside agency used for recruitment? ❑ Yes ❑ No Name ______________

Outside Recruitment Budget Amount $ ______________________

Major Job Responsibilities ______________________________

____

____

Minimum Qualifications ______________________________

____

____

Special Knowledge, Skills and Ability Required ______________________

____

____

Requested by ______________________________ Date ______________

Approved by ______________________________ Date ______________

To be filled out by Human Resources Department.

Date Received______________________________ Date Job Filled ______________

Employee Name ____

22. Personnel Requisition (Management)

Job Title ______________________________

Department ______________________________

Reports to ______________________ ❑ Exempt ❑ Non-Exempt

Recruitment Start Date ______________________

Projected Start Date ______________________

Hiring Salary between __________ and __________ per __________

Bonus Applicable? ❑ Yes ❑ No Amount $ ______________

Other Special Benefits ______________________________

____

Position budgeted for? ❑ Yes ❑ No Amount $ ______________

Outside agency used for recruitment? ❑ Yes ❑ No Name ______________

Outside Recruitment Budget Amount $ ______________

Major Job Responsibilities ______________________________

____

____

____

Minimum Qualifications ______________________________

____

____

____

A successful candidate will possess the following: ______________________________

____

____

____

Number of Subordinates to Supervise ______________

Titles of Subordinates ______________________________

Budget Accountability ______________________________

Assets ______________________________

Special Considerations and Requirements (travel, location, hours, etc.) ______________

____

____

Indicate the level of responsibility and frequency of occurrence for each area of work. Please add areas of work if appropriate. Consider 1 the lowest and 4 the highest. Circle appropriate number.

Area of Work					Comments
Planning/Organizing Others' Work	1	2	3	4	___
Planning/Organizing Own Work	1	2	3	4	___
Leadership	1	2	3	4	___
Training	1	2	3	4	___
Policy Development	1	2	3	4	___
Employee Relations	1	2	3	4	___
Long-Range Planning	1	2	3	4	___
Problem Solving	1	2	3	4	___
Personnel Selection	1	2	3	4	___
Creativity, New Ideas	1	2	3	4	___
Internal Contacts	1	2	3	4	___
Outside Contacts	1	2	3	4	___

Submitted by ______________________ Date ____________

Approved by ______________________ Date ____________

Position Filled Date ____________ Salary ____________

23. Salary Recommendation Form

Employee Name ______________________________

ID # ______________________________

Location ______________________________

Department ______________________________

	Current	Proposed
Title	____________	____________
Salary Grade	____________	____________
Base Rate	____________	____________
Merit Amount	____________	____________
Promotion Amount	____________	____________
Other Amount	____________	____________
Bonus	____________	____________

Effective Date ______________________________

Type of Proposed Increase: ❑ New Hire ❑ Merit ❑ Promotion ❑ Other ____________

Date of Last Increase ____________

Type of Last Increase: ❑ New Hire ❑ Merit ❑ Promotion ❑ Other ____________

Explanation for Proposed Salary Increase ______________________________

____

____

____

Approvals:

Supervisor ______________________________ Date ____________

Manager ______________________________ Date ____________

Division Vice President ______________________________ Date ____________

Human Resources Department ______________________________ Date ____________

24. Job Announcement: Open Position

Job Title ____________________

Department ____________________

Pay Grade ____________________ ❑ Exempt ❑ Non-Exempt

Reports to ____________________

Job Summary ____________________

____

____

____

Job Minimum Qualifications (special skills, education, etc.) ____________________

____

____

____

____

____

____

Interested candidate should contact the Human Resources Department by ____________________

Posted Date ____________________

To be eligible for consideration for the above position you must have been in your current position a minimum of ____________________ months.

25. Job Posting: Open Position

Job Title ____________________

Department ____________________

Pay Grade ____________________ ❑ Exempt ❑ Non-Exempt

Reports to ____________________

Location ____________________

Job Summary ____________________

____

____

____

Duties and Responsibilities ____________________

____

____

____

____

____

____

Minimum Requirements ____________________

____

____

____

Job Posting Date ____________________

All bids must be received by the Human Resources Department within 10 days of the job posting.

26. Job Position Description

Job Title ______________________________

Grade ______________________________

Pay Range ______________________________

Reports to ______________________________

Job Class ______________________________

Location ______________________________

Department ______________________________

Job Summary ______________________________

Duties and Responsibilities ______________________________

Supervision:

Received ______________________________

Given ______________________________

Position Minimum Requirements:

Education ______________________________

Experience ______________________________

Responsibility ______________________________

Initiative ______________________________

____

____

Skills ______________________________

____

____

Physical Requirements ______________________________

____

____

Mental Requirements ______________________________

____

____

Supervision ______________________________

____

____

Equipment Used ______________________________

____

____

Other ______________________________

____

____

Prepared by ______________________ Date ______________

Approved by ______________________ Date ______________

27. Personnel Data Change Form

Effective Date ______________________________

Employee Name (previous name if changed) ____

For Changes Only:

Name ____

Address ____

____

Phone Number ____

Marital Status:

❏ Single

❏ Married

❏ Divorced

Note: An employee is not obligated to report marital status to his or her employer, but the employee may wish to report marital status so the employer can adjust the tax withholding amount.

Signature ____ Date ________________

Please fill out and return to the Human Resources Department.

28. Employee Status Change

Name ______________________________

Employer ID # ______________________________

Department ______________________________

Effective Date ______________________________

Wage/Salary/Title Change:

	Title	Grade	Pay Rate	Increase %
Present	________	________	________	________
Proposed	________	________	________	________

Type of Change: (check appropriate type)

❑ New Hire ❑ Voluntary Resignation

❑ Promotion ❑ Leave of Absence

❑ Other ❑ Sick Leave

❑ Transfer ❑ Layoff

❑ Return from Absence ❑ Disability-Not Work-Related

❑ Termination ❑ Disability-Work-Related

If leave of absence, state duration: from ______________ to ______________

Comments and reasons for change: ______________________________

____

____

____

Submitted by:

Supervisor ______________________ Title ______________ Date ________

Approvals:

Department Manager ______________________ Date ________

Human Resources Manager ______________________ Date ________

Original to Department Manager, copy to Human Resources File.

29. Career Development Worksheet for Management Employee Career Interests

Employee ______________________________ Date ______________

Job Title ____________________ Department ______________ Job Grade ______________

Employees who are satisfied with their present position and do not wish to be considered for other positions should omit Section II when completing this form.

I. Development Goals for the Coming Year:

A. What are your development goals for the coming year? ______________________________

____

____

B. Can you meet these goals, or some of them, through your present work assignment?

C. Indicate any specific training programs, developmental experiences, job assignments or job structure changes that you feel would be beneficial. Please explain.

II. Longer-Range Career Goals:

A. What are your longer-range career aspirations? ______________________________

____

____

B. In your judgment, is your present assignment suitable, given your longer-range aspirations? Please explain.

____

____

____

C. Do you want to be considered for assignment in another function or department? If yes, please specify.

____

____

____

D. What are your main strengths that you would like to have considered in future job assignments?

____

____

____

E. Please describe ways you feel the company could help you prepare yourself for future career opportunities.

____

____

____

III. Location Preferences:

A. Are you willing to relocate now to develop your skills? ❑ Yes ❑ No

B. Will you be willing to relocate within the next five years? If yes, please indicate time frame:

❑ one year ❑ two years ❑ three years ❑ four years ❑ five years

C. Please describe any location restrictions.

____

____

IV. Developmental Progress:

Summarize what you have done this past year to improve work performance and prepare for future responsibilities.

____

____

____

____

____

V. Additional Comments:

____

____

____

____

____

Employee Signature ________________________________ Date ______________

30. Career Development Worksheet for Non-Management Employee Career Interests

Employee ____________________ Date ____________

Job Title ____________________ Job Grade ____________

Department ____________________

Please answer each question wherever you have a preference or an opinion. However, it is not necessary to state a conclusion in each area. Indicate approximate timing where appropriate. This will help us ensure that your personal goals are considered in the career-planning process.

I. Personal Career Goals

A. What are your short- and long-term career aspirations?

____

____

____

B. Do you feel your present job assignment is suitable, given your longer-range aspirations? If so, for how long? If not, please explain.

____

____

____

C. Do you want to be considered for assignment in another function or department? If yes, please specify.

____

____

____

D. What are your current and future plans for self-improvement? (i.e., education, etc.)

____

____

____

E. Please describe ways you feel the company could help you prepare for future career opportunities. What training programs, developmental experiences, job assignments, or job structure changes do you feel would be beneficial?

____

____

____

II. Location Preferences

A. Are you willing to relocate now to develop your skills? ❑ Yes ❑ No

B. Will you be willing to relocate within the next five years? __________ If yes, please indicate time frame:

❑ one year ❑ two years ❑ three years ❑ four years ❑ five years

C. Please describe any location restrictions.

____

____

____

III. Additional Comments

____

____

____

____

____

____

Employee Signature ________________________ **Date** __________

31. Employee Career Development Worksheet Objectives and Results

Employee ______________________________

Job Title ______________________________

Supervisor ______________________________

Period: from ______________ to ______________

Date Written ______________________________

Date Results Reviewed ______________________________

Major Objectives

____

____

____

____

Actions to Achieve Objectives

____

____

____

____

Performance Measures

____

____

____

____

Progress or Outside Influences Uncontrollable by Employee

____

____

____

____

Performance Results

____

____

____

____

32. Employee Incident and Discipline Documentation Form

Employee Information

Name of Employee ____

Employee's Job Title ____

Incident Information

Date/Time of Incident ____

Location of Incident ____

Description of Incident ____

____

____

____

Witnesses to Incident ____

Was this incident in violation of a company policy? ❑ Yes ❑ No

If yes, specify which policy and how the incident violated it. ________________________

____

____

Action Taken

What action will be taken against the employee? ______________________________

____

____

Has the impropriety of the employee's actions been explained to the employee? ❑ Yes ❑ No

Did the employee offer any explanation for the conduct? If so, what was it? ____________________

____

____

Signature of person preparing report ________________________

Date ____

33. Disciplinary Notice

Employee ______________________________

Department ______________________________

❑ Written Warning ❑ Final Warning

1. Statement of the problem (violation of rules, policies, standards, practices, or unsatisfactory performance):

____

____

____

2. Prior discussion or warnings on this subject (oral, written, dates):

____

____

____

____

3. Statement of company policy on this subject:

____

____

____

4. Summary of corrective action to be taken (including dates for improvement and plans for follow-up):

____

____

____

5. Consequences of failure to improve performance or correct behavior:

____

____

____

6. Employee comments: ______________________________

____

____

____

(Continue on reverse if necessary.)

Employee Signature ______________________________ Date ______________

Management Approval ______________________________ Date ______________

Distribution: One copy to Employee, one copy to Supervisor, and original to Personnel File.

34. Employee Performance Review

Name ____________________

Job Title ____________________

Department ____________________

Supervisor ____________________

Date Hired ____________ Last Review Date ____________ This Review Date ____________

The following definitions apply to each factor rated below

Level 6–Far Exceeds Job Requirements
Performance at this level far exceeds the requirements for this position.
Duties and responsibilities are exceptionally met and consistently exceeded.

Level 5–Consistently Exceeds Job Requirements
Performance at this level is always beyond the requirements for this position.
Duties and responsibilities are not only met excellently, but exceeded consistently.

Level 4–Meets and Usually Exceeds Job Requirements
Performance at this level is above the requirements for this position.
Duties and responsibilities are met well and usually exceeded.

Level 3–Consistently Meets Job Requirements
Performance at this level is up to the requirements for this position.
Duties and responsibilities are met consistently and in a satisfactory and acceptable manner.

Level 2–Inconsistent in Meeting Job Requirements
Performance at this level is at the minimum acceptable requirements for this position.
Duties and responsibilities are met marginally.

Level 1–Does Not Meet Job Requirements
Performance at this level is below the minimum acceptable requirements for the position.
Duties and responsibilities are not met in an acceptable manner.

Circle appropriate number.

Quantity of Work Level 1 2 3 4 5 6

Volume of work regularly produced, speed and consistency of output.

Comments ____________________

____

____

Quality of Work Level 1 2 3 4 5 6

Extent to which employee completes assignments.

Comments ____________________

____

____

Job Cooperation Level 1 2 3 4 5 6

Amount of interest and enthusiasm shown in work.

Comments ____

____

____

Ability to Work with Others Level 1 2 3 4 5 6

Extent to which employee interacts effectively with others in doing his/her job.

Comments ____

____

____

Adaptability Level 1 2 3 4 5 6

Extent to which employee is able to perform various assignments within the scope of his/her job duties.

Comments ____

____

____

Communications Level 1 2 3 4 5 6

Extent to which employee communicates effectively with others in doing his/her job.

Comments ____

____

____

Job Knowledge Level 1 2 3 4 5 6

Extent of job information and understanding possessed by employee.

Comments ____

____

____

Initiative Level 1 2 3 4 5 6

Extent to which employee is a self-starter in attaining objectives of his/her job.

Comments ____

____

____

Overall Evaluation of Employee Performance Level 1 2 3 4 5 6

Comments ____

____

____

Attendance ❑ Problem ❑ No Problem

Comments ______________________________

____

____

I. Employee's Career Development

A. Strengths ______________________________

____

____

B. Development Needs ______________________________

____

____

C. Development Plan (including long range) ______________________________

____

____

II. Employee Comments (optional)

General comment about the evaluation of your performance:

____

____

____

____

____

____

Read and acknowledged by:

Employee ______________________________ Date ______________

III. Approvals

Supervisor ______________________________ Date __________

Department Manager ______________________________ Date __________

Human Resources ______________________________ Date __________

President ______________________________ Date __________

35. Time Sheet–Hourly Employees

Employee Name ______________________________

ID # ______________________________

Social Security #

____

Position ______________________________

Department ______________________________

Number ______________________________

Time Period Covered from ______________ to ______________

Day	Date	In	Out	Total Regular	Total Overtime	Total Hours	Approval
Sun							
Mon							
Tues							
Wed							
Thur							
Fri							
Sat							
			Totals				

Employee Signature ______________________ Date ____________

Supervisor Approval ______________________ Date ____________

Legend :

A = Absent
H = Holiday
S = Sick
F = Funeral Leave
J = Jury Duty
V = Vacation

O = Occurrence
P = Personal Leave Approved
T = Tardy
U = Unauthorized Absence
I = Job Injury
LO = Leave of Absence

36. Annual Attendance Record

For Calendar Year ________

Employee Name________________________________ Social Security # ________________

Date of Birth ________________________ Date of Hire ________________________

Position ____________________________ Department ________________________

Day	Jan	Feb	Mar	Apr	May	Jun	Jul	Aug	Sep	Oct	Nov	Dec
1												
2												
3												
4												
5												
6												
7												
8												
9												
10												
11												
12												
13												
14												
15												
16												
17												
18												
19												
20												
21												
22												
23												
24												
25												
26												
27												
28												
29												
30												
31												

Legend:

A = Absent	O = Occurrence	H = Holiday	P = Personal Leave Approved
S = Sick	T = Tardy	F = Funeral Leave	U = Unauthorized Absence
J = Jury Duty	I = Job Injury	V = Vacation	LO = Leave of Absence

Comments and Summary of Attendance:

____

____

37. Request for Leave of Absence Without Pay

Name ______________________________ Social Security # ______________

Address ____

Phone Number ________________ Department ______________________

Position ______________________ Employment Date ________________

Last Day to Work ______________________________

I hereby request a leave of absence without pay, for the purpose indicated:

- ❑ Disability (including pregnancy)
- ❑ Family or Childcare Leave
- ❑ Personal Leave
- ❑ Military Leave
- ❑ Educational Leave
- ❑ Other ______________________________

Start Date ____________________ Return Date ____________________

Purpose ____

I understand that the leave, if granted, may be used only for the purpose described above and use of the leave for any other purpose will be grounds for disciplinary action, up to and including termination.

Employee Signature ________________________ Date __________

Physician's Statement:

If the request for leave is due to medical disability, have your physician complete the following statement:

The above-named is a patient in my care and is expected to be able to resume his/her usual occupation on or about

____

Physician's Address ________________________ Phone Number __________

Physician's Signature ________________________ Date __________

Approval:

Department Manager: ________________

❑ Approved ❑ Denied Reason ______________________________

Manager's Signature ________________________ Date __________

Human Resources Manager

❑ Approved ❑ Denied Reason ______________________________

Manager's Signature ________________________ Date __________

To the Employee: The date of expiration of your leave of absence is the date you are expected to return to work. Request for an extension of leave of absence must be made to the Human Resources Department prior to the return date of your leave. You have the responsibility for maintaining contact, by providing an address and a phone number for contacting you.

38. Request to Inspect Personnel File

Employee Name ______________________________

Date of Request ______________________________

Social Security # ______________________________

Department/Location ______________________________

Work Phone ______________________________

I request an appointment with the Human Resources Department to inspect my personnel file.

I last reviewed my file ______________________________

Signature ______________________________ Date ______________

Appointment is scheduled for:

Date ______________________________

Time ______________________________

Location ______________________________

File review completed (Date) ______________________________

Employee comments regarding information and accuracy of information in the personnel file:

____

____

____

____

____

Human Resources Representative ______________________________ Date ____________

Employee Signature ______________________________ Date ____________

Employee is to complete top section of request form and forward to the Human Resources Department.

Place one completed copy of this form into personnel file upon completion of review.

39. Employee Grievance Form

Date ______________

Name of Employee ____

Department ____

State your grievance in detail, including the date of acts(s) or omissions causing grievance.

____

____

____

Identify other employees with personal knowledge of your grievance.

____

____

State briefly your efforts to resolve this grievance.

____

____

Describe the remedy or solution you would like.

____

____

Employee's Signature ____________________________________ Date _______________

Grievance Team Member–Informal Review

Date Received ____

Actions Taken ____

____

____

Disposition ____

❑ Employee Accepted ❑ Employee Appealed

Assigned Team Member ____ Date Communicated

____

Grievance Team–Formal Review

Date Received ____

Actions Taken ____

____

____

Disposition ______________________________

❑ Employee Accepted ❑ Employee Appealed

Assigned Team Member ______________________________ Date Communicated __________

Grievance Team and Management–Formal Review

Date Received ______________________________

Actions Taken ______________________________

____

____

Disposition ______________________________

❑ Employee Accepted ❑ Employee Appealed

Assigned Team Member______________________________ Date Communicated __________

CHAPTER 3

Employee and Workplace Safety

The safety and security of you and your employees should be your highest business priority. We have included here several documents that can help you achieve the goal of a 100% safe workplace. Post the *Emergency Instructions* in a conspicuous place to advise your employees of safety procedures. Don't be afraid to add information to this form, such as the location of exits, a safe place to congregate outside the premises following an emergency, and specific instructions about machinery that should be turned off in the event of an emergency. The *Employee Telecommuting Memo* highlights several safety issues related to employees who work at home.

If an accident injures an employee, have the employee's supervisor complete the *Supervisor's Report of Work Injury*. This form should be completed as soon as possible following the incident to ensure that the record keeping is complete and accurate. Finally, we have included several Occupational Safety & Health Administration forms: *OSHA Form 300: Log of Work-Related Injuries and Illnesses*, *OSHA Form 300A: Summary of Work-Related Injuries and Illnesses*, and *OSHA Form 301: Injuries and Illnesses Incident Report*. You may be required to fill out these forms in the event of workplace injury. While a complete description of OSHA recordkeeping is beyond the scope of this book, you can find a helpful summary of OSHA compliance on OSHA's Web site at www.osha.gov/dcsp/compliance_ assistance/index.html.

40. Emergency Instructions

These emergency instructions should be posted in a prominent place such as the employee lounge.

Follow these rules in an emergency:

- Stop work and leave the building IMMEDIATELY when the fire alarm sounds or when you are instructed to do so!
- Follow instructions, avoid panic, and cooperate with those responding to the emergency.
- Proceed to the designated or nearest exit.
- Turn off computers, equipment, fans, etc., and close desk drawers.
- Do NOT delay your exit from the building by looking for belongings or other people.
- When leaving the building, go to a clear area well away from the building. Do not obstruct fire hydrants or the responding fire/rescue workers and their equipment.
- Do not re-enter the building until instructed to do so by your supervisor or a fire/rescue worker.

The above rules will be enforced. Periodic fire emergency drills may be conducted. Your life and the lives of others will depend on your cooperation.

If you ever discover a fire:

- Remain calm. Do not shout "Fire!"
- Pull the nearest fire alarm.
- Dial "911" and give the operator the location of the fire–the floor, wing, and room number, if possible.

41. Employee Telecommuting Memo

What follows are some guidelines that we would like our telecommuting employees to follow with respect to their work environment. We want our employees to be safe; these recommendations will ensure the safest home work environment possible. If you have any questions, please contact your manager.

General Lighting

- Use blinds or drapes on windows to eliminate bright light. Blinds should be adjusted during the day to allow light into the room without enabling you to see bright light directly.
- Reorient the workstation so that bright lights aren't in your field of view. Turn off fluorescent light fixtures in your field of view if they're bothersome. (Of course, be considerate of the effect on others who are working nearby.)
- If you use auxiliary desk lighting, it should usually be low wattage and should be directed so that it doesn't directly enter your eyes or directly illuminate the display screen. It's usually inadvisable to put additional lighting on reference documents, because this makes them too bright compared to the screen.

Screen Reflections

- An antireflection screen can be placed over the display. Glass screens perform better than mesh screens. Look for screens that have been approved by the American Optometric Association. (Alternatively, a hood can be purchased and placed over the display to shield it from offending sources; however, hoods often don't perform as well as antireflection screens.)
- Eliminate or cover the sources of the reflections–typically windows and other bright lights behind you.

Flicker Problems

Some people experience a flickering sensation when viewing the screen. If this is bothersome, try turning down the brightness, or use a dark background instead of a light one. If all else fails, using a display with a higher refresh rate might solve the problem. In less than 1% of the population, flickering may trigger epileptic seizures. If this condition applies to you, please immediately notify your supervisor.

Display Characteristics

- Adjust the screen brightness and contrast so that character definition and resolution are maximized. The screen brightness should match the general background brightness of the room. (This is much easier to do with light background screens.)
- Black characters on a white background is probably the best combination. Other combinations can be comfortable as long as the contrast between the characters and the background is high. It's best to avoid dark backgrounds.
- The size of the text should be three times the size of the smallest text you can read. You can test this by viewing the screen from three times your usual working distance; you should still be able to read the text.
- Although 60 Hz is the most common refresh rate, higher refresh rates are preferred. If you need help adjusting your refresh rate, contact your supervisor and we will assist you.
- For color monitors, small dot pitches (less than 0.28 mm) are desirable. If you require a monitor with a higher dot pitch, contact your supervisor and we will assist you.

Workstation Furniture and Arrangement

- Your table should allow for adjusting the keyboard height, have adequate space for both the monitor and reference material, and provide adequate knee space. It's usually best for the keyboard to be 3-5 inches below the standard desktop height of 29 inches; you should not be reaching up to the keyboard.

- Your chair should be easily adjustable in height, provide adjustable lower-back support, and have a flexible, woven seat covering. Five legs provide greater stability than four. Full armrests are not recommended, because they often preclude moving the chair under the table. However, support for the elbow or forearm can relieve strain on the shoulders, arms, and wrists.
- The height of your monitor should be adjustable. The center of the screen should be 10-20 degrees below your straight-ahead gaze (4-9 inches below your eyes, for normal working distances). In most cases, the top of the screen should be just below your eyes. A screen that is higher than these recommendations adversely affects your posture.
- Reference documents should be located close to the screen, with adjustable copy holders. The documents and the screen should be the same distance from your eyes and the brightness of the documents should match that of the screen.

Work Pace

- Take frequent breaks. Get up and walk around at least once an hour. Close your eyes. (People often "forget" to blink when they're concentrating.) Some of the more progressive workplaces even encourage their employees to take naps so that they can be re-energized and be more productive.
- If you feel any physical pain (back pain, headaches, sore wrists, etc.), stop working immediately. Normally these are simply signs of fatigue and can be remedied with sufficient rest or a pain reliever. For 10% of workers, there may be a risk of injury that can easily be prevented or significantly reduced through the use of ergonomic accommodations. If this condition applies to you, please see your human resource specialist to make the necessary accommodations.

Notify

The most important rule of all is to communicate with your superior or manager. If you ever have a question or concern, notify your manager. If you desire an inspection of your workplace, notify your manager.

42. Supervisor's Report of Work Injury

Date of Report ____________________

Injured Employee ____________________ Age __________

Job Title ____________________ Employee Number __________

Location ____________________

Department ____________________

Date of Hire __________ Time in this job (months) __________ Time on this shift (months) __________

Date of Injury __________ Time of Injury __________

Exact Location ____________________

Names of Witnesses ____________________

____

Injury to:

❑ Face or Head ❑ Eyes ❑ Body ❑ Arms ❑ Hands or Fingers

❑ Legs ❑ Toes or Foot ❑ Internal ❑ Lungs

Type of Injury:

❑ Lacerations ❑ Strain or Sprain ❑ Hernia ❑ Fracture

❑ Puncture ❑ Abrasion ❑ Amputation ❑ Burns

❑ Foreign Body ❑ Skin ❑ Gas

Treatment:

❑ First Aid ❑ Nurse ❑ Doctor's Care

❑ Serious ❑ Lost Time ❑ Fatality

Remarks: (Be Specific–e.g., L or R arm, etc.)

____

____

Describe how employee was injured. (What was employee doing? What duty or task?)

____

____

____

What happened that resulted in this injury? (Examples: slipped, fell, was struck.)

____

____

____

What factors do you believe contributed to this accident? (Consider methods, procedures, tools, machines, equipment arrangements, instructions, rules, inherent hazards, skill, experience, materials, and other factors.)

___

___

___

How could such an accident be prevented or avoided?

___

___

___

Investigating Committee (People to be included in accident investigations are listed below.)

1. Injured Employee ___
2. Immediate Supervisor ___
3. Safety Committeeperson ___
4. Shop Steward ___
5. Department Head (or Representative) ___
6. Witnesses ___
7. Safety Department Representative ___
8. Designated Union Safety Representative ___
9. Manager or Appointed Representative ___

Note: Report to be completed by immediate supervisor and turned in to the Safety Department not later than the end of the day following the injury. All lost-time injuries or fatalities must be promptly reported.

Important: All fatalities or accidents resulting in five or more persons being hospitalized must be reported to the appropriate federal or state agency enforcing OSHA regulations within the time limits applicable.

People to be included in accident investigations:

Near Miss/No Injury
The extent of the investigation will be left to the discretion of the supervisor.

Slight (First Aid)
Immediate Investigation
1. Injured Employee
2. Immediate Supervisor

Nurse Case
Immediate Investigation
1. Injured Employee
2. Immediate Supervisor
3. Safety Committeeperson

Doctor Case
Immediate Investigation
1. Injured Employee
2. Immediate Supervisor
3. Safety Committeeperson
4. Shop Steward
5. Department Head (or Representative)
6. Witnesses

Final Investigation
1. Injured Employee
2. Immediate Supervisor
3. Safety Committeeperson
4. Shop Steward
5. Department Head (or Representative)
6. Witnesses
7. Safety Dept. Representative

Lost Time or Fatality

Immediate Investigation

1. Injured Employee
2. Immediate Supervisor
3. Safety Committeeperson
4. Shop Steward
5. Department Head (or Representative)
6. Witnesses
7. Safety Dept. Representative
8. Designated Union Safety Representative

Final Investigation

1. Injured Employee
2. Immediate Supervisor
3. Safety Committeeperson
4. Shop Steward
5. Department Head (or Representative)
6. Witnesses
7. Safety Dept. Representative
8. Designated Union Safety Representative
9. Manager or Appointed Representative

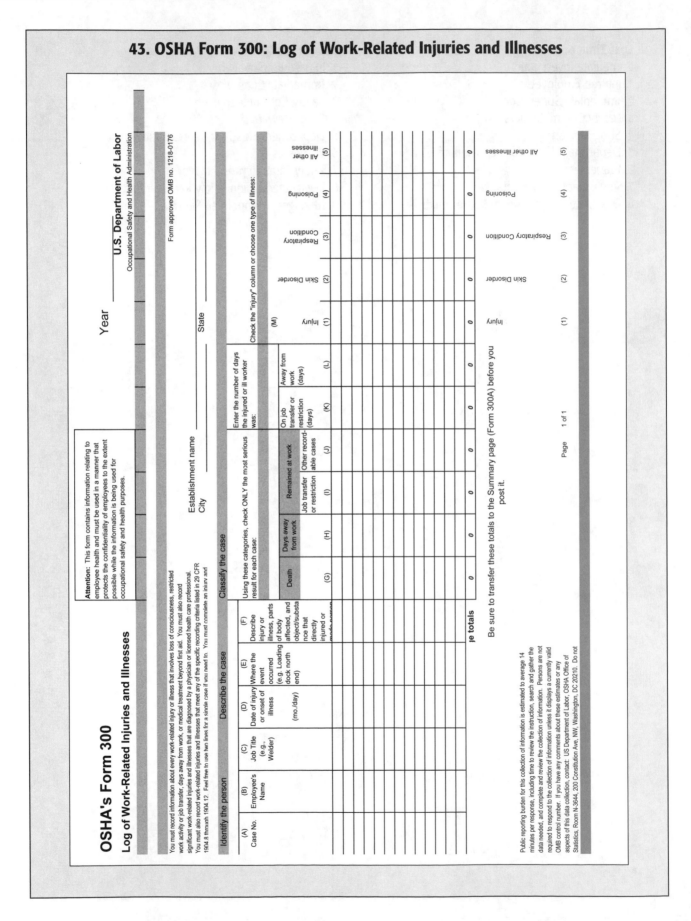

43. OSHA Form 300: Log of Work-Related Injuries and Illnesses

OSHA's Form 300

Log of Work-Related Injuries and Illnesses

Attention: This form contains information relating to employee health and must be used in a manner that protects the confidentiality of employees to the extent possible while the information is being used for occupational safety and health purposes.

Year ____________

U.S. Department of Labor
Occupational Safety and Health Administration

Form approved OMB no. 1218-0176

You must record information about every work-related injury or illness that involves loss of consciousness, restricted work activity or job transfer, days away from work, or medical treatment beyond first aid. You must also record significant work-related injuries and illnesses that are diagnosed by a physician or licensed health care professional. You must also record work-related injuries and illnesses that meet any of the specific recording criteria listed in 29 CFR 1904.8 through 1904.12. Feel free to use two lines for a single case if you need to. You must complete an injury and

Establishment name ____________
City ____________ State ____________

Identify the person		Describe the case				Classify the case										
						Using these categories, check ONLY the most serious result for each case:				Enter the number of days the injured or ill worker was:		Check the "injury" column or choose one type of illness:				
(A) Case No.	(B) Employee's Name	(C) Job Title (e.g., Welder)	(D) Date of injury or onset of illness (mo./day)	(E) Where the event occurred (e.g. Loading dock north end)	(F) Describe injury or illness, parts of body affected, and object/substance that directly injured or made person	Death	Days away from work	Remained at work: Job transfer or restriction	Remained at work: Other record-able cases	On job transfer or restriction (days)	Away from work (days)	(M) Injury	Skin Disorder	Respiratory Condition	Poisoning	All other illnesses
						(G)	(H)	(I)	(J)	(K)	(L)	(1)	(2)	(3)	(4)	(5)
					ɿe totals	0	0	0	0	0	0	0	0	0	0	0

Be sure to transfer these totals to the Summary page (Form 300A) before you post it.

Injury	Skin Disorder	Respiratory Condition	Poisoning	All other illnesses
(1)	(2)	(3)	(4)	(5)

Page 1 of 1

Public reporting burden for this collection of information is estimated to average 14 minutes per response, including time to review the instruction, search and gather the data needed, and complete and review the collection of information. Persons are not required to respond to the collection of information unless it displays a currently valid OMB control number. If you have any comments about these estimates or any aspects of this data collection, contact: US Department of Labor, OSHA Office of Statistics, Room N-3644, 200 Constitution Ave, NW, Washington, DC 20210. Do not

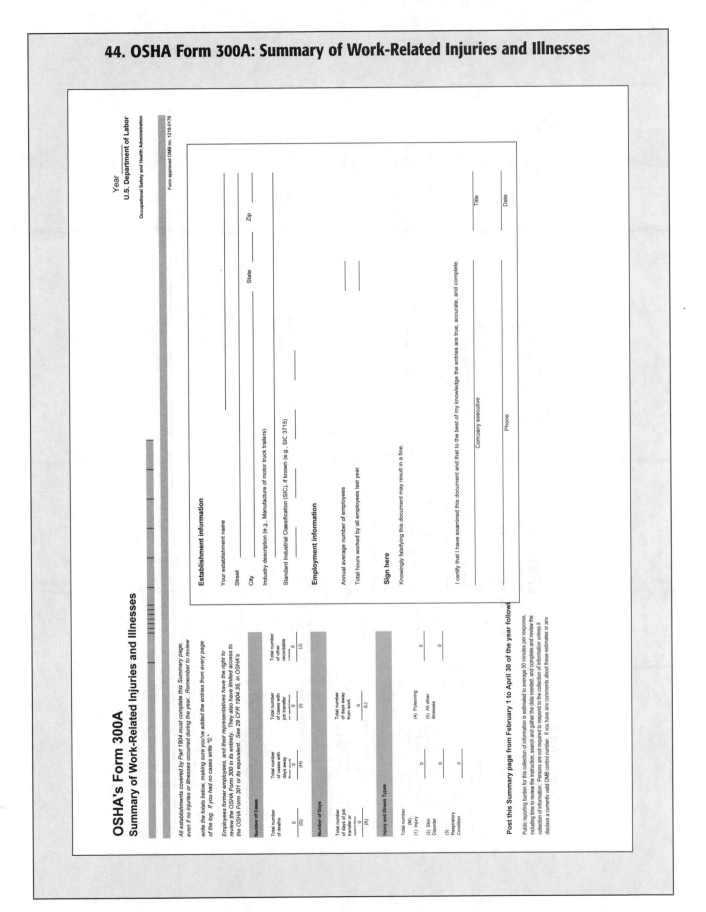

44. OSHA Form 300A: Summary of Work-Related Injuries and Illnesses

OSHA's Form 300A

Summary of Work-Related Injuries and Illnesses

Year ______

U.S. Department of Labor

Occupational Safety and Health Administration

Form approved OMB no. 1218-0176

All establishments covered by Part 1904 must complete this Summary page, even if no injuries or illnesses occurred during the year. Remember to review

write the totals below, making sure you've added the entries from every page of the log. If you had no cases write "0."

Employees former employees, and their representatives have the right to review the OSHA Form 300 in its entirety. They also have limited access to the OSHA Form 301 or its equivalent. See 29 CFR 1904.35, in OSHA's

Number of Cases

Total number of deaths	Total number of cases with days away from work	Total number of cases with job transfer or restriction	Total number of other recordable cases
0	0	0	0
(G)	(H)	(I)	(J)

Number of Days

Total number of days of job transfer or restriction	Total number of days away from work
0	0
(K)	(L)

Injury and Illness Types

Total number (M)

(1) Injury	0	(4) Poisoning	0
(2) Skin Disorder	0	(5) All other illnesses	0
(3) Respiratory Condition	0		

Post this Summary page from February 1 to April 30 of the year followi

Public reporting burden for this collection of information is estimated to average 50 minutes per response, including time to review the instruction, search and gather the data needed, and complete and review the collection of information. Persons are not required to respond to the collection of information unless it displays a currently valid OMB control number. If you have any comments about these estimates or any

Establishment information

Your establishment name ____________

Street ____________

City ____________ State ______ Zip ______

Industry description (e.g., Manufacture of motor truck trailers) ____________

Standard Industrial Classification (SIC), if known (e.g., SIC 3715) ____ ____ ____ ____

Employment information

Annual average number of employees ______

Total hours worked by all employees last year ______

Sign here

Knowingly falsifying this document may result in a fine.

I certify that I have examined this document and that to the best of my knowledge the entries are true, accurate, and complete.

____________ Company executive ______ Title

____________ Phone ______ Date

45. OSHA Form 301: Injuries and Illnesses Incident Report

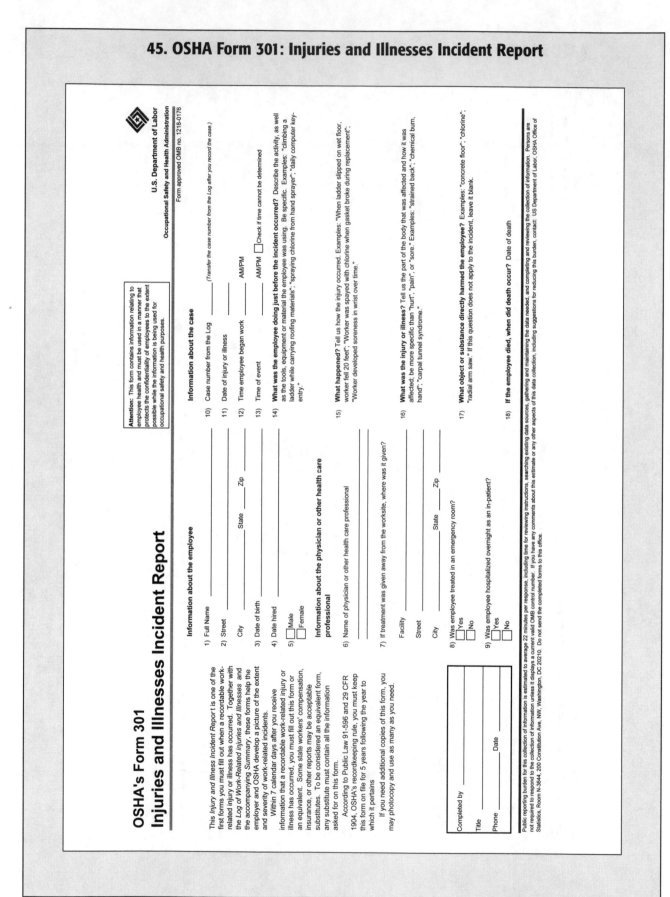

OSHA's Form 301
Injuries and Illnesses Incident Report

Attention: This form contains information relating to employee health and must be used in a manner that protects the confidentiality of employees to the extent possible while the information is being used for occupational safety and health purposes.

U.S. Department of Labor
Occupational Safety and Health Administration

Form approved OMB no. 1218-0176

This *Injury and Illness Incident Report* is one of the first forms you must fill out when a recordable work-related injury or illness has occurred. Together with the *Log of Work-Related injuries and Illnesses* and the accompanying *Summary*, these forms help the employer and OSHA develop a picture of the extent and severity of work-related incidents.

Within 7 calendar days after you receive information that a recordable work-related injury or illness has occurred, you must fill out this form or an equivalent. Some state workers' compensation, insurance, or other reports may be acceptable substitutes. To be considered an equivalent form, any substitute must contain all the information asked for on this form.

According to Public Law 91-596 and 29 CFR 1904, OSHA's recordkeeping rule, you must keep this form on file for 5 years following the year to which it pertains

If you need additional copies of this form, you may photocopy and use as many as you need.

Completed by ____________

Title ____________

Phone ____________ Date ____________

Information about the employee

1) Full Name ____________

2) Street ____________

City ____________ State _____ Zip ______

3) Date of birth ____________

4) Date hired ____________

5) ☐ Male
☐ Female

Information about the physician or other health care professional

6) Name of physician or other health care professional ____________

7) If treatment was given away from the worksite, where was it given?

Facility ____________

Street ____________

City ____________ State _____ Zip ______

8) Was employee treated in an emergency room?
☐ Yes
☐ No

9) Was employee hospitalized overnight as an in-patient?
☐ Yes
☐ No

Information about the case

10) Case number from the Log ________ *(Transfer the case number from the Log after you record the case.)*

11) Date of injury or illness ________

12) Time employee began work ________ AM/PM

13) Time of event ________ AM/PM ☐ Check if time cannot be determined

14) **What was the employee doing just before the incident occurred?** Describe the activity, as well as the tools, equipment or material the employee was using. Be specific. Examples: "climbing a ladder while carrying roofing materials"; "spraying chlorine from hand sprayer"; "daily computer key-entry."

15) **What happened?** Tell us how the injury occurred. Examples: "When ladder slipped on wet floor, worker fell 20 feet"; "Worker was spayed with chlorine when gasket broke during replacement"; "Worker developed soreness in wrist over time."

16) **What was the injury or illness?** Tell us the part of the body that was affected and how it was affected; be more specific than "hurt", "pain", or "sore." Examples: "strained back"; "chemical burn, hand"; "carpal tunnel syndrome."

17) **What object or substance directly harmed the employee?** Examples: "concrete floor"; "chlorine"; "radial arm saw." If this question does not apply to the incident, leave it blank.

18) **If the employee died, when did death occur?** Date of death

Public reporting burden for this collection of information is estimated to average 22 minutes per response, including time for reviewing instructions, searching existing data sources, gathering and maintaining the data needed, and completing and reviewing the collection of information. Persons are not required to respond to the collection of information unless it displays a current valid OMB control number. If you have any comments about this estimate or any other aspects of this data collection, including suggestions for reducing this burden, contact: US Department of Labor, OSHA Office of Statistics, Room N-3644, 200 Constitution Ave, NW, Washington, DC 20210. Do not send the completed forms to this office.

CHAPTER 4

Employee Termination

All employees come to a company looking for a job and many leave looking for a job. This section is brief, but important. When an employee's employment is terminated with your firm, make sure that all is in order before you part ways. The past few decades have witnessed a significant increase in litigation brought by former employees for wrongful termination. While some of the suits are valid, others are groundless and abusive and exploit poor record keeping by employers. Thus, secure all documentation necessary to memorialize the separation and you can more successfully defend a suit brought for wrongful termination.

If an employee chooses to leave voluntarily, have him or her execute the *Voluntary Resignation*. This form serves as a nearly indisputable record of the employee's willing termination of employment. This form may also go a long way to extinguishing an employee's right to charge your business's unemployment insurance for unemployment benefits. The *Employee's Separation Checklist* advises an employee of outstanding issues that must be resolved before separation. *The Manager's Pre-Dismissal Checklist* ensures that all loose ends are well tied before an employee departs. Finally, the *Employee Exit Interview* helps the company and the employee communicate their final thoughts before terminating the employment relationship.

46. Voluntary Resignation

Employee Name ______________________________

Department ______________________________

I voluntarily resign my employment with ______________________________

Effective: Month ____________ Day __________ Year__________

My reasons for leaving are:

____

____

____

____

____

____

____

____

____

____

Forwarding Address: ______________________________

____

____

Employee Signature ______________________________ Date__________

Manager Signature ______________________________ Date__________

47. Employee's Separation Checklist

Employee Name ____

Date of Termination ____

The following items are to have been collected prior to your separation with the company. Please have all these below listed items returned to your manager prior to your separation date. Thank you.

❑ All keys returned.

❑ Company vehicle keys returned.

❑ Company vehicle returned.

❑ Company credit cards returned.

❑ Company phone credit cards returned.

❑ Company equipment (portable phones, beepers, PCs) returned.

❑ COBRA election forms signed and returned.

❑ 401(k) election forms signed and returned.

❑ Profit-sharing election forms signed and returned.

Your files, desk, and work area will be inventoried for all equipment and work utensils given to you by the company.

❑ Desk and working premises inventoried.

48. Manager's Pre-Dismissal Checklist

Employee Name ____________________

Date of Termination ____________________

Collect the following items from the employee prior to separation from the company:

❑ All keys returned.

❑ Company vehicle keys returned.

❑ Company vehicle returned.

❑ Company credit cards returned.

❑ Company phone credit cards returned.

❑ Company equipment (e.g., portable phones, beepers, credit cards, laptop computers) returned.

❑ COBRA election forms signed and returned.

❑ 401(k) election forms signed and returned.

❑ Profit-sharing election forms signed and returned.

❑ Company documents and files inventoried.

❑ Desk and working premises inventoried.

❑ Personnel and Payroll Departments notified of departure.

❑ Final expense report received, reviewed, and approved; expense check prepared.

❑ Final check prepared (including all accrued vacation pay, sick pay, accrued wages, bonus, etc.).

❑ Exit interview prepared.

❑ Exit interview given.

❑ Final checks (payroll and expense) given to terminating employee.

All of the above duties have been completed in a satisfactory manner.

Company has no further liability with the terminating employee.

Manager Signature ____________________ Date __________

49. Employee Exit Interview

Employee Name ______________________________

Title ______________________________

Department ______________________________

Date ______________

What did you like best about your current position?

____

____

____

What did you like least about your current position?

____

____

____

What did you like best about the company?

____

____

____

What did you like least about the company?

____

____

____

What are your feelings toward your supervisor?

____

____

____

Why are you leaving the company at this time? What company and position are you going to?

____

____

____

What are your comments about the company's salary and benefits?

____

____

____

What suggestions do you have for improving your current position and other aspects within the company?

____

____

____

Interviewed by ______________________ Date ____________

Interviewer's remarks

____

____

____

____

____

____

CHAPTER 5

Miscellaneous Personnel Forms

We have included several miscellaneous personnel forms. Unfortunately, not every résumé you receive will be a perfect match. Thus we have included two versions of a *Job Applicant Dismissal*, which you should send to job seekers who don't fit your needs. Of course, you'll want to invite certain applicants for an interview. You can do so with the *Job Applicant Invitation*. The document is safely worded so as not to convey an offer of employment.

You should strongly consider enacting a formal job applicant referral program. Recommendations from current employees are usually your greatest source of new employees. Also, consider the cost of recruitment firms—often a third of a new hire's first-year salary. You can award your current employees with cash or vacation time. Encourage your employees to submit the *Employee Referral* form to the human resources department to recommend candidates for particular positions. We have included an *Applicant Referral Update* for use when one of your employees refers a potential new hire in the context of a job applicant referral program; this form keeps the referring employee up to date on the status of the referral. Finally, the *Employee Referral Award* notifies the referring employee that his or her referral has been accepted.

The *Notice of Established Workday and Workweek* advises your employees of the establishment of or changes to the standard workday and workweek. Direct your employees to use the *Time Log* to record their job activities. The use of this report can help you pinpoint efficiency problems with certain employees and tasks. Use the *Client Time/Expense Sheet* to track activities and expenses for which a client should be billed. If you have employees who are independent contractors, clarify and document that relationship with the *Independent Contractor's Agreement*.

We have included a helpful and descriptive summary of stock option plans, *The Manager's Guide to Employee Stock Option Plans—a Concise Overview*. If your company grants stock options to its employees, the *Stock Option Memorandum to Employees* can help you communicate to your employees the basic principles of stock option plans. Consult a qualified attorney to implement a stock option plan for your company.

50. Job Applicant Dismissal (Version 1)

From: ____

____

____

____

To: ____

____

____

Date: ______________

Dear ______________

Thank you for your time and the interest you've shown in considering a ______________________ position here at our firm. We were fortunate to have interviewed a number of applicants with strong backgrounds such as yours, making our selection process difficult.

We regret to say that we are now concentrating our attention on a limited number of other candidates whose backgrounds appear to be the best match for our firm's needs. Be assured that your résumé and interview have received our full attention. Should another opening present itself in the near future for which you appear qualified, we will contact you immediately.

Your regard for our firm is greatly appreciated. Best wishes for your continued career success.

Thank you.

Yours truly,

51. Job Applicant Dismissal (Version 2)

From: ____

____

____

____

To: ____

____

____

Date ______________

Dear ______________:

Thank you for the interest you've shown in a career opportunity with our firm. We were fortunate to have interviewed a number of applicants with strong backgrounds such as yours, making our selection process difficult.

Be assured that your résumé has received our full attention. While your background is interesting, unfortunately we have no openings that are a match for your skills and experience.

We would like to again thank you for your interest in our firm and wish you continued success in pursuit of your career objectives.

Yours truly,

52. Job Applicant Invitation

From: ____

____

____

____

To: ____

____

____

Date ______________

Dear ____________________

Thank you for the interest you've shown in considering a ______________ position with our firm. Your qualifications have been reviewed by our management team. We feel that your skills could potentially be a good match for the position.

We would like to invite you to visit our firm for an interview to more fully evaluate you as a candidate. This interview is a necessary part of our evaluation process. Please contact ______________ at the telephone number that appears above to arrange the interview. Please plan to spend about an hour with us.

Thank you for your interest and we look forward to meeting with you.

Yours truly,

53. Employee Referral

Date ____________________

Name of Candidate Referred ____________________

For the Position of ____________________

Department ____________________

My relationship and knowledge of this candidate is:

❑ Former Work Peer

❑ Former Supervisor

❑ Former Subordinate

❑ Friend

❑ Other ____________________

My evaluation of this candidate is: (5 equals highest)

Experience	1	2	3	4	5
Job-Related Skills	1	2	3	4	5
Initiative	1	2	3	4	5
Responsibility	1	2	3	4	5
Related Education	1	2	3	4	5
Interpersonal Skills	1	2	3	4	5

Comments and Other Information:

____

____

____

____

____

____

Submitted by ____________________ Date ____________________

Please attach résumé.

54. Applicant Referral Update

To ______________________________

Date ______________

From ______________________________

Thank your for recent referral of ______________________________

For the position of ______________________________

The status of this candidate is:

❑ Job offered but declined

❑ Job offer pending

❑ Currently being interviewed

❑ Résumé on file–no current openings

❑ Not qualified

Thank you for your support and participation in the employee referral program. If any further action is taken regarding this candidate, we will notify you.

55. Employee Referral Award

To ____

Date ________________________

From ____

Congratulations!

We are please to announce that _____________________________________, your recent referral, has been hired effective ___________________________________.

According to the terms of our employee referral program, your award of ___________________ will be processed for you on or about __________________.

Once the referred employee has completed 90 days of continuous, satisfactory employment, the remainder of your award will be immediately processed for you.

You are to be aware that this award may have tax implications for you. The award ❑ is ❑ is not "grossed up" by 20% to offset part or all of the additional taxes that you can incur.

Thank you again for you support and participation in the employee referral program.

Yours truly,

56. Notice of Established Workday and Workweek

In order to arrange fair and consistent work schedules and to determine when overtime payments are due for hours worked beyond 40 in a week or _______ in a day, the following standard workday and workweek has been established:

Workday:

The 24-hour period beginning at ____________________ (time) and ending at ____________________(time).

Workweek:

The seven-day period beginning at ____________________(time) ____________________ (day) and ending at ____________________ (time) ____________________ (day).

This schedule becomes effective ____________________(date).

Please contact your supervisor or the Human Resources Department if you have any questions.

57. Time Log

Name ______________________________

Title ______________________________

Department ______________________________

Date ______________________________

Time	Activity and Result	Total Time Spent

58. Client Time/Expense Sheet

Client Name ______________________________

Associate Name ______________________________

Date	Description of Task or Purchase	Time Used	Expense
Totals			

59. Independent Contractor's Agreement

Date _______________

Dear ____

The following will outline our agreement and summarize the terms of the arrangement that we have discussed.

You have been retained by ______________________________ as an independent contractor for the project of ____.

You will be responsible for successfully completing the above-described project according to specifications and within the policy guidelines discussed.

The project is to be completed by ______________________________ (date) at a cost not to exceed $__________.

You will invoice us for your services rendered at the end of each month.

We will not deduct or withhold any taxes, FICA, or other deductions that we are legally required to make from the pay of regular employees. As an independent contractor, you will not be entitled to any fringe benefits, such as unemployment insurance, medical insurance, pension plans, or other such benefits that would be offered to regular employees.

During this project, you may be in contact with or directly working with proprietary information that is important to our company and its competitive position. All information must be treated with strict confidence and may not be used at any time or in any manner in work you may do with others in our industry.

If you agree to the above terms, please sign and return one copy of this letter for our records. You may retain the other copy for your files.

Agreed:

Independent Contractor ____________________________ Date __________

Company Representative ___________________________ Date __________

60. The Manager's Guide to Employee Stock Option Plans–A Concise Overview

Set forth below is an overview of the tax, accounting, and general business considerations applicable to typical equity-based compensation arrangements. Following the overview are general descriptions of how those considerations apply to three basic types of arrangements: incentive stock options, nonqualified stock options, and restricted stock.

Incentive Stock Options (ISOs) Offer Great Tax Benefits, but Are for Employees Only

An incentive stock option ("ISO") provides for the grant to employees only (not to outside directors, consultants, etc.) of options to acquire stock of the employer and, by satisfying a series of statutory requirements, qualifies for a specified set of tax consequences. To satisfy tax requirements, the plan providing for the grant of the ISOs must be approved by the shareholders within 12 months before or after it is adopted, must specify the aggregate number of shares of employer stock that are available for issuance under the plan, and must specify the employees or class of employee eligible for the plan.

The restrictions applicable to terms of the ISO are as follow:

- The option price must at least equal the fair market value of the stock at the time of grant.
- The option cannot be transferable, except at death.
- There is a $100,000 limit on the aggregate fair market value (determined at the time the option is granted) of stock any employee may acquire during any calendar year. (Any amount exceeding the limit is treated as a nonqualified stock option, as described below.)
- All options must be granted within 10 years of either plan adoption or approval of the plan, whichever is earlier.
- The options must be exercised within 10 years of grant.
- The options must be exercised within three months of termination of employment (extended to one year for disability retirement, with no time limit in the case of death).
- Optimum tax treatment to the employee depends on the employee not making a "Disqualifying disposition" (i.e., the employee does not dispose of the shares within one years after the date of grant of the option or within one year of receipt of the shares).

Modification of an existing option is treated as a grant of a new option, which must meet all of the applicable tax requirements as of the date of the modification. Note that, in the case of a 10% or greater shareholder, the option price must be at least 110% of the fair market value of the stock at the time of the grant and the option period must not exceed five years. The number of options granted to each employee at any one time can be discretionary. The exercisability of options typically vests over time. Vesting can be conditioned on performance, in addition to continued employment. The plan may permit the option price to be paid with other stock held by the employee. If stock received on the previous exercise of another ISO is used to exercise an ISO, the disposition of the previously held shares will be nontaxable unless it is a disqualifying disposition.

Tax Consequences of ISOs

For the employer:

No compensation deduction is ever allowed for an ISO, unless the employee makes a disqualifying disposition, in which case the employer receives a deduction equal to the employee's income inclusion for the year in which the disqualifying disposition occurs. Under current rules, the employer is not required to withhold income or employment taxes, even in the case of a disqualifying disposition.

For the employee:

There is no taxable income to the employee at the time of the grant or timely exercise. However, the difference between the value of the stock at exercise and the exercise price is an item of adjustment for purposes of the dreaded alternative minimum tax ("AMT"). In the absence of a disqualifying disposition, gain or loss when the stock is later sold is long-term capital gain or loss. Gain or loss is the difference between the amount realized from the sale and the tax basis (i.e., the amount paid on exercise). In the case of a disqualifying disposition, the employee is treated as having ordinary income subject to tax in an amount equal to the lesser of (i) the difference between the amount realized on the disposition and the exercise price or (ii) the difference between the fair market value of the stock on the date the ISO is exercised and the exercise price. Any gain in excess of the amount taxed as ordinary income will be treated as a long- or short-term capital gain, depending on whether the stock was held for more than 12 months.

Nonqualified Stock Options (NSOs): The Leftovers

In general, nonqualified stock options ("NSOs"), unlike ISOs, are not subject to specific tax eligibility requirements–an NSO is just a plain old option. Thus, any option that is not an ISO is by default an NSO.

The term "nonqualified" means just that–if the option does not qualify as an ISO, it's a stock option that enjoys no special tax treatment. NSOs are typically granted with an exercise price approximating the value of the stock at the time of grant, although they are frequently issued at some discount from such value. Like ISOs, NSOs may become exercisable as they vest over time, conditioned on continued employment or specific performance criteria. Unlike ISOs, NSOs can be issued to anyone, employee or otherwise.

Tax Consequences of NSOs

For the employer:

In general, the employer receives a deduction equal to (and at the same time as) the employee's income inclusion. The employer is required to withhold income and employment taxes on the employee's income amount.

For the employee:

In general, there is no taxable income to the employee at the time of the grant. However, the difference between the value of the stock at exercise and the exercise price is ordinary income to the employee at the time of exercise. The income recognized on exercise is subject to income tax withholding and to employment taxes. When the stock is later sold, the gain or loss is capital gain or loss (calculated as the difference between the sales price and tax basis, which is the sum of the exercise price and the income recognized at exercise).

Accounting Treatment of ISOs and NSOs

Generally, under traditional rules, there is no charge to earnings for accounting purposes, unless the option is granted with an option price of less than the fair market value of the stock, determined at the date of the grant (the measurement date). For companies contemplating an IPO within the foreseeable future, the valuation of stock option grants can be particularly important, as the SEC commonly questions the exercise prices of options granted in the period before the IPO.

Certain conditions, however, may result in an earnings charge if there is a stock value/exercise price disparity at some other measurement date. The exercise of an option with stock already held can result in the earnings charge being calculated at the exercise date if the stock used to exercise the option has been held less than six months. Withholding of stock upon exercise will not result in a new measurement date if the withheld stock is limited to the minimum withholding tax payable by the employee. Withholding of more shares can result in the exercise date becoming a new measurement date for the withheld shares. A cash bonus to pay withholding taxes can result in the exercise date becoming a new measurement date for the option as well as the cash bonus itself.

Under rules adopted by the Financial Accounting Standards Board, companies are "encouraged" to account for equity-based compensation awards based on the fair value of the awards; companies that do not do so nonetheless must disclose such fair value in notes to their financial statements. We believe that most public companies choose the latter approach.

The accounting treatment of option grants to non-employees has recently changed. Grants to non-employees (other than grants to non-employee directors, who for this purpose are treated as employees) will now incur a compensation expense for the company, even if the option price is set at the fair market value of the stock at the time of the grant.

	Incentive Stock Option (ISO)	**Nonqualified Stock Option (NSO)**
Tax Qualification Requirements?	Many	None
Who Can Receive?	Employees Only	Anyone
How Taxed for Employee?	There is no taxable income to the employee at the time of the grant or timely exercise. However, the difference between the value of the stock at exercise and the exercise price is an item of adjustment for purposes of the alternative minimum tax ("AMT"). When the stock is later sold, the gain or loss is long-term capital gain or loss (calculated as the difference between the amount realized from the sale and the tax basis, which is the amount paid on exercise). Disqualifying disposition destroys favorable tax treatment.	The difference between the value of the stock at exercise and the exercise price is ordinary income. The income recognized on exercise is subject to income tax withholding and to employment taxes. When the stock is later sold, the gain or loss is capital gain or loss (calculated as the difference between the sales price and tax basis, which is the sum of the exercise price and the income recognized at exercise).

61. Stock Option Memorandum to Employees

What follows is an explanation of the current stock option plans offered by ____________________. Please bear in mind that stock option plans are powerful but complicated devices. Thus, to maximize the benefit to you personally, you should educate yourself about stock options. This memo is meant to be an overview and summary.

What Is a Stock Option? How Do Options Work?

A stock option gives an employee the right to buy a certain number of shares in a company at a fixed price for a certain number of years. The price at which the option is provided is called the "grant" or "strike" price and is usually the market price at the time the options are granted (usually the first day of employment).

Employees who have been granted stock options hope that the share price will go up and that they will be able to make substantial gains by exercising (purchasing) the stock at the grant price and then selling the stock at the (hopefully) higher current market price. The difference between the grant price and the current market price is called the "spread."

A stock option "vests" when the employee earns the right to exercise the option. Typically, an employee's options begin vesting one year after employment begins and continue vesting until three or four years after employment begins. This gradual vesting is called a "vesting schedule." When the vesting schedule is complete, the options are said to be fully vested.

The Two Principal Types of Options

There are two principal kinds of stock option programs, each with unique rules and tax consequences: incentive stock options (ISOs) and nonqualified stock options (NSOs).

Incentive Stock Options (ISOs)

These are also known as "qualified" stock options because they qualify to receive special tax treatment. IMPORTANT: With ISOs, no income tax is due at grant or exercise–rather, the tax is deferred until you sell the stock. This is a valuable benefit to employees. The Company offers ISOs to eligible employees.

Upon sale, the entire option gain (the initial spread at exercise plus any subsequent appreciation) is taxed at long-term capital gains rates, provided you sell at least two years after the option is granted and at least one year after you exercise. The current long-term capital gains rate is 20% (a much lower rate than the 28% to 39% bracket for ordinary income–a huge tax savings). If you don't meet the one- and two-year holding period requirements, the sale is a "disqualifying disposition" and you are taxed as if you had held NSOs (see below).

A warning applies here: the spread at exercise is considered a preference item for purposes of calculating the alternative minimum tax (AMT), increasing taxable income for AMT purposes. The AMT is hopelessly complicated and Congress is actually considering making changes to the law. You need not worry about the AMT until exercise. Also, a disqualifying disposition can help you avoid this tax.

Nonqualified Stock Options (NSOs)

The taxation of NSOs is not as beneficial for employees as ISOs. You are required to pay ordinary income tax on the difference ("spread") between the grant price and the stock's market value when you purchase ("exercise") the shares. Companies get to deduct this spread as a compensation expense.

After that, any subsequent appreciation in the stock is taxed at capital gains rates when you sell. Keep the stock for more than a year and you'll have a long-term capital gain, taxed at a top rate of 20%; hold it for one year or less and your gain is short-term, taxed at higher, ordinary income tax rates. Nonqualified options can be granted at a discount to what is then the stock's market value. They also are "transferable" to children and charity, provided your company permits it.

How to Exercise Stock Options

There are three basic ways to exercise stock options: cash, stock swap, and "cashless exercise."

Cash: This is the most straightforward way. You give your employer money and get stock certificates in return. But what happens, when it's time to exercise the option, if you don't have enough cash to buy the option shares and pay any resulting tax?

Stock swap: Some employers let you exercise stock options by trading company stock you own already. If, for example, your company stock sells for $20 a share and you have an ISO to buy 1,000 additional shares at $10, you can either paying $10,000 in cash or exchange 500 shares you already own for the 1,000 new shares. (This strategy has the extra benefit of limiting your holdings of company stock.) If the stock you're swapping is ISO shares, you must have held them for the required one- and two-year holding periods; otherwise, the exchange is treated as a sale and you incur tax.

Cashless exercise: To exercise a stock option this way, you borrow the money you need from a stockbroker and simultaneously sell at least enough shares to cover your costs, including taxes and commissions. You receive any balance in cash or stock.

There is an important restriction on your ability to sell shares under any of the plans: the shares that you are granted are not registered with the Securities and Exchange Commission and so they're "restricted" from resale. Restricted shares must be held for one year before they can be sold.

When to Exercise Stock Options

Conventional thinking is that you should wait until your options are about to expire before you exercise them, to allow the stock to appreciate and maximize your gain. However, many employees can't wait that long. One study found that the typical employee cashed out of his or her options within six months of becoming eligible to do so—and thus sacrificed an estimated $1 in future value for every $2 realized.

CHAPTER 6

Sales and Revenue Analysis Tools

The forms in this section are all designed to increase your company's sales. The *Sales Call Log* is a log for use by salespersons; it serves as a record of telephone conversations with customers and prospects. The *Client/Prospect Contact Log* is a related form that summarizes the calls and contacts made to a particular prospect. The *Sales Prospect File* is the best log for use by salespersons in industries where the sales are made through incoming calls and during advertising campaigns.

The *Customer Satisfaction Survey* lets you learn from your most valuable critics-your customers. The *Customer Service Request* helps you effectively gather, track, follow, and respond to customer service inquiries.

Use the *Product Information* form to keep a unified and complete description of all of your products and services. The *Order Card* is a handy and simple card that you can include in mailings and facsimile advertisements. It enables your customers to quickly and easily place orders for your products and services. Use the *Work Order/ Request for Quote* form when your customers request custom goods and services. The *Sales Order Form* is a familiar receipt/invoice form.

The *Daily Sales Recap* is an internal sales tracking mechanism; it enables you and your staff to see a day-by-day analysis of your company's sales. The *Month-to-Month Sales Comparison Log* enables your staff to compare sales performance on a month-to-month basis.

The *Cash Receipts Control Log* is an effective tracking mechanism for cash-based businesses; the form may also serve to prevent employee theft and loss. Ensure that the cash on hand at the end of each business day reconciles with the amount on the *Cash Receipts Control Log.*

62. Sales Call Log

Number ______________________________ Date__________________

Name of Company ______________________________

Contact ______________________________ Phone __________________

Type of Call: ❑ Customer ❑ Prospect

Comments

____

____

Purpose of Call

____

____

Opening Conversation

____

____

____

Sales Story

____

____

____

Benefits to Customer

____

____

____

Objections or Resistance Response

____

____

Closing Conversation

____

____

____

When to Follow Up

____

____

63. Client/Prospect Contact Log

Sales Representative ______________________

Company ______________________

Contact(s) ______________________

Address ______________________

Phone ______________________

Date	Comments	Next Call/Contact?	Sale?

64. Sales Prospect File

❑ New Prospect ❑ Current Client ❑ Follow-up Date ____________

Company Name ____________

Contact ____________

Title ____________

Address ____________

____

Phone ____________

Source of Initial Contact

❑ Call-in ❑ Direct Mail ❑ Referral–by Whom? ____________

Current Supplier ____________

Approximate Monthly Sales Volume ____________

Action Taken to Follow-up

____

____

____

Sales Calls History

Comments

____

____

____

____

____

General Comments

____

____

____

____

____

____

65. Customer Satisfaction Survey

Your input is valuable to us and we are constantly looking for ways to improve the quality of our products and services. Please take a few minutes to fill out the few questions below. Please return this survey by fax at ______________________ or in the envelope provided.

Please LIST "Outstanding," "Good," "Average," "Needs Improvement," or "Unacceptable" and comment in the area provided:

Products	Outstanding	Good	Average	Needs Improvement	Unacceptable
Services and Support	**Outstanding**	**Good**	**Average**	**Needs Improvement**	**Unacceptable**
Delivery	**Outstanding**	**Good**	**Average**	**Needs Improvement**	**Unacceptable**
Ordering and Billing	**Outstanding**	**Good**	**Average**	**Needs Improvement**	**Unacceptable**
Employees	**Outstanding**	**Good**	**Average**	**Needs Improvement**	**Unacceptable**

Comments

____

____

____

____

____

Thank you. You are a valued customer!

66. Customer Service Request

Customer Service Request	
Customer	Date
Contact	Originator
	Department
Telephone	Telephone
Customer Complaint:	
Person Assigned for Resolution:	
Recommended Action/Action Taken:	
Customer Follow-up Notes: Issue Resolved: ❑ Yes	

67. Product Information

Product ______________________________

Brand Name ______________________________

ID # ______________________________

Product Description

____

____

____

Features

____

____

____

Applications

____

____

____

Technical Specifications

____

____

____

Materials Required

____

____

____

Distributors

____

____

____

Required Lead Time ______________

Prepared by ______________________ Date ______________

Approved by ______________________ Date ______________

68. Order Card

Yes! I'd like to make an order. Please send me:

Quantity	Item Description	Price per Unit	Extended Price
________	________________________________	__________	__________
________	________________________________	__________	__________
________	________________________________	__________	__________
________	________________________________	__________	__________

❑ Payment Enclosed ❑ Bill Me Total __________ $__________

Name ________________________________ Phone ______________

Address ____

City ________________________________ State ______________ZIP

✂...

Yes! I'd like to make an order. Please send me:

Quantity	Item Description	Price per Unit	Extended Price
________	________________________________	__________	__________
________	________________________________	__________	__________
________	________________________________	__________	__________
________	________________________________	__________	__________

❑ Payment Enclosed ❑ Bill Me Total __________ $__________

Name ________________________________ Phone ______________

Address ____

City ________________________________ State ______________ZIP

✂...

Yes! I'd like to make an order. Please send me:

Quantity	Item Description	Price per Unit	Extended Price
________	________________________________	__________	__________
________	________________________________	__________	__________
________	________________________________	__________	__________
________	________________________________	__________	__________

❑ Payment Enclosed ❑ Bill Me Total __________ $__________

Name ________________________________ Phone ______________

Address ____

City ________________________________ State ______________ZIP

69. Work Order/Request for Quote

Overview

Customer Name ______________________________

Customer Address ______________________________

Contact Person ______________________________

Phone ____________________

Project Description ______________________________

____

____

Specific Instructions

Materials and Quantities to Be Used

____

____

____

____

Additional Outside Services Required

____

____

____

____

Comments

____

____

____

____

Sample of Design or Sketch of Design

Pricing ______________________________

____

Submitted by ____________________ Date ____________

70. Sales Order Form

Customer Name ______________________________ Date ______________

Phone ______________________________

Address ______________________________

City ______________________________ State______________ ZIP ____________

Ship to Address ______________________________

City ______________________________ State______________ ZIP ____________

Special Instructions

____

____

____

____

Item Number	Description	Quantity	Unit Price	Extended Price

Gross Total ____________

Tax ____________

Freight ____________

Labor ____________

Total Due ____________

Order Taken by ______________________________

71. Daily Sales Recap

For the Month of ________________, __________

Date	Taxable Sales	Nontaxable Sales	Total Sales
1			
2			
3			
4			
5			
6			
7			
8			
9			
10			
11			
12			
13			
14			
15			
16			
17			
18			
19			
20			
21			
22			
23			
24			
25			
26			
27			
28			
29			
30			
31			
TOTAL			

72. Month-to-Month Sales Comparison Log

For Year ______________

Month	Taxable Sales	Nontaxable Sales	Total Sales
January	______	______	______
February	______	______	______
March	______	______	______
April	______	______	______
May	______	______	______
June	______	______	______
July	______	______	______
August	______	______	______
September	______	______	______
October	______	______	______
November	______	______	______
December	______	______	______

73. Cash Receipts Control Log

Period ______________________________

Date	Check Amount	Customer ID	Reference No.
________	$________	________	________
________	$________	________	________
________	$________	________	________
________	$________	________	________
________	$________	________	________
________	$________	________	________
________	$________	________	________
________	$________	________	________
________	$________	________	________
________	$________	________	________
________	$________	________	________
________	$________	________	________
________	$________	________	________
________	$________	________	________
________	$________	________	________
________	$________	________	________
________	$________	________	________
________	$________	________	________
________	$________	________	________
________	$________	________	________
________	$________	________	________
________	$________	________	________
________	$________	________	________
________	$________	________	________
________	$________	________	________
________	$________	________	________
________	$________	________	________

Reconciled to Daily Cash Deposit by ______________________________ Date __________

Authorized by ______________________________ Date __________

CHAPTER 7

Credit, Billing, and Collection Tools

The forms presented in this section are designed to help you and your company receive payment for the goods and services you and your company provide. The forms include credit application forms, credit terms documentation, past due reminder and demand letters, and invoices/statements.

Your company will have an easier time with the challenges of billing and collections if it formalizes its credit application process and consistently applies the credit application process to every customer who comes knocking. When a new customer appears, you should begin by asking the customer to complete *Authorization to Release Credit Information.* This authorization form gives your company the authority to make inquiries with credit reporting bureaus without fear of consequence. Never submit a credit inquiry to a credit reporting bureau without written authorization. You'll also ask your new customer to complete either the *Business Credit Application* or, if the customer is an individual, the *Personal Credit Application*. These credit application forms are invaluable. Not only do they help you evaluate your customer for creditworthiness, but also they serve to obtain information that can make the collection process easier in the event that your customer defaults on the credit arrangements. The *Credit Approval Form* is an internal tracking mechanism that collects certain information gleaned from the credit inquiry process and ensures that all necessary staff authorize the approval of credit for each customer.

Once your organization has agreed to extend credit to a customer, you should document the credit terms by having your customer submit a signed copy of the *Credit Terms Agreement*. This is another powerful protection device that can give you significant leverage if a customer defaults on those credit terms.

Naturally, you can increase the speed at which your customers pay and the reliability with which they pay if you make it fast and easy to pay. The *EasyPay Automatic Payment Agreement* is a notice and agreement signed by your customer that enables you to make automatic withdrawals from either your customer's bank or your customer's credit card. Once this agreement is in place, your customers are far more likely to pay on time and in full.

The *Response to Request for Adjustment of Account* is a letter that your credit or collections department would send to a customer who has formally requested an adjustment to his or her account.

The next four forms in this section address the unfortunate but all too common circumstance of a late-paying or nonpaying customer. The four letters escalate both in tone and consequences. The *Credit Terms Reminder Letter* is a bland and polite reminder for the habitually late-paying customer. We have included two *Past Due Reminder Letters*, which you should promptly issue when a customer fails to pay after 30 and 45 days, respectively. You should always endeavor to not allow your receivables to age: studies have shown that uncollected customer balances become far less likely to be collected if they are allowed to age beyond 60, 90, and 120 days. The last collection letter is the *Past Due Demand Letter*. This is your last resort when handling a nonpaying customer; the letter terminates the credit privileges of the errant customer and threatens legal and collection action.

It is important to recognize the difference between *invoices* and *statements*. Invoices are individual billing notices; typically, one invoice is delivered to a customer for each order. Statements are billing summaries; typically, a statement is delivered to a customer periodically. The statement will summarize billing and payment activity and will reference each individual invoice. If you invoice your customers, you should issue monthly statements as well. We have included two forms of invoices. Use the *Job Invoice* when you provide both materials and labor to your customers; use the *Customer Invoice* when you provide only goods or only services. Use the *Customer Statement* to advise your customers of billing and payment activity.

The *Request for Payment* form is a simple invoice best used for a one-time customer for whom you do not wish to set up a full-blown account. Use the *Short Pay Inquiry Form* when a customer fails to pay the full amount of an invoice.

74. Authorization to Release Credit Information

From:

____

____

____

____

To:

____

____

____

____

Date ______________

Dear ______________________________,

Thank you for your recent interest in establishing credit with our company. Please sign the authorization to release information agreement below and complete the enclosed form. Then send them to us with your most recent financial statements. We will contact your credit and bank references. Then we will contact you regarding your credit terms with our company.

Thank you.

Signature

Credit Manager

We have recently applied for credit with ______________________________.
We have been requested to provide information for their use in reviewing our creditworthiness. Therefore, I authorize the investigation of me and my firm, ______________________________, and its related credit information.

The release in any manner of all information by you is authorized whether such information is of record or not.

I do hereby release all persons, agencies, firms, companies, etc. from any damages resulting from providing such information.

This authorization is valid for 30 days from the date of my signature below. Please keep a copy of my release request for your files. Thank you for your cooperation.

Signature ______________________________ Date ______________

75. Business Credit Application

From:

____

____

____

Thank you for your interest in our company's products and services. We appreciate your business and look forward to a long and prosperous business relationship.

Please complete the credit application and return it to the above address, attention Credit Department. Please note our credit terms. You will be advised shortly of your credit status with our company. Thank you.

Credit Application

Business Legal Name____

Business Trade Name____

Web Site Address ____

Business Address Information

Address ____

City/Town ____

State/Province _______________________ Zip ____________________

Check one:

Sole Proprietorship ______ Partnership ______ Corporation ______ LLC ______ Other________

Federal Tax ID Number _________________

Contact Person _____________________ Title ____________________

Contact Person _____________________ Title ____________________

Phone (_____)______________ Ext _____ Fax (_____)____________

E-mail Address _________________________ Dept __________________

Hours of Operation ____

Names of Authorized Account Users _______________________________

Do you require an Invoice? Yes _______ No _______

Invoice Preferred?

Weekly invoice and monthly statement _______ Open item statement _______

Billing Address Information (If different from above)

Address ____

City/Town ____

State/Province ___________________________ ZIP _________________

Contact Persons _________________________ Title _________________

Phone (______)____________________ Ext ______ Fax (______)____________

E-mail Address ______________________________ Dept ________________

Other Location Information (i.e., Local Contacts)

Additional Location ____

Address ____

City/Town ____

State/Province ______________________________ ZIP ______________

Contact Persons ___________________________ Title ______________

Phone (______)____________________ Ext ______ Fax (______)____________

E-mail Address ___________________________ Dept ________________

Hours of Operation ____

Preferred Billing Date ____

Names of Authorized Users _______________________________________

Doing Business as (DBA) Names ___________________________________

Bank References

Bank Name ____

Account Number ____

City/Town ____

State/ Province _________ Phone (_____) _______________ Ext ________

Bank Officer ____

Bank Name ____

Account Number ____

City/Town ____

State/ Province _________ Phone (_____) _______________ Ext ________

Bank Officer ____

Trade or Supplier Credit References (Must provide at least 3)

Name ____

Address ____

Person to Contact ____

City/Town ____

State/Province ______________________________ ZIP ______________

Phone (______)____________________ Ext ______ Fax (______)____________

Name ______________________________

Address ______________________________

Person to Contact ______________________________

City/Town ______________________________

State/Province ______________ ZIP __________

Phone (____)__________ Ext _____ Fax (____)__________

Name ______________________________

Address ______________________________

Person to Contact ______________________________

City/Town ______________________________

State/Province ______________ ZIP __________

Phone (____)__________ Ext _____ Fax (____)__________

Names of Principals: Owners, Officers, Partners

Name ______________________________

Address ______________________________

City/Town ______________________________

State/Province ______________ ZIP __________

Phone (____)__________ Ext _____ Fax (____)__________

Title ______________ Social Security # _____-_____-_____

Name ______________________________

Address ______________________________

City/Town ______________________________

State/Province ______________ ZIP __________

Phone (____)__________ Ext _____ Fax (____)__________

Title ______________ Social Security # _____-_____-_____

Please attach additional pages if you have more than two principals.

I certify that I am authorized to sign and submit this application for and on behalf of the applicant. I also certify that the foregoing information is true and correct to the best of my knowledge.

______________________________ ______________________________

Name (Please Print or Type) Title

______________________________ ______________________________

Signature Date

76. Personal Credit Application

From:

____

____

____

Thank you for your interest in our company's products and services. We appreciate your business and look forward to a long and prosperous business relationship.

Please complete the credit application and return it to the above address, attention Credit Department. Please note our credit terms. You will be advised shortly of your credit status with our company. Thank you.

Credit Application

Personal Information:

Name____

Address ____

City/Town ____

State/Province ___________________________ ZIP _______________________

Social Security Number _______-________-_______

Phone (______)_________________ Ext ______ Fax (______)_______________

E-mail Address ___________________________ Date of Birth___________________

Do you ❑ Own ❑ Rent Monthly Housing Payment Amount $_______________

Prior Addresses for the Last 5 Years:

Address ______________________________________ City State ZIP: _______________________

Address ______________________________________ City State ZIP: _______________________

Employment:

Employer ____

Address ____

Occupation_____________________________

Contact to verify employment______________________ Phone # (______)_________________

Length of Employment____________________ Monthly Gross Salary ____________________

Credit References:

Bank Name __________________________ Account Number __________________________

City/Town ____

State/ Province ________ Phone (______) _______________ Ext ________

Bank Officer ____

Credit Card Type ____________ Number ____________________ Exp. Date ________________

Credit Card Type________________ Number ______________________ Exp. Date ____________________

I certify that I am authorized to sign and submit this application for and on behalf of the applicant. I also certify that the foregoing information is true and correct to the best of my knowledge.

__________________________________ __________________________

Name (Please Print or Type) Date

____

Signature

77. Credit Approval Form

To be completed by the Credit Department.

Company Name (Applicant)______________________________

Company Address ______________________________

Contact Name ______________________________

Phone Number ______________________________

Bank References Notes ______________________________

____

____

Credit References Notes ______________________________

____

____

Approximate Amount of Business Anticipated per Month (as per Sales Manager) $ _______________

Credit Terms ____________________

Credit Limit ____________________

Any Special Instructions ______________________________

____

____

Prepared by ______________________________

Approvals:

Credit Manager ____________________ Date ____________

Sales Manager ____________________ Date ____________

Controller ____________________ Date ____________

General Manager ____________________ Date ____________

78. Credit Terms Agreement

I, the "Applicant," hereby agree to the following credit terms agreement in connection with my application for credit terms from ______________________________ ("Company"). I, Applicant, agree as follows:

1. Applicant represents that the information supplied with the credit application and all associated documentation is in all respects complete, accurate, and truthful. Applicant agrees to notify Company promptly, in writing, of any substantive changes in the information Applicant has provided.
2. Applicant agrees to pay in full for goods and services rendered (without deduction or setoff) on or before the earlier of the 30th day of the month following the date of billing or the due date started on each billing to the order of Company. Any amounts not paid when due shall be assessed a service charge at the rate of ____% per year (____% per month) or the highest rate allowed by law.
3. If Applicant's account is placed or given to an attorney for collection, Applicant shall pay any and all expenses of collection and attempted collection, court costs, and reasonable attorney's fees in addition to other amounts due. The failure of Company to charge interest on Applicant's account or pursue any other remedy available to it shall not constitute Company's waiver of any rights.
4. The acceptance of this application by Company does not constitute an agreement to extend credit to Applicant or to provide services to Applicant. Company, in its absolute discretion, may set and/or modify credit limits from time to time or terminate credit, with or without notice to Applicant.
5. In the event Applicant or any affiliate of Applicant (i.e., a company or other entity under common control) defaults in the payment of any sums due to Company, all other amounts due from Applicant or any affiliate shall be immediately due and payable, including any amount due for freight in transit. Also, in the event of such default, to the extent allowed under applicable law, Company is hereby authorized by Applicant to take possession of any freight then being shipped by Applicant and hold the same until payment is made, with all the rights of a secured party under the Uniform Commercial Code, as applicable in the State of Company's headquarters.
6. Applicant agrees that Company may set off against monies due it from Applicant or any affiliate any monies owed by Company to Applicant or any affiliate. Applicant agrees that he/she will not set off against any amounts due Company or claimed to be due to Applicant from Company.
7. If any one or more of the above terms becomes invalid or illegal in any respect, such term or terms shall be waived and the validity, legality, and enforceability of the remaining terms shall not be affected.
8. All disputes related to underlying charges must be submitted to Company no later than 30 days following date of billing. Any billing not challenged within 60 days will be deemed accepted and it is agreed will not thereafter be subject to dispute by Applicant. Adjustments must be submitted to Company in writing. All adjustments must reference either an invoice number or an air waybill number, or both numbers, for which the adjustment is being made.
9. I have read, I understand, and I accept the above terms, and I have provided true information to the best of my knowledge. I understand you will rely on the information provided herein in determining whether to extend credit and the limits thereof and that you may wish to periodically update the information given herein. For the purpose of obtaining credit from Company, Applicant hereby authorizes Company or its agents to investigate the Applicant's personal, partnership, or corporate credit and financial responsibility.

____
Applicant

______________________________ ______________
Name (Please Print or Type) Title

______________________________ ______________
Signature Date

79. EasyPay Automatic Payment Agreement

Here's How It Works:

When you enroll in EasyPay, we deduct funds automatically from your local checking account or credit card account to pay your bill. Your bill will be paid for you on time and automatically. You won't have to worry about missing a payment if you are away on a business trip or vacation. You'll continue to receive your monthly statement and you'll have 15 days from the billing date to review it before your bank pays the amount due. If you feel there is a problem with your bill, simply call us at ________________. Of course, you can always dispute a bill with us even if the bill was paid automatically–we are always here to listen. You can notify us if you wish to discontinue EasyPay at any time.

It's Easy to Start EasyPay:

Simply complete the attached form and return it with your next payment. Enclose an original check marked "Void" or a photocopy of a check from the checking account you wish to have debited or, if you wish to have your credit card account billed automatically, just fill out the form below. Your next bill will show "No Payment Due" and your financial institution will show the appropriate debit on your monthly statement.

Why wait? Just fill out the form and send it in with your next payment.

EasyPay Authorization Agreement

I hereby authorize ________________________ ("Company") to deduct funds from my checking account/credit card account listed below to pay my Company bills. I understand that these automatic payments may be cancelled if I notify Company in writing prior to the next billing date.

____

(Please Print) Name of Your Bank or Credit Card Company

____ ____________________

Your Name as Shown on Financial Institution Records Your Daytime Phone

____

Address in Our Records

____ ____________________

Your Signature as Shown on Financial Institution Records Today's Date

To Charge a Bank Account: please attach an original check on which you've written "VOID" or a photocopy of a check from your checking account and return it along with this form with your next payment. Deposit slips cannot be accepted.

To Charge a Credit Card: please fill out the following:

____

Type: VISA/MasterCard/American Express Card Number Exp. Date

____

Credit Card Billing Address

80. Response to Request for Adjustment of Account

From:

____

____

____

____

To:

____

____

____

____

Date ______________

Dear Customer:

Thank you for writing us regarding an error or adjustment to your account with our firm.

We have received your request and are currently researching your account and its history. We should complete our research shortly and make any necessary adjustment on your next statement. Understand that the accuracy of your account is of vital importance to us and that we will give this matter our highest attention.

Yours truly,

81. Credit Terms Reminder Letter

From:

____

____

____

____

To:

____

____

____

____

Date _______________

Dear _________________________________:

Thank you for your recent order with our firm. As a reminder to your Purchasing and Accounts Payable Departments, our credit terms are as follows: ____.
If you have any questions about your credit terms or our policies, please feel free to contact us.

Thank you for adhering to our credit policy. We hope our business relationship is a long and prosperous one.

Thank you again.

82. Past Due Reminder Letter

From:

____

____

____

____

To:

____

____

____

____

Date _______________

Dear Customer:

Please take note that your account is still past due in the amount of $ _______________________. We sent you a statement a short time ago, which was not acted upon by you. Please submit payment immediately to avoid further charges to your account. We want to continue our relationship with you, but we need your cooperation and your payment to do so.

Thank you for your attention to this matter.

83. Past Due Reminder Letter

From:

____

____

____

____

To:

____

____

____

____

Date _______________

Dear Customer:

Please take note that your account is still past due in the amount of $ _______________________. We sent you a statement a short time ago, which was not acted upon by you. Please submit payment immediately.

Your failure to pay the amount due on your account is a violation of the terms of your credit agreement with us. We therefore will suspend your account in seven days from the date of this letter if we do not receive payment. Once we suspend your account, it is unlikely that we will reactivate credit terms on your account.

We sincerely hope that you submit payment in full.

Thank you.

84. Past Due Demand Letter

From:

____

____

____

____

To:

____

____

____

____

Date _______________

Dear Customer:

This matter requires your immediate attention. Please take note that your account is still past due in the amount of $_______________________. We sent you a statement a short time ago, and several reminders, upon which you have not acted. This is our final request for payment and we ask that you submit payment immediately.

We had sincerely hoped that we could continue to do business with you, but your failure to pay your outstanding bill has made that impossible. We have suspended your credit privileges with our company.

Furthermore, if we do not receive payment immediately, we will turn this matter over for collection to a collection agency or attorney, or both. Please review your credit agreement. We will be seeking interest and we may also seek court costs and fees and attorney's fees to the extent permitted by law.

We sincerely hope that you submit payment in full to avoid the course of action that we have outlined here.

Thank you.

85. Job Invoice

Buyer

Date	Your Order #	Our Order #	Sales Rep	FOB	Ship Via	Terms	Tax ID

Materials			
Quantity	Material	Unit Price	Amount
		Total Materials	

Labor			
Date	Hours/Tasks	Rate	Amount
		Total Labor	
		Total Materials and Labor	

86. Customer Invoice

Buyer

Date	Your Order #	Our Order #	Sales Rep	FOB	Ship Via	Terms	Tax ID

Quantity	Item	Units	Description	Discount %	Taxable	Unit Price	Total
						Balance	

87. Customer Statement

Buyer

Statement Date	Statement #

Reference	Date	Item/Code	Description	Amount	Balance
				Balance	

Codes: C = Credit Memo P = Payment A = Discount Allowed
D = Debit Memo I = Invoice F = Finance Charge

88. Request for Payment

From:

____

____

____

____

To:

____

____

____

____

Date ______________

Dear Customer:

We have received your order and promptly processed the order according to your instructions. Please send the amount listed below immediately. Payment is expected in the form of a check, money order, VISA, or MasterCard. Please place the reference number on your payment. We appreciate your interest in our product/service and your prompt attention to this matter.

Thank you.

Accounting Department

Amount $ ______________________ Reference # ______________________

From:

Check payment $ ______________ Check # ______________

To Charge a Credit Card: please fill out the following:

____

Type: VISA/MasterCard/American Express Card Number Exp. Date

____

Credit Card Billing Address

____

____

____

____

89. Short Pay Inquiry Form

From:

____

____

____

____

To:

____

____

____

____

Date _______________

Dear Customer:

We recently received payment from you for our invoice # _________________. Thank you.

However, the amount that you submitted fell short of the amount of the invoice. We were unable to determine why. Below please tell us the reason for the short pay so that we may review our records and determine if the short pay is acceptable.

Thank you.

Accounting Department

Amount of short-paid $ ______________________ Reference # _______________________

From __________________________________

Reason for short payment ____

____

CHAPTER 8

Contracts and Agreements

The surest way to maintain clear understandings with your customers and vendors is to document your arrangements in written agreements. We have included here several useful and universal contracts and agreements.

Use the *Bill of Sale* to record the terms of a simple sale of goods or property. The *Unsecured Promissory Note* is simply a legal document that documents a promise to pay money at a future date. Use this document to memorialize simple business or personal loans. The *Secured Promissory Note and Security Agreement* is a legal document that memorializes a loan, but it goes a step farther: it grants to the lender the right to repossess property in the event the loan is not repaid. The *Secured Promissory Note and Security Agreement* gives the lender much greater rights and power than the *Unsecured Promissory Note.*

The *Simple Commercial Lease* is a straightforward rental agreement for commercial (non-residential) property. The *Consulting Services Agreement* is a general and universal agreement suitable for nearly all types of consulting services firms. Simply customize the agreement to cover the particular services that you offer. The *Multimedia Development Contract* is a contract suitable for use by Web developers, programmers, and print and graphic designers. Keep in mind, however, that you will need to customize the *Multimedia Development Contract* to cover the particular services that you offer.

The *Mutual Nondisclosure Agreement* is an agreement whereby two parties agree to maintain the confidentiality of information that they share in the context of business discussions or negotiations. The *Mutual Nondisclosure Agreement* is common in many industries where parties will discuss technology, work product, trade secrets, and competitive secrets in the context of negotiations. Finally, the *Mutual Compromise Agreement and Mutual Release* is an agreement to finally and forever settle a dispute between two parties. Use this agreement to finalize the resolution of conflicts and lawsuits between you and third parties.

90. Bill of Sale

BILL OF SALE

This Bill of Sale is made on this ______ day of 20___ between ________________________________ ("Seller") and ______________________________ ("Buyer").

Seller, in exchange for consideration of $__________, the receipt of which funds is acknowledged, hereby do grant, sell, transfer, and deliver to Buyer the following goods: ____.

Buyer shall have full rights and title to the goods described above.

Seller is the lawful owner of the goods and the goods are free from all encumbrances. Seller has good right to sell the goods and will warrant and defend the right against the lawful claims and demands of all persons.

____
Signature of Seller

____
Signature of Buyer

91. Unsecured Promissory Note

UNSECURED PROMISSORY NOTE

Amount: $____________________

Date: __________________

For value received, ________________________________ ("Borrower") hereby covenants and promises to pay to ______________________________ ("Lender") __________________________________ Dollars ($__________.00) in lawful money of the United States of America, together with interest thereon computed from the date hereof at the rate of ten percent (10%) per annum, on an actual day/365 day basis. All interest, principal, and other costs hereunder shall be due and payable to the holder ("Holder") of this Promissory Note (this "Note") on or before ____________________ (the "Due Date").

Payments of principal and interest will be made in legal tender of the United States of America. Borrower shall have the right to prepay without penalty all or any part of the unpaid balance of this Note at any time. Borrower shall not be entitled to re-borrow any prepaid amounts of the principal, interest, or other costs or charges. All payments made pursuant to this Note will be first applied to accrued and unpaid interest, if any, then to other proper charges under this Note, and the balance, if any, to principal.

This Note shall be paid as follows: monthly payments of $_____________ shall be made upon this Note on the first day of each month, commencing with the date of ________________, and shall continue until ____________ (the "Repayment Date"), at which time all sums due hereunder shall be paid.

Notwithstanding anything in this Note to the contrary, the entire unpaid principal amount of this Note, together with all accrued but unpaid interest thereon and other unpaid charges hereunder, will become immediately all due and payable without further notice at the option of the Holder if Borrower fails to timely make any payment hereunder when such payment becomes first due and such failure continues for a period of ten days after written notice from Holder to Borrower.

If any amount payable to Holder under this Note is not received by Holder on or before the Due Date, then such amount (the "Delinquent Amount") will bear interest from and after the Due Date until paid at an annual rate of interest equal to the greater of (i) fifteen percent (15%) or (ii) the maximum rate then permitted by law (the "Default Rate"). If the maximum rate then permitted by law is lower than 15%, the maximum legal rate shall be the Default Rate.

All rights, remedies, undertakings, obligations, options, covenants, conditions, and agreements contained in this Note are cumulative and no one of them will be exclusive of any other. Any notice to any party concerning this Note will be delivered as set forth in the Financing Agreement.

Borrower for itself and its legal representatives, successors, and assigns expressly waives presentment, protest, demand, notice of dishonor, notice of nonpayment, notice of maturity, notice of protest, presentment for the purpose of accelerating maturity, and diligence in collection, and consents that Holder may extend the time for payment or otherwise modify the terms of payment or any part or the whole of the debt evidenced hereby.

The prevailing party in any action, litigation, or proceeding, including any appeal or the collection of any judgment concerning this Note, will be awarded, in addition to any damages, injunctions, or other relief, and without regard to whether or not such matter be prosecuted to final judgment, such party's costs and expenses, including reasonable attorneys' fees, and Lender shall be entitled to recover all of its attorneys' fees and costs should Lender place this Note in the hands of an attorney for collection.

____ ("Borrower")

Signature ________________________________

Date ____________________________________

92. Secured Promissory Note and Security Agreement

SECURED PROMISSORY NOTE

Amount: $____________________

Date: ________________________

For value received, ___________________________________ ("Borrower") hereby covenants and promises to pay to ____________________________________ ("Lender") ____________________________________ Dollars ($__________) in lawful money of the United States of America, together with interest thereon computed from the date hereof at the rate of ten percent (10%) per annum, on an actual day/365 day basis. All interest, principal, and other costs hereunder shall be due and payable to the holder ("Holder") of this Promissory Note (this "Note") on or before ____________________ (the "Due Date").

Payments of principal and interest will be made in legal tender of the United States of America. Borrower shall have the right to prepay without penalty all or any part of the unpaid balance of this Note at any time. Borrower shall not be entitled to re-borrow any prepaid amounts of the principal, interest, or other costs or charges. All payments made pursuant to this Note will be first applied to accrued and unpaid interest, if any, then to other proper charges under this Note, and the balance, if any, to principal.

This Note is secured by a security interest in Borrower's assets, as more particularly described in the Security Agreement attached to this Note.

This Note shall be paid as follows: monthly payments of $_____________ shall be made upon this Note on the first day of each month, commencing with the date of _____________________, and shall continue until ___________ (the "Repayment Date"), at which time all sums due hereunder shall be paid.

Notwithstanding anything in this Note to the contrary, the entire unpaid principal amount of this Note, together with all accrued but unpaid interest thereon and other unpaid charges hereunder, will become immediately all due and payable without further notice at the option of the Holder if Borrower fails to timely make any payment hereunder when such payment becomes first due and such failure continues for a period of ten days after written notice from Holder to Borrower.

If any amount payable to Holder under this Note is not received by Holder on or before the Due Date, then such amount (the "Delinquent Amount") will bear interest from and after the Due Date until paid at an annual rate of interest equal to the greater of (i) fifteen percent (15%) or (ii) the maximum rate then permitted by law (the "Default Rate"). If the maximum rate then permitted by law is lower than 15%, the maximum legal rate shall be the Default Rate.

All rights, remedies, undertakings, obligations, options, covenants, conditions, and agreements contained in this Note are cumulative and no one of them will be exclusive of any other. Any notice to any party concerning this Note will be delivered as set forth in the Financing Agreement.

Borrower for itself and its legal representatives, successors, and assigns expressly waives presentment, protest, demand, notice of dishonor, notice of nonpayment, notice of maturity, notice of protest, presentment for the purpose of accelerating maturity, and diligence in collection and consents that Holder may extend the time for payment or otherwise modify the terms of payment or any part or the whole of the debt evidenced hereby.

The prevailing party in any action, litigation, or proceeding, including any appeal or the collection of any judgment concerning this Note, will be awarded, in addition to any damages, injunctions, or other relief, and without regard to whether or not such matter be prosecuted to final judgment, such party's costs and expenses, including reasonable attorneys' fees, and Lender shall be entitled to recover all of its attorneys' fees and costs should Lender place this Note in the hands of an attorney for collection.

______________________________ ("Borrower")

Signature ______________________________

SECURITY AGREEMENT ACCOMPANYING SECURED PROMISSORY NOTE

Date____________________

This Security Agreement is made on this ______ day of ______________ between ______________________________ ("Borrower") and ______________________________ ("Lender").

1. Security Interest. Borrower grants to Lender a "Security Interest" in the following property (the "Collateral"):

____

____

____

____

____

The Security Interest shall secure the payment and performance of Borrower's promissory note of given date herewith in the principal amount of ______________ Dollars ($_________) and the payment and performance of all other liabilities and obligations of Borrower to Lender of every kind and description, direct or indirect, absolute or contingent, due or to become due, now existing or hereafter arising.

2. Covenants. Borrower hereby warrants and covenants:
   a. The parties intend that the collateral is and will at all times remain personal property despite the fact and irrespective of the manner in which it is attached to realty.
   b. The Borrower will not sell, dispose, or otherwise transfer the collateral or any interest therein without the prior written consent of Lender, and the Borrower shall keep the collateral free from unpaid charges (including rent), taxes, and liens.
   c. The Borrower shall execute alone or with Lender any Financing Statement or other document or procure any document, and pay the cost of filing the same in all public offices wherever filing is deemed by Lender to be necessary.
   d. Borrower shall maintain insurance at all times with respect to all collateral against risks of fire, theft, and other such risks and in such amounts as Lender may require. The policies shall be payable to both the Lender and the Borrower as their interests appear and shall provide for ten (10) days' written notice of cancellation to Lender.
   e. The Borrower shall make all repairs, replacements, additions, and improvements necessary to maintain any equipment in good working order and condition. At its option, Lender may discharge taxes, liens, or other encumbrances at any time levied or placed on the collateral, may pay rent or insurance due on the collateral, and may pay for the maintenance and preservation of the collateral. Borrower agrees to reimburse Lender on demand for any payment made or any expense incurred by Lender pursuant to the foregoing authorization.
3. Default. The Borrower shall be in default under this Agreement if it is in default under the Note. Upon default and at any time thereafter, Lender may declare all obligations secured hereby immediately due and payable and

shall have the remedies of a Lender under the Uniform Commercial Code. Lender may require the Borrower to make it available to Lender at a place that is mutually convenient. No waiver by Lender of any default shall operate as a waiver of any other default or of the same default on a future occasion. This Agreement shall inure to the benefit of and bind the heirs, executors, administrators, successors, and assigns of the parties. This Agreement shall have the effect of an instrument under seal.

________________________________ ("Borrower")

Signature __________________________

Date______________________________

93. Simple Commercial Lease

This Commercial Lease is hereby made between ____________________, the "Lessor," and ____________, the "Lessee," concerning the following property: ____________________________________, the "Premises."

Lessee hereby leases from Lessor the Premises.

1. Term and Rent. Lessor will lease the above Premises for an initial term of _________ years and ____________ months, beginning on ________________, 20_____, and ending on ___________, 20______, as provided herein at the monthly rent of $ ____________________, payable in equal installments in advance on the first day of each month for that month's rental, during the term of the lease. All rental payments shall be made to Lessor, at the following address: ____________ ____.
2. Use. Lessee shall use and occupy the Premises for ______________________. The Premises shall be used for no other purpose. Lessor represents that the Premises may lawfully be used for such purpose.
3. Care and Maintenance of Premises. Lessee acknowledges that the Premises are in good order and repair, unless otherwise indicated herein. Lessee shall, at his own expense and at all times, maintain the Premises in good and safe condition, including electrical wiring, plumbing and heating installations, and any other system or equipment upon the Premises and shall surrender the same, at termination hereof, in as good a condition as received, normal wear and tear excepted. Lessee shall be responsible for all repairs required, excepting the roof, exterior walls, structural foundations, and the following: __________________________________, which shall be maintained by Lessor. Lessee shall also maintain in good condition such portions adjacent to the Premises, such as sidewalks, driveways, lawns, and shrubbery, which would otherwise be required to be maintained by Lessor.
4. Alterations. Lessee shall not, without first obtaining the written consent of Lessor, make any alterations, additions, or improvements, in, to, or about the Premises.
5. Ordinances and Statues. Lessee shall comply with all statutes, ordinances, and requirements of all municipal, state, and federal authorities now in force, or which may hereafter be in force, pertaining to the Premises, occasioned by or affecting the use thereof by Lessee.
6. Assignment and Subletting. Lessee shall not assign this lease or sublet any portion of the Premises without prior written consent of the Lessor, which shall not be unreasonably withheld. Any such assignment or subletting without consent shall be void and, at the option of the Lessor, may terminate this lease.
7. Utilities. All applications and connections for necessary utility services on the demised Premises shall be made in the name of Lessee only, and Lessee shall be solely liable for utility charges as they become due, including those for sewer, water, gas, electricity, and telephone services.
8. Entry and Inspection. Lessee shall permit Lessor or Lessor's agents to enter upon the Premises at reasonable times and upon reasonable notice, for the purpose of inspecting the same, and will permit Lessor, at any time within sixty (60) days prior to the expiration of this lease, to place upon the Premises any usual "To Let" or "For Lease" signs and permit persons desiring to lease the same to inspect the Premises thereafter.
9. Possession. If Lessor is unable to deliver possession of the Premises at the commencement hereof, Lessor shall not be liable for any damage caused thereby, nor shall this lease be void or voidable, but Lessee shall not be liable for any rent until possession is delivered. Lessee may terminate this lease if possession is not delivered within ten (10) days of the commencement of the term hereof.
10. Indemnification of Lessor. Lessor shall not be liable for any damage or injury to Lessee, or any other person, or to any property, occurring on the demised Premises or any part thereof, and Lessee agrees to hold Lessor harmless from any claims for damages, no matter how caused.

11. Insurance. Lessee, at his expense, shall maintain public liability insurance including bodily injury and property damage insuring Lessee and Lessor with minimum coverage as follows:______________________________
____

    Lessee shall provide Lessor with a Certificate of Insurance showing Lessor as additional insured. The Certificate shall provide for a ten-day written notice to Lessor in the event of cancellation or material change of coverage. To the maximum extent permitted by insurance policies that may be owned by Lessor or Lessee, Lessee and Lessor, for the benefit of each other, waive any and all rights of subrogation that might otherwise exist.

12. Eminent Domain. If the Premises or any part thereof or any estate therein, or any other part of the building materially affecting Lessee's use of the Premises, shall be taken by eminent domain, this lease shall terminate on the date when title vests pursuant to such taking. The rent, and any additional rent, shall be apportioned as of the termination date, and any rent paid for any period beyond that date shall be repaid to Lessee. Lessee shall not be entitled to any part of the award for such taking or any payment in lieu thereof, but Lessee may file a claim for any taking of fixtures and improvements owned by Lessee and for moving expenses.

13. Destruction of Premises. In the event of a partial destruction of the Premises during the term hereof, from any cause, Lessor shall forthwith repair the same, provided that such repairs can be made within sixty (60) days under existing governmental laws and regulations, but such partial destruction shall not terminate this lease, except that Lessee shall be entitled to a proportionate reduction of rent while such repairs are being made, based upon the extent to which the making of such repairs shall interfere with the business of Lessee on the Premises. If such repairs cannot be made within said sixty (60) days, Lessor, at his option, may make the same within a reasonable time, this lease continuing in effect with the rent proportionately abated as aforesaid, and in the event that Lessor shall not elect to make such repairs that cannot be made within sixty (60) days, this lease may be terminated at the option of either party. In the event that the building in which the demised Premises may be situated is destroyed to an extent of not less than one-third of the replacement costs thereof, Lessor may elect to terminate this lease whether the demised Premises be injured or not. A total destruction of the building in which the Premises may be situated shall terminate this lease.

14. Lessor's Remedies on Default. If Lessee defaults in the payment of rent, or any additional rent, or defaults in the performance of any of the other covenants or conditions hereof, Lessor may give Lessee notice of such default and if Lessee does not cure any such default within sixty (60) days, after the giving of such notice (or if such other default is of such nature that it cannot be completely cured within such period, if Lessee does not commence such curing within such sixty (60) days and thereafter proceed with reasonable diligence and in good faith to cure such default), then Lessor may terminate this lease on not less than thirty (30) days' notice to Lessee. On the date specified in such notice, the term of this lease shall terminate and Lessee shall then quit and surrender the Premises to Lessor, but Lessee shall remain liable as hereinafter provided. If this lease shall have been so terminated by Lessor, Lessor may at any time thereafter resume possession of the Premises by any lawful means and remove Lessee or other occupants and their effects. No failure to enforce any term shall be deemed a waiver.

15. Common Area Expenses. In the event the Premises are situated in a shopping center or in a commercial building in which there are common areas, Lessee agrees to pay his pro-rata share of maintenance, taxes, and insurance for the common areas.

16. Attorney's Fees. In case suit should be brought for recovery of the Premises, or for any sum due hereunder, or because of any act which may arise out of the possession of the Premises, by either party, the prevailing party shall be entitled to all costs incurred in connection with such action, including a reasonable attorney's fee.

17. Notices. Any notice that either party may or is required to give shall be given by mailing the same, postage prepaid, to Lessee at the Premises, or Lessor at the address shown below [give address], or at such other places as may be designated by the parties from time to time.

18. Heirs, Assigns, Successors. This lease is binding upon and inures to the benefit of the heirs, assigns, and successors in interest to the parties.
19. Subordination. This lease is and shall be subordinated to all existing and future liens and encumbrances against the property.
20. Entire Agreement. The foregoing constitutes the entire agreement between the parties and may be modified only by a writing signed by both parties. The following Exhibits, if any, have been made a part of this lease before the parties' execution hereof:

Signed this ________ day of ____________________, 20____.

____
Signature of Lessor

____
Signature of Lessee

94. Consulting Services Agreement

CONSULTING SERVICES AGREEMENT

This Consulting Services Agreement (this "Agreement") is hereby made between ____________________ ("Client") and ____________________ ("Consultant"). Consultant agrees to provide the "Services," as more fully defined below, to Client and Client agrees to pay to Consultant the Consultant Services Fee, as more fully defined below.

1. Definitions. The following definitions shall apply to this Agreement.
   a. The "Services Fee Payment Schedule" (if applicable) shall include the compensation outlined in Exhibit A, and shall be paid according to the terms outlined in the table attached to this Agreement as Exhibit B.
   b. The "Agreement Term" shall begin with the Commencement Date and shall end with the Termination Date.
   c. The "Commencement Date" shall be the later of (i) the last date upon which a party executes this Agreement or (ii) the first date upon which Services are rendered.
   d. The "Termination Date" shall be any of the following: (i) the one-year anniversary of the Commencement Date or (ii) the date of receipt by either party of a Termination Notice.
2. Services. Consultant shall perform the duties and tasks outlined in the table attached to this Agreement as Exhibit C (the "Services"). The Services may include a development schedule and milestones.
3. Payment. Client shall pay the "Consulting Services Fee" as outlined in the table attached to this Agreement as Exhibit A, and shall pay such Consulting Services Fee according to the "Services Fee Payment Schedule" (if applicable) as outlined in the table attached to this Agreement as Exhibit B.
4. Termination. Either party may without cause terminate this Agreement by delivering to the other party written notice via U.S. Mail, facsimile, or personal delivery (but not by electronic mail transmission) expressing a desire to terminate this Agreement (a "Termination Notice"). Termination shall be effective immediately upon receipt of a Termination Notice.
5. Representations and Warranties. The parties to this Agreement make the following representations and warranties.
   a. Both parties represent and warrant to the other party that they have the full power to enter into this agreement without restriction.
   b. This Agreement shall not establish an employer/employee relationship between the parties. Consultant shall be an independent contractor and shall not enjoy the benefits normally afforded to employees provided either by Client's policy or by law.
   c. Consultant shall not include in the Material (as defined in Paragraph 5, below) any copyrights, trade secrets, trademarks, service marks, patents, or other property that to the Consultant's knowledge would infringe on the rights of third parties.
   d. Consultant shall not be an agent or representative of Client, except as specifically defined in this Agreement. Consultant shall have no authority to, and shall not attempt to, bind Client to contracts with third parties.
6. Confidential Information. Neither party shall, at any time, either directly or indirectly, use for its own benefit, nor shall it divulge, disclose, or communicate any information received from the other party that has been identified as Confidential. Both parties agree to execute standard nondisclosure agreements in connection with this Agreement.
7. Copyrights. Consultant, in the absence of any agreement to the contrary, agrees to irrevocably assign and convey to Client all rights, title, and interest to the copyrights, trade secrets, trademarks, service marks, patents, or

other property created or to be created in connection with the performance of the Services (the "Material"). Client shall be deemed the author of such material and the Material shall be a "work for hire" as defined in 17 U.S.C. § 201 and the cases interpreting it.

8. Limitation of Damages. NEITHER PARTY SHALL BE LIABLE TO THE OTHER PARTY FOR ANY INCIDENTAL, CONSEQUENTIAL, SPECIAL, OR PUNITIVE DAMAGES OF ANY KIND OR NATURE, INCLUDING, WITHOUT LIMITATION, THE BREACH OF THIS AGREEMENT OR ANY TERMINATION OF THIS AGREEMENT, WHETHER SUCH LIABILITY IS ASSERTED ON THE BASIS OF CONTRACT, TORT, OR OTHERWISE, EVEN IF EITHER PARTY HAS BEEN WARNED OR WARNED OF THE POSSIBILITY OF ANY SUCH LOSS OR DAMAGE.

9. General Provisions. This Agreement constitutes the entire agreement of the parties and supersedes all prior understandings and agreements of the parties, whether oral or written. If any provision of this Agreement shall be held to be invalid or unenforceable for any reason, (i) the remaining provisions shall continue to be valid and enforceable; or (ii) if by limiting such provision it would become valid and enforceable, then such provision shall be deemed to be written, construed, and enforced as so limited. This Agreement shall be governed by the laws of the State of California. This Agreement is to be performed in (and venue shall lie exclusively in) ____________________ County, ____________________. This Agreement shall not be strictly construed against any party to this Agreement. Any controversy or claim arising out of or relating to this Agreement, or the breach thereof, shall be resolved by either (i) adjudication in a small claims court (subject to jurisdictional limitations) or (ii) in binding arbitration administered under the rules of the American Arbitration Association in accordance with its applicable rules.

Date ____________ Date ____________

______________________________ ______________________________

Consultant Client

Exhibit A: The "Consulting Services Fee" shall include the following payments and shall be according to the terms outlined herein:

The "Consulting Services Fee" shall include:

$__________________, payable per hour for the time that Consultant devotes to the performance of the Services and for which written itemization for individual tasks is provided to Client (the "Hourly Rate"). The Hourly Rate shall be recorded in increments of time no greater than 1/10 of an hour (6 minutes). Payment shall be made within 15 days of the receipt of a written invoice by Client.

The "Consulting Services Fee" shall include:

$__________________, payable in cash, by negotiable draft(s), or by transfer(s) to Client's bank account, according to the Services Fee Payment Schedule, which appears as Exhibit B.

Exhibit B: The "Services Fee Payment Schedule" shall include the following payments and according to the terms outlined herein:

The "Consulting Services Fee" shall be paid as follows:

$__________________ shall accrue to the consultant upon the completion of each calendar month of service. Partial months shall be prorated on a daily basis. Payment shall be made within 15 days following the later of (a) the end of any applicable calendar month or (b) the submission of a written invoice to Client.

Exhibit C: The "Services" to be performed under the Agreement shall include the following:

Describe services to be performed.

95. Multimedia Development Contract

MULTIMEDIA DEVELOPMENT CONTRACT

This agreement is entered into by and between ____________________("Client") and ____________________ ("Developer") (together, the "Parties").

The effective date of this agreement is ______________ ("Effective Date").

Recitals

WHEREAS, Developer offers the following services and related services: digital media design and development, corporate identity design and development, print design, Web site design and development, interactive kiosk design and development, CD-ROM design and development, logo design and development, computer graphics design and development.

WHEREAS, Client wishes to have Developer provide services for compensation.

NOW, THEREFORE, in consideration of the promises and mutual covenants and agreements set forth herein, Client and Developer agree as follows:

Definitions

"Existing Client Content" means the material provided by Client to be incorporated into the Product.

"Developer Tools" means the software tools of general application, whether owned or licensed to Developer, which are used to develop the Product.

"Development Schedule" shall be, only when applicable, as set forth in Schedule B to this Agreement, which lists the deliverable items contracted for ("Deliverables") and the deadlines for their delivery.

"Error" means, only when applicable, any failure of a Deliverable or Product to (i) meet the Specifications, if any, or (ii) to properly operate.

"Payment Schedule" shall be set forth in Schedule C to this Agreement and is the schedule by which payments under this agreement shall be made.

"Product" means the material that is the subject of this agreement, as further described in paragraph 1.1, below.

"Specifications" for the product, only when applicable, shall be set forth in Schedule A.

DEVELOPMENT AND DELIVERY OF DELIVERABLES, PAYMENT

1.1. Developer agrees to develop, on behalf of Client, the following (the "Product"): (describe what you are making, e.g., interactive Kiosk, educational CD-ROM, Web site, etc.).

1.2. Developer shall use his best efforts to develop each Deliverable and/or Product in accordance with the Specifications, if any.

1.3. All development work will be performed by Developer or his employees or by approved independent contractors who have executed confidentiality agreements, where appropriate.

1.4. Developer shall deliver all Deliverables and/or Product within the times specified in the Development Schedule and in accordance with the Specifications, if any.

1.5. Developer agrees to comply with all reasonable requests of Client as to the manner of delivery of all Deliverables, which may include delivery by electronic means.

1.6. Client agrees to pay according to the Payment Schedule.

1.7. If the Client, following the execution of this Agreement, alters the Specifications, or alters the nature and/or scope of the project as described in paragraph 1.1, or requests additional work, Developer reserves the right, upon notification to the Client, to (i) modify the Payment Schedule or (ii) charge Client on an hourly basis for the additional time at the rate of $____________ per hour.

1.8. Except as expressly provided in this Agreement or in a later writing signed by the Client, Developer shall bear all expenses arising from the performance of its obligations under this Agreement.

1.9. Except as expressly provided in this Agreement, this Agreement does not include any maintenance work on the Product or later enhancements to the product.

TESTING AND ACCEPTANCE

2.1. All Deliverables shall be thoroughly tested by Developer (if applicable) and all necessary corrections as a result of such testing shall be made, prior to delivery to Client.

2.2. When applicable, in the event that a Deliverable or Product delivered to Client has an Error, Client shall notify Developer within 7 days of delivery or shall waive its objections. Upon notification to Developer, Developer shall have 7 days to make a correction to the Deliverable or Product and present the repaired Deliverable or Product to Client. If the Payment Schedule calls for work under this Agreement to be paid by piece rate, time spent correcting Errors is to be included in the amounts in the Payment Schedule. If the Payment Schedule calls for work under this Agreement to be paid by hourly rate, time spent correcting Errors shall be billed to Client according to the hourly rate in the Payment Schedule.

COPYRIGHTS

3.1. Client will retain copyright ownership of Existing Client Content.

3.2. Developer will retain copyright ownership of the following material ("Developer's Components") to be created in the development of the Product and to include any and all of the following:

a. Developer's existing tools, such as (source code, pre-existing code, scripts, stock images–basically your tools that you bring to the project: these should be non-negotiable items and should appear here in every contract.)

b. Content created in connection with development of the Product, including: (simply insert the components that you are creating to which you wish to retain the rights–HTML code, source code, Java code, computer code in any language, images, animations, scripts, script code, text, logos).

3.3. Client will retain copyright ownership of, and Developer agrees to irrevocably assign and convey to Client all rights, title, and interest in the same, the following material ("Client's Components") to be created in the development of the Product and to include any and all of the following: (HTML code, source code, Java code, computer code in any language, images, animations, scripts, script code, text, logos–simply insert the components that you are creating to which you wish to give the rights).

3.4. Developer will retain copyright ownership of any copyrights not specifically granted to either party by this Agreement ("Non-specified Components").

3.5. Developer, however, grants to Client a royalty-free, worldwide, perpetual, irrevocable, non-exclusive license, with the right to sublicense through multiple tiers of sub-licensees, to use, reproduce, distribute, modify, publicly perform, and publicly display the Developer's Components and Non-specified Components in any medium and in any manner, unless such rights are specifically limited by this Agreement. This license includes the right to modify such copyrighted material.

3.6. Client, however, grants to Developer a royalty-free, worldwide, perpetual, irrevocable, non-exclusive license, to use, reproduce, distribute, modify, publicly perform, and publicly display its Existing Client Content and Client's Components (if any) for the sole and limited purpose of use in Developer's portfolio as self-promotion and not for direct commercial sale.

3.7. For the purposes of this agreement, "copyright" shall be deemed to include copyrights, trade secrets, patents, trademarks, and other intellectual property rights.

3.8. If any third party content or Developer Tools are used in the development of the Product, Developer shall be responsible for obtaining and/or paying for any necessary licenses to use third party content.

CONFIDENTIALITY

4.1. The terms of this Agreement, Existing Client Content, and other sensitive business information are confidential ("Confidential Information"). Developer and Client agree, except as authorized in writing, not to disclose to any third party Confidential Information. Developer agrees to return to Client promptly, upon completion of the Product, all Existing Client Content.

WARRANTIES, COVENANTS, AND INDEMNIFICATION

5.1. Developer represents and warrants to Client the following: (i) Developer has the full power to enter into this agreement without restriction, (ii) except with respect to Existing Client Content, and properly licensed materials, the performance, distribution, or use of the Product will not violate the rights of any third parties, and (iii) Developer agrees to defend, hold harmless, and indemnify Client and its representatives from and against all claims, defense costs, judgments, and other expenses arising out of the breach of the foregoing warranties.

5.2. Client represents and warrants to Developer the following: (i) Client has the full power to enter into this agreement without restriction, (ii) the performance of this Agreement will not violate the rights of any third parties, and (iii) Client agrees to defend, hold harmless, and indemnify Developer and its representatives from and against all claims, defense costs, judgments, and other expenses arising out of the breach of the foregoing warranties.

TERMINATION

6.1. If Developer fails to correct an Error according to paragraph 2.2 after 3 attempts, Client may terminate this agreement without making any further payments according to the Payment Schedule.

6.2. No termination of this Agreement by any party shall affect Developer's rights to receive his hourly rate for all time spent producing Deliverables and/or Product.

MISCELLANEOUS PROVISIONS

7.1. This Agreement contains the entire understanding and agreement of the parties, supersedes all prior written or oral understandings or agreements, and may not be altered, modified, or waived except in a signed writing.

7.2. EXCEPT AS PROVIDED ABOVE WITH RESPECT TO THIRD PARTY INDEMNIFICATION, NEITHER PARTY SHALL BE LIABLE TO THE OTHER PARTY FOR ANY INCIDENTAL, CONSEQUENTIAL, SPECIAL, OR PUNITIVE DAMAGES OF ANY KIND OR NATURE, INCLUDING, WITHOUT LIMITATION, THE BREACH OF THIS AGREEMENT OR ANY TERMINATION OF THIS AGREEMENT, WHETHER SUCH LIABILITY IS ASSERTED ON THE BASIS OF CONTRACT, TORT, OR OTHERWISE, EVEN IF EITHER PARTY HAS BEEN WARNED OR WARNED OF THE POSSIBILITY OF ANY SUCH LOSS OR DAMAGE.

____

Developer

____

Client

Schedule A

Specifications

(This will depend on the job, obviously, and may not apply to all jobs.)

Schedule B

Development Schedule

(This will depend on the job, obviously, and may not apply to all jobs.)

Schedule C

Payment Schedule

(For hourly rate:)

Developer shall be paid on an hourly basis, and his rates and billing procedures are as follows: Charges are $____________ per hour. The minimum billing increment is six minutes or 1/10 of an hour. Time spent on individual tasks is rounded up to the next 10th of an hour.

(For piece rate:)

Deliverables	Due Date	Payment Due
Down payment (1/3)	__________	$________
Milestone 1	__________	$________
Milestone 2	__________	$________
Final Completion	__________	$________
Total Payment	__________	$________

96. Mutual Nondisclosure Agreement

This agreement is made effective on _______________ (date) by and between _______________________________ (first party) and ___________________________________ (second party) (collectively, the "Parties"), to ensure the protection and preservation of the confidential and/or proprietary nature of information disclosed or made available or to be disclosed or made available to each other. For the purposes of this agreement, each Party shall be deemed to include any subsidiaries, internal divisions, agents, and employees. Any signing party shall refer to and bind the individual and the entity that he or she represents.

Whereas the Parties desire to ensure the confidential status of the information that may be disclosed to each other.

Now, therefore, in reliance upon and in consideration of the following undertakings, the Parties agree as follows:

1. Subject to limitations set forth in paragraph 2, all information disclosed to the other party shall be deemed to be "Proprietary Information." In particular, Proprietary Information shall be deemed to include any information, marketing technique, publicity technique, public relations technique, process, technique, algorithm, program, design, drawing, mask work, formula, test data research project, work in progress, future development, engineering, manufacturing, marketing, servicing, financing, or personal matter relating to the disclosing party, its present or future products, sales, suppliers, clients, customers, employees, investors, or business, whether in oral, written, graphic, or electronic form.

2. The term "Proprietary Information" shall not be deemed to include information that (i) is now, or hereafter becomes, through no act or failure to act on the part of the receiving party, generally known or available information, (ii) is known by the receiving party at the time of receiving such information as evidenced by its records, (iii) is hereafter furnished to the receiving party by a third party, as a matter of right and without restriction on disclosure, (iv) is independently developed by the receiving party without reference to the information disclosed hereunder, or (v) is the subject of a written permission to disclose provided by the disclosing party.

   Not withstanding any other provision of this Agreement, disclosure of Proprietary Information shall not be precluded if such disclosure:

   (a) is in response to a valid order of a court or other governmental body of the United States or any political subdivision thereof,

   (b) is otherwise required by law, or,

   (c) is otherwise necessary to establish rights or enforce obligations under this agreement, but only to the extent that any such disclosure is necessary.

   In the event that the receiving party is requested in any proceedings before a court or any other governmental body to disclose Proprietary Information, it shall give the disclosing party prompt notice of such request so that the disclosing party may seek an appropriate protective order. If, in the absence of a protective order, the receiving party is nonetheless compelled to disclose Proprietary Information, the receiving party may disclose such information without liability hereunder, provided, however, that such party gives the disclosing party advance written notice of the information to be disclosed and, upon the request and at the expense of the disclosing party, uses its best efforts to obtain assurances that confidential treatment will be accorded to such information.

3. Each party shall maintain in trust and confidence and not disclose to any third party or use for any unauthorized purpose any Proprietary Information received from the other party. Each party may use such Proprietary Information in the extent required to accomplish the purpose of the discussions with respect to the subject. Proprietary Information shall not be used for any purpose or in any manner that would constitute a violation on law regulations, including without limitation the export control laws of the United States of America. No other rights or licenses to trademarks, inventions, copyrights, or patents are implied or granted under this Agreement.

4. Proprietary Information supplied shall not be reproduced in any form except as required to accomplish the intent of this Agreement.
5. The responsibilities of the Parties are limited to using their efforts to protect the Proprietary Information received with the same degree of care used to protect their own Proprietary Information from unauthorized use or disclosure. Both Parties shall advise their employees or agents who might have access to such Proprietary Information of the confidential nature thereof and that by receiving such information they are agreeing to be bound by this Agreement. No Proprietary Information shall be disclosed to any officer, employee, or agent of either party who does not have a need for such information for the purpose of the discussions with respect to the subject.
6. All Proprietary Information (including all copies thereof) shall remain the property of the disclosing party and shall be returned to the disclosing party after the receiving party's need for it has expired, or upon request of the disclosing party, and in any event, upon completion or termination of this Agreement. The receiving party further agrees to destroy all notes and copies thereof made by its officers and employees containing or based on any Proprietary Information and to cause all agents and representatives to whom or to which Proprietary Information has been disclosed to destroy all notes and copies in their possession that contain Proprietary Information.
7. This Agreement shall survive any termination of the discussion with respect to the subject and shall continue in full force and effect until such time as Parties mutually agree to terminate it.
8. This Agreement shall be governed by the laws of the United States of America and as those laws that are applied to contracts entered into and to be performed in all states. Should any revision of this Agreement be determined to be void, invalid, or otherwise unenforceable by any court or tribunal of competent jurisdiction, such determination shall not affect the remaining provisions of this Agreement, which shall remain in full force and effect.
9. This Agreement contains final, complete, and exclusive agreement of the Parties relative to the subject matter hereof and supersedes any prior agreement of the Parties, whether oral or written. This Agreement may not be changed, modified, amended, or supplemented except by a written instrument signed by both Parties.
10. Each party hereby acknowledges and agrees that, in the event of any breach of this Agreement by the other party, including, without limitations, the actual or threatened disclosure of a disclosing party's Proprietary Information without the prior express written consent of the disclosing party, the disclosing party will suffer an irreparable injury such that no remedy at law will afford it adequate protection against or appropriate compensation for such injury. Accordingly, each party hereby agrees that the other party shall be entitled to specific performance of a receiving party's obligations under this Agreement as well as further injunctive relief as may be granted by a court of competent jurisdiction.
11. The term of this agreement is for two (2) years, commencing on the "Effective Date."

AGREED TO:

Signature ______________________________

Printed Name ___________________________

Date __________

AGREED TO:

Signature ______________________________

Printed Name ___________________________

Date __________

97. Mutual Compromise Agreement and Mutual Release

THIS MUTUAL COMPROMISE AGREEMENT AND MUTUAL RELEASE ("Agreement") is entered into as of ______________________, by and between ______________________________ ("Debtor") and ______________________________ ("Creditor") (collectively "Parties or Party"). For the purposes of the Agreement, "Party" includes subsidiaries and parents of a Party and includes individuals serving as directors, officers, employees, agents, consultants, and advisors to or of a Party.

A. BACKGROUND

1. Debtor and Creditor entered into an agreement or series of agreements (the "Contract") whereby Debtor provided a series of services to Creditor for an agreed-upon fee.
2. Since the time of entering into the Contract, the Parties have determined that a settlement of the mutual obligations between them is appropriate and would best serve the interests of all of the Parties. This Agreement is intended to express the Parties' intent to equitably settle the obligations arising from or related to the Contract.

B. AGREEMENT

NOW, THEREFORE, IN CONSIDERATION OF THE FOLLOWING, THE FOREGOING, THE MUTUAL COVENANTS, PROMISES, AGREEMENTS, REPRESENTATIONS, AND RELEASES CONTAINED HEREIN, AND IN EXCHANGE FOR OTHER GOOD AND VALUABLE CONSIDERATION, THE RECEIPT, SUFFICIENCY, AND ADEQUACY OF WHICH IS HEREBY ACKNOWLEDGED, THE PARTIES HEREBY AGREE AS FOLLOWS:

1. Settlement.
   a. Debtor shall pay the following amounts to Creditor: ______________________, such payment to be made no later than ______________________ date.
   b. Debtor shall owe no further liability or obligation to Creditor in connection with any services.
2. Confidentiality. Debtor and Creditor shall keep the terms of the Agreement confidential and shall not disclose such terms to any other Party except as is necessary for the proper conduct of the disclosing Party's business.
3. No Other Payments. No additional funds shall be required to be paid or transferred by Creditor to Debtor or by Debtor to Creditor.
4. Nature and Effect of Agreement and Conditions Thereon. This Agreement consists of a compromise and settlement by the Parties of claims arising from the Contract described in Section A, Paragraph 2, above, and a release given by the Parties relinquishing their claims against the other. By executing this Agreement, the Parties intend to and do hereby extinguish the obligations heretofore existing between them and arising from that dispute.

   The nature and effect of this agreement, and the enforcement of any of the provisions found herein, is strictly conditioned upon the actions described in Paragraph 1. The shares must bear the medallion guaranteed signature of an authorized officer of the entity whose name appears on the face of the certificate and the shares must be accompanied by a resolution of the board authorizing transfer of the shares.
5. Admissions. This Agreement is not, and shall not be treated as, an admission of liability by either Party for any purpose, and shall not be admissible as evidence before any tribunal or court.
6. Compromise Agreement. The Parties hereby compromise and settle any and all past, present, or future claims, demands, obligations, or causes of action for compensatory or punitive damages, costs, losses, expenses, and compensation, whether based on tort, contract, or other theories of recovery, which the Parties have or which may later accrue to or be acquired by one Party against the other, the other's predecessors and successors in interest, heirs, and assigns, past, present, and future officers, directors, shareholders, agents, employees, parent and subsidiary organizations, affiliates, and partners, arising from the subject matter of the claim described in

Section A, Paragraph 2, above, and agree that this compromise and settlement shall constitute a bar to all such claims. The Parties agree that this compromise and settlement shall constitute a bar to all past, present, and future claims arising out of the subject matter of the action described in Section A, Paragraph 2, above.

7. Release and Discharge. The Parties hereby release and discharge the other, the other's predecessors and successors in interest, heirs, and assigns, past, present, and future officers, directors, shareholders, agents, employees, parent and subsidiary organizations, affiliates, and partners from, and relinquish, any and all past, present, or future claims, demands, obligations, or causes of action for compensatory or punitive damages, costs, losses, expenses, and compensation, whether based on tort, contract, or other theories of recovery, which the Parties have or which may later accrue to or be acquired by one Party against the other arising from the subject of the claim described in Section A, Paragraph 2, above.

8. Unknown Claims. The Parties acknowledge and agree that, upon execution of the release, this Agreement applies to all claims for damages or losses that either Party may have against the other, whether those damages or losses are known or unknown, foreseen or unforeseen, and in the event that this Agreement is deemed executed in California, the Parties thereby waive application of California Civil Code Section 1542.

   The Parties certify that each has read the following provisions of California Civil Code Section 1542: "A general release does not extend to claims which the creditor does not know or suspect to exist in his favor at the time of executing the release, which if known by him must have materially affected his settlement with the debtor."

   The Parties understand and acknowledge that the significance and consequence of this waiver of California Civil Code Section 1542 is that even if one Party should eventually suffer additional damages arising out of the facts referred to in Section A, Paragraph 2, above, that Party will not be able to make any claim for these damages. Furthermore, the Parties acknowledge that they intend these consequences even as to claims for damages that may exist as of the date of this release but that the damaged or harmed Party does not know exist and that, if known, would materially affect that Party's decision to execute this release, regardless of whether the damaged Party's lack of knowledge is the result of ignorance, oversight, error, negligence, or any other cause.

9. Conditions of Execution. Each Party acknowledges and warrants that its execution of this compromise agreement and release is free and voluntary.

10. Representation of Understanding. All Parties and signatories to this Agreement acknowledge and agree that the terms of this Agreement are contractual and not mere recital, and all Parties and signatories represent and warrant that they have carefully read this Agreement, have fully reviewed its provisions with their attorneys, know and understand its contents, and sign the same as their own free acts and deeds. It is understood and agreed by all Parties and signatories to this Agreement that execution of this Agreement may affect rights and liabilities of substantial extent and degree and, with the full understanding of that fact, they represent that the covenants and releases provided for in this Agreement are in their respective best interests.

11. Construction. The provisions of this Agreement shall not be construed against either Party.

12. Entire Agreement. This Agreement constitutes the entire agreement between the Parties and signatories and all prior and contemporaneous conversation, negotiations, possible and alleged agreements, and representations, covenants, and warranties, express or implied, or written, with respect to the subject matter hereof, are waived, merged herein, and superseded hereby. There are no other agreements, representations, covenants, or warranties not set forth herein. The terms of this Agreement may not be contradicted by evidence of any prior or contemporaneous agreement. The Parties further intend and agree that this Agreement constitutes the complete and exclusive statement of its terms and that no extrinsic evidence whatsoever may be introduced in any judicial or arbitration proceeding, if any, involving this Agreement. No part of this Agreement may be amended or modified in any way unless such amendment or modification is expressed in writing signed by all Parties to this Agreement.

13. Counterparts. This Agreement may be executed in multiple counterparts, each of which shall be deemed an

original but all of which together shall constitute one and the same instrument. When all of the Parties and signatories have executed any copy hereof, such execution shall constitute the execution of this Agreement, whereupon it shall become effective.

14. Governing Law. THIS AGREEMENT WILL BE GOVERNED AND CONSTRUED IN ACCORDANCE WITH THE LAW OF THE STATE OF ______________________________ AND THE UNITED STATES OF AMERICA, WITHOUT REGARD TO CONFLICT OF LAW PRINCIPLES. This Agreement shall not be strictly construed against any Party to this Agreement. Any controversy or claim arising out of or relating to this Agreement, or the breach thereof, shall be resolved by arbitration administered under the rules of the American Arbitration Association in accordance with its applicable rules. Such arbitration shall take place within San Mateo County, California, and shall be binding upon all Parties, and any judgment upon or any an award rendered by the arbitrator may be entered in any court having jurisdiction thereof.
15. Binding Effect. The provisions of this Agreement shall be binding upon and inure to the benefit of each of the Parties and their respective successors and assigns. Nothing expressed or implied in this Agreement is intended, or shall be construed, to confer upon or give any person, partnership, or corporation, other than the Parties, their successors and assigns, any benefits, rights, or remedies under or by reason of this Agreement, except to the extent of any contrary provision herein contained.
16. Authority. The Parties hereto represent and warrant that they possess the full and complete authority to covenant and agree as provided in this Agreement and, if applicable, to release other Parties and signatories as provided herein. If any Party hereto is a corporation or limited liability company, the signatory for any such corporation or limited liability company represents and warrants that such signatory possesses the authority and has been authorized by the corporation or limited liability company to enter into this Agreement, whether by resolution of the board of, upon the instruction by an authorized officer of, as authorized in the bylaws of the corporation on whose behalf the signatory is executing this Agreement, or otherwise.
17. Severability. If any provision of this Agreement is held by a court to be unenforceable or invalid for any reason, the remaining provisions of this Agreement shall be unaffected by such holding.
18. Exchanges by Fax. The exchange of a fully executed Agreement in counterparts or otherwise by fax shall be sufficient to bind the Parties to the terms and conditions of this Agreement.

IN WITNESS WHEREOF, the Parties and signatories execute this Agreement on the dates indicated.

______________________________, "Debtor"

Date ____________________

Signature ______________________________

______________________________, "Creditor"

Date __________________

Signature ______________________________

CHAPTER 9

Corporate Governance Forms

A corporation's shareholders, directors, officers, and managers must observe particular formalities in a corporation's operation and administration. For example, decisions regarding a corporation's management must often be made by formal vote and must be recorded in the corporate minutes. Shareholders and directors are typically directed by state law to hold annual meetings. Meetings of shareholders and directors must be properly noticed and must meet quorum requirements. We have included the most useful and common corporation governance forms here.

The *Notice of Special/Annual Meeting of Shareholders* is a formal notice to the shareholders of a corporation announcing a meeting of shareholders and advising of the date, time, and place of the meeting. The *Minutes of Annual or Special Meeting of Shareholders* form is a sample of the written record that you should prepare following an annual or special meeting of the shareholders of a corporation. The *Minutes of Annual/Special Meeting of Directors* form is a sample of the written record that you should prepare following an annual or special meeting of the board of directors of a corporation. Finally, the *Action of Corporation Directors by Written Consent* is a consent form used by directors when they take unanimous action by written consent instead of through a formal special meeting. This less formal consent process is often used by smaller corporations because it is faster and more convenient than noticing and holding a formal meeting.

98. Notice of Special/Annual Meeting of Shareholders

NOTICE OF SPECIAL/ANNUAL MEETING OF SHAREHOLDERS OF SUPERCORP, INC.

Pursuant to a call made by shareholders, notice is hereby given that a (special or annual) meeting of the Shareholders of SuperCorp, Inc. will be held on __________, (date), at ______________ (time), at ____________________________ (address), to consider and act on the following:

(Insert matters to be considered, such as "A proposal that John Jones be removed from the board of directors" or "To discuss the company's past fiscal year performance.")

Date ____________________

____

Corporate Secretary

99. Minutes of Annual or Special Meeting of Shareholders

MINUTES OF (ANNUAL/SPECIAL) MEETING OF SHAREHOLDERS OF SUPERCORP, INC.

The shareholders of SUPERCORP, INC., held a (special/annual) meeting on __________ (date), at ______________ (time), at __________________ (place).

The following shareholders were present at the meeting, in person or by proxy, representing shares as indicated:

John Jones, 100,000 shares
John Smith, 100,000 shares
John Miller, 75,000 shares

Also present were Michael Spadaccini, attorney to the corporation, and Lisa Jones, an employee of the corporation.

The (president, chairperson of the board, secretary, etc.) of the corporation called the meeting to order and announced that he would chair the meeting and that a quorum was present and that the meeting was held pursuant to a written notice of meeting given to all shareholders of the corporation. A copy of this notice was ordered inserted into the minute book immediately preceding the minutes of this meeting.

The minutes of the previous meeting of shareholders were then read and approved. The minutes were then inserted into the minute book of the corporation.

The chairperson then announced that the election of directors was in order. The chairperson called the matter to a vote, noting that each shareholder had nominated himself to serve. Directors were then elected to serve until the next annual meeting of stockholders and until their successors were duly elected and qualified, as follows:

John Jones
John Smith
John Miller

The chairperson then announced a proposal to change the corporation's fiscal year from December 31 to June 30. The chairperson advocated the change because he felt that the June 30 fiscal year would more closely reflect the seasonality of the corporation's sales. While John Smith and John Miller agreed with this point, they noted that the administrative work associated with the change would strain the organization, so they would not support the change. Thus, the matter was not brought to a vote. The chairperson noted that the board would bring the matter up at next year's meeting, and John Smith and John Miller agreed that was suitable.

The chairperson then announced a proposal for the company to obtain a credit line from a local bank. All the directors agreed that it the company should pursue a credit line of up to $500,000 and that the credit line could be secured with the company's inventory. The chairperson noted that he had discussed the credit line with two banks and both were interested in having the company apply. The chairperson then brought the matter to a vote; the directors voted unanimously to pursue the credit line and to authorize the corporation to open the credit line.

There being no further business to come before the meeting, on the motion duly made, seconded, and adopted, the meeting was adjourned.

I, the Secretary of the Corporation, attest that the foregoing minutes are a true and accurate description of the matters and votes brought before the corporation at the above-captioned meeting.

____
Corporate Secretary

100. Minutes of Annual/Special Meeting of Directors

MINUTES OF MEETING OF THE DIRECTORS OF SUPERCORP, INC.

The directors of SUPERCORP, INC. held (an annual or a special) meeting on __________ (date), at __________ (time), at ______________ (place).

The following directors were present at the meeting:

John Jones
Jane Smith
Lisa Miller, who also serves as Chairperson of the Board

Also present were Michael Spadaccini, attorney to the corporation, and Lisa Jones, a shareholder.

The Chairperson called the meeting to order and announced that the meeting was held pursuant to a written waiver of notice and consent to the holding of the meeting. The waiver and consent was presented to the meeting and, on a motion duly made, seconded, and carried, was made a part of the records and ordered inserted into the minute book immediately preceding the records of this meeting.

The directors agreed to dispense with the reading of the minutes of the last meeting.

The directors then considered the acceptance of the resignation of Lisa Jones as corporate secretary. The directors, with John Jones abstaining from the vote, voted to accept the resignation of Lisa Jones.

The directors then considered the sale of a piece of property owned by the Corporation, specifically a parcel of land at 701 Riford Road in Glen Ellyn, Illinois, of 1/4 acre. A buyer has offered $30,000 for the land. The directors agreed that the offer should be accepted.

The directors considered the election of officers to serve until the next annual meeting of directors. The directors unanimously voted to elect the following persons to the corresponding positions:

John Jones, President and CEO
Jane Smith, Treasurer and CFO
Lisa Miller, Corporate Secretary

"The directors then considered the acceptance of the resignation of Lisa Jones as corporate secretary. The directors, with John Jones abstaining from the vote, voted to accept the resignation of Lisa Jones."

There being no further business to come before the meeting, the meeting was duly adjourned.

I, the Corporate Secretary, hereby attest that the foregoing is a true and accurate transcription of the matters discussed and resolved by the board of directors of the Corporation.

____
Corporate Secretary

101. Action of Corporation Directors by Written Consent

ACTION OF DIRECTOR(S) BY WRITTEN CONSENT TO APPROVE STOCK OPTION PLAN AND TO ISSUE SHARES OF STOCK

The undersigned, the director(s) of EVOLUTION WATER COMPANY, INC., agree unanimously to the following:

RESOLVED, that the undersigned directors waive notice of a special meeting of directors pursuant to the Corporation's bylaws and hereby agree that the following actions and resolutions be taken by this written consent.

RESOLVED, that the "Evolution Water Company Stock Option Plan" presented to the undersigned directors and attached to this written consent as an exhibit is hereby adopted by the corporation.

RESOLVED FURTHER, that the officers of this corporation be, and they hereby are, authorized to sell and issue to the following persons the number of shares of capital stock of this corporation and for the consideration indicated opposite each name:

NAME	NUMBER OF SHARES	$ PER SHARE	TYPE AND AMOUNT OF CONSIDERATION
John Jones	100,000	$0.75	$75,000 in cash

Date ____________

____
Melissa Bess, Director

____
Brian Bess, Director

CHAPTER 10

Business Operation Tools

Controlling business operations is essential to generating a profit and meeting your business expectations. This section provides you with a range of worksheets to develop and control key operation issues, production schedules, and costing.

The *Vendor Information Sheet* helps you compile and maintain complete information on current and potential vendors. Use this form initially to confirm approval of new vendors. When deciding among the goods or services of several vendors, use the *Vendor Price and Comparison Analysis* to compare the offerings of each.

If your business conducts manufacturing operations, use the *Daily Production Planning/Schedule* to formalize your production goals. Use the *Production Completion Notice* to internally notify departments (sales and billing, especially) of the completion of an order.

The *Marketing Department Budget Recap* helps you analyze the sales, margins, and marketing expenses for your products or services. The *Sales Price Estimate* helps you budget and calculate the expenses you'll incur in the production of goods; this calculation helps you determine a sales price for your production with an adequate profit margin. The *Job Costing Report* helps you budget and calculate the expenses you'll incur in the completion of a job or project; this calculation helps you determine your profit. The *Job Costing Comparison Report* is an analytical tool that compares your estimated and actual revenues, material costs, and labor costs.

The *Ratio Analysis Worksheet* is a powerful analytical and budgeting tool. It helps you analyze key financial ratios by comparing your current year ratios with prior year ratios. The *Ratio Analysis Worksheet* can pinpoint trouble areas in your business and reveal areas where your business operations are improving.

The *Commission Report Worksheet* helps you compile sales and commission information for your sales staff, but it can also serve an analytical function by comparing the performances of sales staff members.

The *Production Efficiency Worksheet* analyzes the hour-by-hour performance of production facilities or production lines.

102. Vendor Information Sheet

Name of Firm ______________________________ Phone ______________

Address ____

____

Headquarters Office ______________________________

❑ Corporation ❑ Partnership ❑ Individual ❑ Other ____________

Date Business Started ____________________

President/Principal Owner ______________________________

Other Officers ____

____

Has this company provided products or services to our company before? ❑ Yes ❑ No

If so, when and what type? ____

____

List current customers and their approximate purchase value ______________________________

____

List trade references (name, phone) ____

____

List bank references (name, branch, phone) ____

____

Completed by ______________________________ Date ______________

Approved by ______________________________ Date ______________

103. Vendor Price and Comparison Analysis

Item Description ______________________________ Item # ______________

Enter quantity here and price per item below.

Vendor Name	____	____	____	____	Lead Time	Other Factors
______________	$____	$____	$____	$____	________	________
______________	$____	$____	$____	$____	________	________
______________	$____	$____	$____	$____	________	________
______________	$____	$____	$____	$____	________	________
______________	$____	$____	$____	$____	________	________
______________	$____	$____	$____	$____	________	________
______________	$____	$____	$____	$____	________	________
______________	$____	$____	$____	$____	________	________
______________	$____	$____	$____	$____	________	________
______________	$____	$____	$____	$____	________	________
______________	$____	$____	$____	$____	________	________
______________	$____	$____	$____	$____	________	________
______________	$____	$____	$____	$____	________	________
______________	$____	$____	$____	$____	________	________
______________	$____	$____	$____	$____	________	________
______________	$____	$____	$____	$____	________	________
______________	$____	$____	$____	$____	________	________

Comments

104. Daily Production Planning/Schedule

Date ____________ Shift ____________ Plant ______________________________

Product Description	Product I.D.#	Quantity
1. ______________________	____________	________
______________________	____________	________
______________________	____________	________
2. ______________________	____________	________
______________________	____________	________
______________________	____________	________
3. ______________________	____________	________
______________________	____________	________
______________________	____________	________
4. ______________________	____________	________
______________________	____________	________
______________________	____________	________
5. ______________________	____________	________
______________________	____________	________
______________________	____________	________
6. ______________________	____________	________
______________________	____________	________
______________________	____________	________
7. ______________________	____________	________
______________________	____________	________
______________________	____________	________
8. ______________________	____________	________
______________________	____________	________
______________________	____________	________
9. ______________________	____________	________
______________________	____________	________
______________________	____________	________
10. ______________________	____________	________
______________________	____________	________
______________________	____________	________

105. Production Completion Notice

Customer I.D.# ________________ Sales Order # ______________ Production Order # _______________

Scheduled Completion Date ____________________ Actual Date __________________________

Scheduled Shipping Date ______________________ Actual Date __________________________

Signed by ___________________________ Date _________________

Description of changes made to original sales order:

____

____

____

____

____

____

____

____

____

____

____

____

____

____

____

106. Marketing Department Budget Recap

For the Reporting Period of ______________________

Product A ______________________

Product B ______________________

Product C ______________________

Product D ______________________

		Product A	Product B	Product C	Product D	Total
Gross Sales		$______	$______	$______	$______	$______
Discounts & Returns	–	$______	$______	$______	$______	$______
Net Sales	=	$______	$______	$______	$______	$______
Cost of Goods Sold	–	$______	$______	$______	$______	$______
Gross Margin	=	$______	$______	$______	$______	$______
Marketing Expenses:						
Sales Department Expense		$______	$______	$______	$______	$______
Delivery	+	$______	$______	$______	$______	$______
Warehousing	+	$______	$______	$______	$______	$______
Advertising	+	$______	$______	$______	$______	$______
Sales Promotion	+	$______	$______	$______	$______	$______
Marketing Research	+	$______	$______	$______	$______	$______
Development Cost	+	$______	$______	$______	$______	$______
Total Marketing Expense	=	$______	$______	$______	$______	$______
Gross Margin		$______	$______	$______	$______	$______
Total Marketing Expense	–	$______	$______	$______	$______	$______
Profit	=	$______	$______	$______	$______	$______

107. Sales Price Estimate

For Job #/Name ______________________________

Materials:	Quantity	x Unit Cost	= Extended
Raw Materials - A ______________________	__________	$__________	$__________
Raw Materials - B ______________________	__________	$__________	$__________
Raw Materials - C ______________________	__________	$__________	$__________
Raw Materials - D ______________________	__________	$__________	$__________
Total Raw Materials			$__________
Labor:	Time	x Rate	= Extended
Set Up Labor	__________	$__________	$__________
Direct Labor	__________	$__________	$__________
Post Labor	__________	$__________	$__________
Benefit Factoring (Add benefit/hour for the hours of employees included in Labor)	__________	$__________	$__________
Total Labor			$__________

Other Costs:		Costs
Outside Services		$__________
Delivery	+	$__________
Burden Rate (Overhead expense directly related to each unit produced)	+	$__________
Other ______________________________	+	$__________
Other ______________________________	+	$__________
Total Other Costs	=	$__________
Total Raw Materials + Total Labor + Total Other Costs = Total Job Cost	=	$__________
Total Job Cost x Your Desired Profit Margin ________% = Total Price of Job	=	$__________

108. Job Costing Report

Description ______________________________

Job Number ______________________________

Start Date ______________________

Completion Date ______________________

Invoice #	Transaction Description	Amount		Revenues:
________	________________	________		$________
________	________________	________	+	$________
________	________________	________	+	$________
________	________________	________	+	$________
________	________________	________	+	$________
________	________________	________	+	$________
Total Revenues			=	$________
Material and Outside Services Costs:				
	________________			$________
	________________		+	$________
	________________		+	$________
	________________		+	$________
	________________		+	$________
Total Materials & Services			=	$________
Labor Cost:				
____________	________________			$________
____________	________________		+	$________
____________	________________		+	$________
____________	________________		+	$________
____________	________________		+	$________
____________	________________		+	$________
Total Labor			=	$________
Total Materials and Services + Total Labor = Total Costs			=	$________
Total Revenues - Total Costs = Profit			=	$________

109. Job Costing Comparison Report

Description ______________________________

Job Number ______________________________

Start Date ______________

Completion Date ______________

Revenues:

Invoice #	Transaction Description	Amount	– Estimated	= Difference
________	______________	$________	$________	$________
________	______________	$________	$________	$________
________	______________	$________	$________	$________
________	______________	$________	$________	$________
________	______________	$________	$________	$________
________	______________	$________	$________	$________
Total Revenues		$________	$________	$________

Material and Outside Services:

______________	$________	$________	$________
______________	$________	$________	$________
______________	$________	$________	$________
______________	$________	$________	$________
______________	$________	$________	$________
______________	$________	$________	$________
Total Materials and Services	$________	$________	$________

Labor Cost:

______________	$________	$________	$________
______________	$________	$________	$________
______________	$________	$________	$________
______________	$________	$________	$________
______________	$________	$________	$________
______________	$________	$________	$________
Total Labor	$________	$________	$________
Total Materials and Services + Total Labor = Total Costs	$________	$________	$________
Total Revenues - Total Costs = Profit	$________	$________	$________

110. Ratio Analysis Worksheet

For the Month Ending ______________________

Current Ratio = Current Assets ÷ Current Liabilities

Current Ratio = ________________ ÷ _______________ = This Year

Current Ratio = ________________ ÷ _______________ = Last Year

Inventory Turnover = Cost of Goods Sold ÷ Inventory

Inventory Turnover = ________________ ÷ _______________ = This Year

Inventory Turnover = ________________ ÷ _______________ = Last Year

Total Asset Turnover = Net Sales ÷ Total Assets

Total Asset Turnover = ________________ ÷ _______________ = This Year

Total Asset Turnover = ________________ ÷ _______________ = Last Year

Average Collection Period = Accounts Receivable ÷ Average Credit Sales/Day

Average Collection Period = ________________ ÷ _______________ = This Year

Average Collection Period = ________________ ÷ _______________ = Last Year

Long-Term Debt to Equity = Long-Term Debt ÷ Stockholders' Equity

Long-Term Debt to Equity = ________________ ÷ _______________ = This Year

Long-Term Debt to Equity = ________________ ÷ _______________ = Last Year

Total Debt to Total Assets = Total Liabilities ÷ Total Assets

Total Debt to Total Assets = ________________ ÷ _______________ = This Year

Total Debt to Total Assets = ________________ ÷ _______________ = Last Year

Earnings per Share = Earnings after Tax less Dividends ÷ Number of Common Shares Outstanding

Earnings per Share = ________________ ÷ _______________ = This Year

Earnings per Share = ________________ ÷ _______________ = Last Year

111. Commission Report Worksheet

Name of Salesman:

#1 ______________________________

#2 ______________________________

#3 ______________________________

#4 ______________________________

#5 ______________________________

#6 ______________________________

#7 ______________________________

#8 ______________________________

		Salesman #1	Salesman #2	Salesman #3	Salesman #4
Monthly Net Sales		$________	$________	$________	$________
Less Adjustments		$________	$________	$________	$________
Net Sales Applicable	=	$________	$________	$________	$________
Commission Rate	x	________	________	________	________
Commission Due	=	$________	$________	$________	$________

		Salesman #5	Salesman #6	Salesman #7	Salesman #8
Monthly Net Sales		$________	$________	$________	$________
Less Adjustments		$________	$________	$________	$________
Net Sales Applicable	=	$________	$________	$________	$________
Commission Rate	x	________	________	________	________
Commission Due	=	$________	$________	$________	$________

112. Production Efficiency Worksheet

Date ______________ Shift ____________________ Supervisor ______________________________

Comments ____

Standard Output is 100% capacity of output for production line. Actual Output ÷ Standard Output = % Efficient

	Hour									
	1	2	3	4	5	6	7	8	9	10
Line 1 Product										
Actual Output/Hour										
Cumulative Output										
Standard Output/Hour										
Standard Cumulative										
% Efficient/Hour										
Comments										

	Hour									
	1	2	3	4	5	6	7	8	9	10
Line 2 Product										
Actual Output/Hour										
Cumulative Output										
Standard Output/Hour										
Standard Cumulative										
% Efficient/Hour										
Comments										

	Hour									
	1	2	3	4	5	6	7	8	9	10
Line 3 Product										
Actual Output/Hour										
Cumulative Output										
Standard Output/Hour										
Standard Cumulative										
% Efficient/Hour										
Comments										

	Hour									
	1	2	3	4	5	6	7	8	9	10
Line 4 Product										
Actual Output/Hour										
Cumulative Output										
Standard Output/Hour										
Standard Cumulative										
% Efficient/Hour										
Comments										

CHAPTER 11

Basic Accounting

This section addresses monitoring and controlling your entity's general ledger activity from chart of accounts to general journal. It is extremely important to maintain the integrity of the general ledger—the underlying source of all of your financial reports. Of course, most businesses today use financial accounting software to record financial transactions. Conveniently, this software maintains the general ledger and general ledger transactions automatically. However, you must still have a sound understanding of underlying accounting principles to operate your financial software properly. If your chart of accounts is improperly created or maintained, your general ledger will be inaccurate.

We begin this section with *A Brief Explanation of Accounting*, a summarized overview of essential accounting principles. This overview will help you develop the foundation of your accounting system: the chart of accounts.

The *Chart of Accounts Maintenance* helps you develop your chart of accounts. Classify your most common transactions into short descriptions in a logical order. Classify each chart of accounts entry as one of the following: asset, liability, capital/equity, income, or expense.

The *General Journal* and *Journal Transactions* are forms with which you can record and classify your financial transactions.

113. A Brief Explanation of Accounting

Accounting for Transactions

For most companies, financial statements summarize hundreds of transactions. Bookkeeping records these transactions and then provides the figures for the financial statements.

Double Entry

All accounting systems are based on the principle of double entry, which ensures that the books will always be in balance, according to the fundamental accounting equation:

Assets = Liabilities + Owners' Equity.

Every financial transaction must be recorded in at least two accounts. For every change in value of an account on one side of the accounting equation, there must be a balancing change in the value of one or more accounts on the other side. If not, then the books will not be in balance and the financial statements based on those books will be incorrect.

Double entry accounting, which has been around since the late 15th century, traditionally serves two purposes. One, it ensures a trail of transactions: it shows where every amount of money comes from and where it goes. Two, it helps prevent errors in math, because every number is entered into multiple accounts, so there are multiple totals to compare.

Debits and Credits

If you understand how debits and credits work, you'll understand the whole accounting system.

The terms "debit" and "credit" refer to an increase or a decrease created by a transaction. Which is which depends on the type of account.

Account Type	Normal Balance	To Increase Account Enter	To Decrease Account Enter
Asset	Debit	Debit	Credit
Liability	Credit	Credit	Debit
Capital	Credit	Credit	Debit
Income	Credit	Credit	Debit
Expense	Debit	Debit	Credit

Every accounting entry in the general ledger contains both a debit and a credit. For every entry, the debits must equal the credits; if not, then the entry is out of balance.

Here are four simple transactions as examples.

Example 1
A customer buys merchandise for $500 cash.
Debit (increase) Cash (asset) by $500.
Credit (increase) Sales (income) by $500.

Example 2
A customer charges merchandise for $300.
Credit (increase) Sales (income) by $300.
Debit (increase) Accounts Receivable (asset) by $300

Example 3
You pay a utilities bill of $200.
Credit (decrease) Cash (asset) by $200.
Debit (increase) Expenses (expense) by $200.

Example 4
A customer pays a bill of $400.
Debit (increase) Cash (asset) by $400.
Credit (decrease) Accounts Receivable (asset) by $400.

For each transaction there is a debit and a credit—a double entry—and the debit and the credit are equal, in balance.

Accounts

The first step in setting up an accounting system is to decide what accounts you want to use to track your transactions. In the examples above, the accounting system uses Cash, Sales, Accounts Receivable, and Expenses. Other common accounts are Inventory, Office Supplies, Accounts Payable, and Payroll. Some will be very specific to your business, depending on type and size and complexity, and some will be generic accounts that are used by any business.

Each account should have a concise name and a number according to its type (assets, liabilities, capital, income, or expenses) and its classification within that type. The accounts are listed in a logical, numerical sequence in the chart of accounts.

Accounts should always be listed in the chart of accounts in the following order: assets, liabilities, capital, income, and expenses. Within each type, the order should follow a standard logic. For assets: current, fixed, and others. For liabilities: current and long-term. For capital: paid-in capital, owner's draw, and company's retained earnings. It's wise to allow gaps in your numbering sequence to allow for adding accounts later.

Here's an example of a chart of accounts:

100 Petty Cash
100-199 Asset Accounts
101 Cash in Bank (checking account)
102 Cash on Hand
110 Accounts Receivable
120 Inventory—Raw Materials
123 Inventory—Work in Process
126 Inventory—Finished Goods
130 Prepaid Expenses
135 Notes Receivable
150 Land
152 Buildings
154 Machinery and Equipment
156 Vehicles
158 Office Furniture and Equipment
160 Leasehold Improvements
172 Accumulated Depreciation—Buildings
174 Accumulated Depreciation—Machinery and Equipment
176 Accumulated Depreciation—Vehicles
178 Accumulated Depreciation—Office Furniture and Equipment
180 Operating Deposits
182 Other Assets

185 Goodwill
200-299 Liability Accounts
200 Accounts Payable
210 Payroll Tax Payable–Federal
212 Payroll Tax Payable–State
215 Sales Tax Payable
220 401(k) Deductions Payable
222 Health Insurance Payable
225 Short-Term Debt Payable
230 Other Current Liabilities
240 Bank Loans
250 Mortgage Loans
260 Other Long-Term Debt
300-399 Equity Accounts
300 Paid-In Capital
305 Draw
310 Retained Earnings–Prior Year
315 Retained Earnings–Current Year
400-499 Revenue Accounts
400 Nontaxable Sales
405 Taxable Sales
410 Finance Charge Income
500-599 Cost of Goods Sold
500 Cost of Goods Sold
600-699 Expense Accounts
600 Advertising
602 Vehicle Expense
605 Cleaning and Maintenance
610 Commissions
615 Insurance
620 Legal and Accounting
625 Interest Expense
630 Repairs
635 Dues and Subscriptions
640 Licenses, Fees, and Taxes
645 Utilities
650 Rent
660 Wages
666 Employer Payroll Taxes
669 Employee Benefits
675 Travel and Entertainment
680 Promotions
685 Contributions
690 Depreciation Expense
695 Interest Income

Accounting Cycle

The accounting cycle is the sequence of procedures used to track financial transactions and to report the financial effect of those transactions.

Here's an overview of the cycle.

- A transaction occurs.
- A document of the transaction (source document) goes to accounting.
- The source document is analyzed to journalize the transaction.
- The journals are posted to the general ledger.
- A trial balance is prepared.
- Financial statements are prepared.

Transactions and Source Documents

Business transactions occur in various ways, but they all generate paperwork–cash receipts, credit card receipts, cash register tapes, cancelled checks, return slips, customer invoices, purchase orders, supplier invoices, check stubs or copies, time cards, deposit slips, payment stubs for interest, notes for loans, and so on. Each source document should include at least the date, the amount, a description of the transaction, and, when practical, the name and address of the other party.

These source documents are essential to your accounting system. They are records of transactions and provide information necessary to track financial operations. They should be stored for future reference, whether to be used in analyzing your financial statements or, in case of an audit, to support those statements.

Some recurring transactions may not generate any paper source document, such as depreciation expenses, bank transfers or charges that do not involve checks, and cost of doing business for which an invoice has yet to be received or paid. For such transactions, the source document must be generated, by means of a depreciation schedule, a bank reconciliation statement, or an accrued expense schedule.

General Journal

When a transaction is journalized, it is recorded in the general journal, the "book of original entry." The general journal is basically a chronological list of transactions, each with an explanation, possibly a reference number, and an indication of the accounts affected (debited and credited) and the amounts.

General Ledger

The next step is to post (transfer) the entry to the general ledger, which is a book of transaction accounts. The general ledger simplifies analysis of the effects of transactions on accounts and is the basis for compiling financial statements.

Each page of the general ledger should have a heading with the transaction account number and description and the following columns: date of the journal posting, journal posting reference description, and debit and credit.

The entries from the general journal are transferred to the appropriate account pages in the general ledger. Each account can be balanced at any time: the debits are totaled, the credits are totaled, and the difference is calculated.

Closing at Month End and Preparing the Financial Statements

At the end of the month, the general ledger is closed after all transactions have been posted to the appropriate journals. Then, the account totals from the journals are transferred to the general ledger accounts. Next, the general ledger accounts are totaled, to arrive at a preliminary ending balance for each account.

A preliminary trial balance is prepared. All general ledger account balances are transferred to a trial balance, which is a listing of all accounts and their balances. The total debits should equal total credits.

Certain adjustments must be made before the books can be closed, to account for items that are not recorded in daily transactions. These adjusting entries are handled basically like any other entries: they're analyzed, journalized, and posted. Then the accounts affected by the adjustments are balanced again and an adjusted trial balance is prepared, using the adjusted balances of each general ledger account. Again, total debits must equal total credits.

The working trial balance ensures that the books are in balance. It's a listing of all of the transaction accounts on a spreadsheet, each with its month-end balance, either a debit or a credit, next to the description. There are also two columns for debit or credit items for the balance sheet and two columns for debit or credit items for the income statement. After the first two columns of the working trial balance are "balanced," the figures are transposed to the column for the balance sheet or the column for income statement.

Next, the debits and credits are transposed from the working trial balance to the appropriate sections of the balance sheet or the income statement. The balance sheet shows the company's financial position. The income statement shows all revenue earned during the period, less all expenses incurred in generating that revenue.

After preparing the financial statements, it's necessary to ready the general ledger for the next accounting period. To do this, the revenue and expense accounts are cleared out and the net income or loss is transferred to an account such as Retained Earnings or Owners' Equity. This is done by making closing entries in the general journal.

After the closing entries, all revenue and expense accounts will have a zero balance. Then, a final trial balance is prepared, to help ensure that all general ledger account balances are correct for the beginning of the new accounting period. Since all revenue and expense accounts have been closed out to zero, this trial balance will contain only balance sheet accounts.

This is a simplified, generic explanation of the accounting cycle. It will vary according to the needs of the company and the procedures it uses. Most of these procedures are automated in many companies. However, it's still good to understand the accounting basics.

114. Chart of Accounts Maintenance

Account	Description	Account Type	Ratio Group	Consolidation Account

Account Type: I = Income E = Expense A = Asset L = Liability O = Equity

Ratio Group: For financial ratio relationship groups listed on form 110, *Ratio Analysis Worksheet*.

Consolidation Account: Use to consolidate one or more accounts, such as all cash accounts into one cash account.

Entered by ______________________________ Date ____________

Authorized by ____________________________ Date ____________

115. General Journal

For the Month of ____________

Journal #	Date	Description	Account	Debit Amount	Credit Amount
			Totals	$	$

Prepared by ________________________________ Date ____________

Approved by ________________________________ Date ____________

116. Journal Transactions

For the Month of ____________________

Batch #	Batch Control	Period	Journal	Batch Type (N, R, M)	Reverse (Y, N)

Account	Sub	Ref #	Date	Transaction Description	Debit Amount	Credit Amount
				Totals	$	$

Batch Type: N = Nonrecurring R = Recurring M = Manual

Entered by ____ Date ______________

Authorized by ____ Date ______________

CHAPTER 12

Cash Disbursements and Purchasing

This section offers tools that streamline and control your purchasing procedures. The *Purchase Order* is likely familiar; use it to place orders with vendors. You and your employees can use the *Expense Report* both internally and in connection with expenses billable directly to clients. The *Petty Cash Voucher* helps you keep track of funds spent from the petty cash account. The *Check Requisition* is an internal control and record-keeping tool; instruct your staff members to use this form to request checks for purchases.

109. Purchase Order

From:

____

____

____

____

To:

____

____

____

____

Purchase Order Number ____________________

Please supply and deliver the goods or services specified below to the address above. The stated goods or services shall be delivered no later than ________________.

This order is subject to the following conditions: ____

____

Item #	Quantity	Description	Net Unit Price	Total
			Net Total Price	$

Invoices, quoting the order number, should be submitted for payment to:

Signed ____

Name ____

Title ____

This order is not valid unless it is signed.

Please acknowledge receipt of this order.

110. Expense Report

Period covered: From ______________ To ______________					
Name	Dept/Sales Office	Report Date	Date of Trip	From / /	To / /
Business Purpose		Account No.			

Day	Date	Transportation (Air, Rail, Taxi, Limousine, Bus, Car Rental, etc.)	Automobile Expense (Gas Mileage, Tolls, Parking) ***	Lodging	Meals (Itemize Business: Breakfast/ Lunch/Dinner)	Entertain- ment	Misc.***	Totals
Sunday								
Monday								
Tuesday								
Wednesday								
Thursday								
Friday								
Saturday								
Totals								

Automobile Expenses***				Entertainment and Business Meals Only***				
Date	Location	Mileage, Gas, Parking, Repairs, Service	Amount	Date	Entertained (name, company, title)	Place	Business Purpose	Amount

Miscellaneous Expenses***			Expense Summary		Instructions
Date	Detail	Amount	Total Expenses Reported	Amount	Deduct from my advance
					Mail to:

Employee Signature	Date
Approved By	Date

111. Petty Cash Voucher

Account	Description	Amount
	Total Cash Amount	$
Received by	Authorized by	

Account	Description	Amount
	Total Cash Amount	$
Received by	Authorized by	

Account	Description	Amount
	Total Cash Amount	$
Received by	Authorized by	

Account	Description	Amount
	Total Cash Amount	$
Received by	Authorized by	

112. Check Requisition

Requestor	Date of Request	Date Check Needed by

Make Payable to	Description of Item Needed	Amount
	Total Cash Amount	$

Authorized by	Date

Requestor	Date of Request	Date Check Needed by

Make Payable to	Description of Item Needed	Amount
	Total Cash Amount	$

Authorized by	Date

Requestor	Date of Request	Date Check Needed by

Make Payable to	Description of Item Needed	Amount
	Total Cash Amount	$

Authorized by	Date

Requestor	Date of Request	Date Check Needed by

Make Payable to	Description of Item Needed	Amount
	Total Cash Amount	$

Authorized by	Date

CHAPTER 13

Inventory Movement and Valuation Tools

This section will guide you in managing and evaluating your inventory. Maintaining the accuracy and integrity of your inventory system is important, but so are identifying and correcting all causes of variances.

Use the *In-House Stock Requisition* form to request inventory internally. This form will serve as a written record of both the request and the delivery from inventory. When you ship goods to a customer, you should accompany the goods with a *Shipping Verification*. Request that a signed copy of the *Shipping Verification* be returned to you and instruct your carrier to secure a signed copy on your behalf. This document serves as your proof of delivery of the shipment.

Use the *Physical Inventory Count Sheet* when performing a physical count of your inventory. The *Physical Inventory Gain or Loss* form enables you to track inaccuracies and shrinkage to your inventory by comparing your *book count*—the amount of inventory shown in your records—and your *physical count*—the amount of inventory shown by an inspection.

Substantial differences between book count and physical count can mean poor record keeping, entry errors, and, in some cases, employee theft. The *Raw Material Shrinkage Report* helps calculate and track losses due to shrinkage of inventory. This tool can help you pinpoint problem areas.

The *Physical Inventory Valuation Report* will determine your total physical inventory value. Simply enter the quantity of each item based on a physical inventory count and multiply the quantity by the cost per unit to determine the value. The *Book Inventory Valuation Report* works the same way as the *Physical Inventory Valuation Report,* except that you use the book count of inventory. The advantage of the *Book Inventory Valuation Report* is that it does not require a full physical inventory count. The obvious disadvantage, however, is that book inventory counts are typically less accurate than physical inventory counts. The *Physical vs. Book Inventory Cost Variance Report* reveals the differences between the book value and the physical value of your inventory.

The *Inventory Status Sheet* helps you maintain an accurate physical count of individual items. Use the *Authorization to Destroy Inventory* to secure approval before disposing of inventory and to notify appropriate personal of the inventory change. Use the *Property Loss Report* whenever your business suffers loss to its inventory or property. Be sure to fill the form out completely and as soon as possible after the loss. A promptly completed *Property Loss Report* will carry more evidentiary weight with insurance adjusters.

121. In-House Stock Requisition

Requisition # __________

From ____

Job Reference Number ______________________ Date Needed ____________

Department ____

Location ____

Description of items requested from in-house stock:

Quantity	Item Number	Description	Quantity Issued	Date Issued	Initials

Requested by	Date
Approved by	Date

122. Shipping Verification

From:

____
____
____
____

Shipper ____________________ Date ____________________

Ship to:

Carrier

Quantity Shipped	Item Number	Description

Proof of shipment received:

Signature of Receiving Clerk Date

123. Physical Inventory Count Sheet

Sheet #		Location	
Item Number	**Description**	**Quantity**	**Location**
Counted by		Date	

124. Physical Inventory Gain or Loss

For the Period Ending:

Item Number	Description	Book Count	Physical Count	Difference

Prepared by	Date
Reviewed by	Date

125. Raw Material Shrinkage Report

For the Period Ending:

Item Number	Description	Cost per Unit	Quantity Lost	Total Value Lost

All shrinkage losses greater than $__________ per item are to be explained below.

____

____

____

____

Prepared by ______________________________________ Date __________

Reviewed by ______________________________________ Date __________

126. Physical Inventory Valuation Report

For the Period Ending:

Item Number	Description	Quantity	Cost per Unit	Total Value
			Total Value	$

Prepared by	Date
Reviewed by	Date

127. Book Inventory Valuation Report

For the Period Ending:

Item Number	Description	Quantity	Cost per Unit	Total Value
			Total Value	$

Prepared by	Date
Reviewed by	Date

128. Physical vs. Book Inventory Cost Variance Report

For the Period Ending:

Item Number	Description	Book Value	Physical Value	Difference
			Total Value	$

Prepared by	Date
Reviewed by	Date

129. Inventory Status Sheet

Item Description				Item Number		
Quantity on Hand	Quantity Ordered	Date Ordered	Unit Cost	Quantity Received	Date Received	Usage

Quantity on Hand: The present quantity of inventory per book inventory report
Quantity Ordered: The quantity of item ordered from vendor
Date Ordered: The date item was ordered from vendor
Unit Cost: The unit cost of item per vendor
Quantity Received: The quantity of item received from vendor
Date Received: The date item was received from vendor
Usage: The actual usage of item in production or sales

Add Quantity on Hand to Quantity Received and subtract Usage to get next Quantity on Hand

130. Authorization to Destroy Inventory

Date ______________

Reason for Request to Destroy Inventory

____

____

____

____

Item Number	Description	Quantity to Be Destroyed

Prepared by	Date
Reviewed by	Date

Copy to: Inventory Control, Accounting, Warehouse Manager, and Files.

131. Property Loss Report

Department	Date
Completed by	Date

Cause of Loss	**Type of Loss**
❏ Theft	❏ Property Damage
❏ Vandalism	❏ Inventory
❏ Burglary	❏ Money/Cash
❏ Tools and Equipment	❏ Tools and Equipment
❏ Fire/Arson	❏ Employee Time
❏ Accident/Damage	❏ Business Interruption
❏ Unexplained	❏ Other:
❏ Other:	

Type of Loss	Description	Value Lost

Date and Time Loss Occurred ____________________

Date and Time Loss Reported ____________________

❏ Police Report Made Report ID # ____________

List Police Department Contacts and Notes ____________________

Besides the property loss, were there any other consequences of the loss? ____________

Could this loss have been avoided? ❏ Yes ❏ No

If Yes, how? ____________________

Other Comments, Notes: ____________________

CHAPTER 14

Financial Reports

This section offers a full range of financial reports and supporting schedules that will help you quickly produce accurate financial reports for your business. Many of the forms are interactive spreadsheet files that will calculate most of the figures for you.

The *Period-End Closing and Analysis* is a control tool that will greatly increase the accuracy and integrity of your financial statements. You can use this form to close out the month, the quarter, and the year. The *Actual vs. Budget Income Statement* is an interactive computer spreadsheet file that calculates the variance between budgeted income statement items and actual income statement items. You'll find a copy of the file on the disk included with this volume. Enter the actual and budgeted items and the worksheet calculates the dollar variance for each item.

The seven *Balance Sheet Support Schedules* help you accumulate information for individual balance sheet items. These can be real money-savers; they make it unnecessary for your accountant or auditor to accumulate the information on his or her own. The *Balance Sheet Support Schedule—Cash Balance* accumulates information on cash accounts. The *Balance Sheet Support Schedule—Marketable Securities* accumulates information on stocks, bonds, and other marketable instruments. The *Balance Sheet Support Schedule—Accounts Receivable* aggregates accounts receivable information. The *Balance Sheet Support Schedule—Inventory* accumulates information on inventory. The *Balance Sheet Support Schedule—Prepaid Expenses* amortizes prepaid expenses and aggregates period-end totals. The *Balance Sheet Support Schedule—Accounts Payable* summarizes and accumulates accounts payable information. The *Balance Sheet Support Schedule—Notes Payable* accumulates information on notes and loan obligations.

The *Cash Flow Forecast—12 Month* is an interactive spreadsheet that forecasts sales, expenses, and available cash for a 12-month period. The *Cash Flow Forecast—Five Year* does the same for a five-year period. The files are on the disk included with this volume. Simply enter your anticipated sales and expenses and the worksheet calculates the surplus or deficit and the running cash balance.

The *Income Statement—12 Month* is an interactive spreadsheet that accumulates and totals income statement items for a 12-month period. The *Income Statement—Quarterly* calculates the same data for four quarters. The files are on the disk included with this volume. Enter your sales and expenses and the worksheet records the information and calculates the total annual balance for all items.

The *Quarterly Balance Sheet* is an interactive spreadsheet that accumulates and totals balance sheet items for four quarters. The *Year-End Balance Sheet* calculates the same data at the end of your year. The files are on the disk included with this volume. Enter your assets and liabilities and the worksheet records the information and calculates the total balance for all items.

132. Period-End Closing and Analysis

Using this form will increase the level of accuracy and integrity of the financial statements and general ledger. Use to ensure that all month-end tasks have been completed and reviewed.

1. Cash in Banks	Done by	Date	Reviewed by	Date
All bank accounts reconciled from month-end balance per the bank statement to the general ledger balance, with all unusual reconciling items investigated and resolved. (Ensure that, prior to reconciliation, the general ledger balance has been updated to reflect all quarterly entries.)				
Bank reconciliations prepared by an employee who is independent from the cash receipts and disbursements functions.				
Bank reconciliations initialed and dated by the preparer.				
Bank reconciliation reviewed by manager, as evidenced by his/her initials and date.				
2. Accounts Receivable—Trade				
General ledger balance reconciled to balance per detailed accounts receivable aging. All reconciling items investigated and resolved, with journal entries prepared as required.				
All customer account receivable balances have been reviewed for collectibility, giving proper consideration to: • All significant past due accounts • All disputed invoices and erroneous billings • All unissued credits				
The allowance for doubtful accounts has been determined as the sum of the specific and general reserves and has been treated as an offset of current trade receivables. The journal entry to record the specific reserve for disputed invoices, erroneous credits, and doubtful accounts and the general reserve has been made against bad debt expense: • Debit bad debt expense • Credit allowance for doubtful accounts				
All specific invoices determined to be uncollectible have been written off against the allowance for doubtful accounts by the following entry: • Debit allowance for doubtful accounts • Credit accounts receivables–trade				
The approval for the write-offs of uncollectible accounts has been made by individuals who do not have direct access to incoming cash receipts or to the accounts receivable ledgers.				
3. Other Receivables (Including notes)				
All other receivables are supported by account analyses and have been evaluated as to collectibility. Adjustments have been made as required.				

4. Inventory	Done by	Date	Reviewed by	Date
Physical inventory of supplies and materials taken and compared with stock status. Any discrepancies are to be identified, researched, and corrected for the following inventory items: • Raw Materials • Finished Goods • Other				
The physical inventory reconciliation worksheets between physical and stock status report are to be reviewed and approved by manager, as evidenced by his/her initials and date.				
Determine that the stock status report properly reflects month-end quantities on hand and current unit costs.				
Update the inventory cost summary spreadsheet with the following information: • Beginning year inventory value by item and category • Current month-end inventory value by item and category • Determine inventory value difference between beginning inventory values and current month-end values • Journal entry prepared to record inventory • Reverse the prior period's inventory entry				
Record inventory using the net inventory amount obtained in earlier mentioned step, as follows: • Debit/credit inventory account • Credit/debit cost of costs sold (If difference between beginning and current month valuations is positive, debit inventory and credit cogs; if difference is negative, debit COGS and credit inventory.)				
Attach supporting schedules to the journal entry sheet.				
5. Prepaid Expenses				
Changes in account balances have been analyzed and composition of account balances listed on support schedules, which agree with general ledger for each account: • Prepaid state income taxes? • Prepaid IRS • Prepaid insurance				
6. Property, Plant, and Equipment				
Journal entry prepared to record depreciation expense for the current month from prepared detail property records, as follows: • Debit depreciation expense • Credit accumulated depreciation for each account: ❑ Equipment ❑ Automobiles ❑ Leasehold improvements				

6. Property, Plant, and Equipment (continued)	Done by	Date	Reviewed by	Date
Review and ensure that cost and general ledger agree with detailed records of fixed assets for each account: • Equipment • Automobiles • Leasehold improvements				
Changes in asset costs (additions and disposals) are substantiated by vendor invoices or cash receipts. Gain or loss computed and recorded after taking into account related accumulated depreciation.				
7. Deposits and Other Assets				
Changes in account balances have been analyzed and composition of account balances listed on support schedules, which agree with general ledger for each account.				
8. Accounts Payable				
Accounting department completed matching of invoices received by month-end to open receivers (merchandise received by month-end and included in inventory, for which invoices have not been received), prepared accounts payables vouchers, and processed through A/P system. (Cut-off procedures for accounts payables must coincide with those for inventory.)				
Prepare schedules listing open receivers and other open payables.				
Merchandise recap schedule prepared from accounts payable schedules, listing accruals, returns for credits, merchandise returns, merchandise returns deducted from payments, holding for credit, overage, and freight applicable for the month.				
Journal entry prepared to record above prepared schedules: • Debit applicable cost of sales or expense account • Credit accounts payables				
Journal entry prepared reversing prior month accrual for open receivers and other accounts payables adjustments.				
Check registers issued by accounts payables covering the period between month-end and date of the accounts payable expense. Distribution report reviewed to determine what checks were issued subsequent to month-end.				
Journal entry prepared to record above: • Debit cash • Credit accounts payable				
Accounts payable per detailed listing, reconciled to the general ledger balance. All discrepancies are to be identified, researched, and corrected.				

9. Accrued Expenses	Done by	Date	Reviewed by	Date
All accounts analyzed and composition of account balance schedules in agreement with the general ledger balances: • Federal tax payable • State income tax payable • Payroll tax payable • Workers comp payable • Sales tax payable • Other taxes payable • City tax payable • Accrued wages payable				
Inquiries made regarding services received for which invoices not received (e.g. legal, accounting, consulting, etc). Proper journal entries prepared to record such expenses in the month that the services were received, as follows: • Debit various expense accounts • Credit various accrued expense accounts				
Amount of accrued payroll expense determined by obtaining the payroll recap for the first payroll subsequent to month-end and prorating the total to the month prior to and subsequent to month-end. Journal entry prepared as follows: • Debit payroll expense by department • Credit accrued wages payable				
10. Other Liabilities				
General ledger balances in agreement with the detailed support schedules and amortization schedules. Any discrepancies should be identified, researched, and corrected.				
Evaluate propriety of short-term versus long-term general ledger balances and classify accordingly.				
11. Sales				
Total monthly sales–including gross, sales tax, discounts, and net–have been accumulated from the accounts receivable subsystem into a monthly sales journal, cash receipts, and discounts taken journal.				
12. Other Income				
Interest-bearing investments reviewed and interest earned through month-end but not received is accrued as follows: • Debit interest income receivable • Credit interest income				
13. Work in Progress				
Review open orders file. Prepare list of open orders reflecting all related costs incurred with open orders (jobs).				

13. Work in Progress (continued)	Done by	Date	Reviewed by	Date
Prepare appropriate journal entry to match costs with revenues from above mentioned schedule, as follows: • Debit work in progress • Credit various cost of sales, wages, and other related expense accounts				
Prepare reversing entry of prior month's work in progress entry, as follows: • Debit various cost of sales, wages, and other related expense accounts • Credit work in progress				
14. Commissions				
Review open job orders, ensuring that all closed jobs are recorded closed.				
Review job costing detail reports, ensuring that total revenues and related costs tie out to revenues and costs reflected in preliminary trial balance. If any discrepancies, identify, research, and correct as appropriate.				
Summarize the month's closed job cost detail reports by number of closed jobs, revenues, and related costs from above reconciliation.				
Generate and review commission recap schedule by salesperson, to ensure that closed jobs, revenues less sales tax, and related costs tie out to the summarized job costing detail reports.				
Extend net sales less related expenses at commission rate ____% for each salesperson by closed job. Total and cross-foot commission recap schedule.				
Accrue commissions expense by the following journal entry: • Debit commission expense • Credit accrued commissions				
15. Income Taxes				
Quarterly tax provisions and tax liability calculated based upon pro rata share of annualized net income, giving consideration to tax payments made, net operating loss carry forwards, etc.				

133. Actual vs. Budget Income Statement

For the Period:	Actual	Budget	Variance-$
Sales			
Sales			$0.00
Other			$0.00
Total Sales	**$0.00**	**$0.00**	**$0.00**
Less Cost of Goods Sold			
Materials			$0.00
Labor			$0.00
Overhead			$0.00
Other			$0.00
Total Cost of Goods Sold	**$0.00**	**$0.00**	**$0.00**
Gross Profit	**$0.00**	**$0.00**	**$0.00**
Operating Expenses			
Salaries and wages			$0.00
Employee benefits			$0.00
Payroll taxes			$0.00
Rent			$0.00
Utilities			$0.00
Repairs and maintenance			$0.00
Insurance			$0.00
Travel			$0.00
Telephone			$0.00
Postage			$0.00
Office supplies			$0.00
Advertising/Marketing			$0.00
Professional fees			$0.00
Training and development			$0.00
Bank charges			$0.00
Depreciation			$0.00
Miscellaneous			$0.00
Other			$0.00
Total Operating Expenses	**$0.00**	**$0.00**	**$0.00**
Operating Income	**$0.00**	**$0.00**	**$0.00**
Interest Income (expense)			$0.00
Other Income (expense)			$0.00
Total Nonoperating Income (expense)	**$0.00**	**$0.00**	**$0.00**
Income (Loss) Before Taxes	**$0.00**	**$0.00**	**$0.00**
Income Taxes			**$0.00**
Net Income (Loss)	**$0.00**	**$0.00**	**$0.00**

134. Balance Sheet Support Schedule–Cash Balance

For the Period:			
Bank Account Detail Description		Balance, This Month, This Year	Balance, This Month, Prior Year
Bank Name	Account		
	Total Cash Balances	$	$

Detail totals must agree with Cash on Balance Sheet.

This table reflects bank balances that comprise the cash balance on a company's balance sheet. This is a detailed report often used in CPA review. If management prepares this report before CPA review, CPA fees can be dramatically reduced.

Prepared by ______________________________ Date __________

Reviewed by ______________________________ Date __________

135. Balance Sheet Support Schedule–Marketable Securities

For the Period:			
Marketable Securities Detail Description		Balance, This Month, This Year	Balance, This Month, Prior Year
Investment Type	Description		
	Total Marketable Securities Balance	$	$

Detail totals must agree with Marketable Securities on Balance Sheet.

This table reflects bank balances that comprise the marketable securities balance on a company's balance sheet. This is a detailed report often used in CPA review. If management prepares this report before CPA review, CPA fees can be dramatically reduced.

Prepared by ______________________________ Date __________

Reviewed by ______________________________ Date __________

136. Balance Sheet Support Schedule–Accounts Receivable

For the Period:		
Accounts Receivable	Balance, This Month, This Year	Balance, This Month, Prior Year
Balance per Accounts Receivable Detail:		
Current		
Over 30 days		
Over 60 days		
Over 90 days		
Total Accounts Receivable Balance	$	$

Detail totals must agree with Accounts Receivables on Balance Sheet.

Prepared by ______________________________ Date ____________

Reviewed by ______________________________ Date ____________

137. Balance Sheet Support Schedule–Inventory

For the Period:		
Inventory	Balance, This Month, This Year	Balance, This Month, Prior Year
Balance per Inventory Detail:		
Raw Materials		
Work in Progress		
Finished Goods		
Other		
Total Inventory Balance	$	$

Detail totals must agree with Inventory on Balance Sheet.

Prepared by ______________________________ Date ____________

Reviewed by ______________________________ Date ____________

138. Balance Sheet Support Schedule–Prepaid Expenses

For the Period:		
Prepaid Expenses	Balance, This Month, This Year	Balance, This Month, Prior Year
Balance per Prepaid Expenses Amortization Schedules:		
Prepaid Insurance		
For the Period _____/_____ to _____/_____ Total of Payments Months in Period Monthly Amortized Amount Remaining Periods	 ÷ = X	
Total Prepaid Insurance Balance	$	$
Prepaid Worker's Compensation		
For the Period _____/_____ to _____/_____ Total of Payments Months in Period Monthly Amortized Amount Remaining Periods	 ÷ = X	
Total Prepaid Worker's Compensation Balance	$	$
Prepaid Other		
Description: For the Period _____/_____ to _____/_____ Total of Payments Months in Period Monthly Amortized Amount Remaining Periods	 ÷ = X	
Total Prepaid Other Balance	$	$
Grand Total All Prepaid Expense Balances	$	$

Detail totals must agree with Prepaid Expenses on Balance Sheet.

Prepared by ____ Date ____________

Reviewed by ____ Date ____________

139. Balance Sheet Support Schedule–Accounts Payable

For the Period:		
Accounts Payable	Balance, This Month, This Year	Balance, This Month, Prior Year
Beginning Balance		
Purchases		
Disbursements		
Adjustments		
Ending Balance		
Total Accounts Payable Balance	$	$

Detail totals must agree with Accounts Payable on Balance Sheet.

Prepared by ______________________________ Date __________

Reviewed by ______________________________ Date __________

140. Balance Sheet Support Schedule–Notes Payable

For the Period:		
Notes Payable	Balance, This Month, This Year	Balance, This Month, Prior Year
Note 1 Description:		
Beginning Balance		
Principal Payments		
Adjustments		
Note 1 Balance	$	$
Note 2 Description:		
Beginning Balance		
Principal Payments		
Adjustments		
Note 2 Balance	$	$
Note 3 Description:		
Beginning Balance		
Principal Payments		
Adjustments		
Note 3 Balance	$	$
Note 4 Description:		
Beginning Balance		
Principal Payments		
Adjustments		
Note 4 Balance	$	$
Total Notes Payable Balance	$	$

Detail totals must agree with Notes Payable on Balance Sheet.

Prepared by ______________________________ Date ____________

Reviewed by ______________________________ Date ____________

141. Cash Flow Forecast–12-Month

Period/Month:	1	2	3	4	5	6	7	8	9	10	11	12	Total
Receipts													
Cash sales													0
Collections from credit sales													0
Other													0
Total Receipts	**0**	**0**	**0**	**0**	**0**	**0**	**0**	**0**	**0**	**0**	**0**	**0**	**0**
Payments													
Cash purchases													0
Payments to creditors													0
Salaries and wages													0
Employee benefits													0
Payroll taxes													0
Rent													0
Utilities													0
Repairs and maintenance													0
Insurance													0
Travel													0
Telephone													0
Postage													0
Office supplies													0
Advertising													0
Marketing/promotion													0
Professional fees													0
Training and development													0
Bank charges													0
Miscellaneous													0
Owner's drawings													0
Loan repayments													0
Tax payments													0
Capital purchases													0
Other													0
Total Payments	**0**	**0**	**0**	**0**	**0**	**0**	**0**	**0**	**0**	**0**	**0**	**0**	**0**
Cashflow Surplus (+) or Deficit (-)	**0**	**0**	**0**	**0**	**0**	**0**	**0**	**0**	**0**	**0**	**0**	**0**	**0**
Start Cash (Owner's Equity+Loans-Start Up)	**0**	**0**	**0**	**0**	**0**	**0**	**0**	**0**	**0**	**0**	**0**	**0**	**0**
Closing Cash Balance	**0**	**0**	**0**	**0**	**0**	**0**	**0**	**0**	**0**	**0**	**0**	**0**	**0**

Note: This form is available on the accompanying CD as an Excel template.

142. Cash Flow Forecast–Five-Year

Period/Month:	1	2	3	4	5	Total
Receipts						
Cash sales						0
Collections from credit sales						0
Other						0
Total Receipts	**0**	**0**	**0**	**0**	**0**	**0**
Payments						
Cash purchases						0
Payments to creditors						0
Salaries and wages						0
Employee benefits						0
Payroll taxes						0
Rent						0
Utilities						0
Repairs and maintenance						0
Insurance						0
Travel						0
Telephone						0
Postage						0
Office supplies						0
Advertising						0
Marketing/promotion						0
Professional fees						0
Training and development						0
Bank charges						0
Miscellaneous						0
Owner's drawings						0
Loan repayments						0
Tax payments						0
Capital purchases						0
Other						0
Total Payments	**0**	**0**	**0**	**0**	**0**	**0**
Cashflow Surplus (+) or Deficit (-)	**0**	**0**	**0**	**0**	**0**	**0**
Start Cash (Owner's Equity+Loans-Start Up)	**0**	**0**	**0**	**0**	**0**	
Closing Cash Balance	**0**	**0**	**0**	**0**	**0**	

Note: This form is available on the accompanying CD as an Excel template.

143. Income Statement–12-Month

Period/Month:	1	2	3	4	5	6	7	8	9	10	11	12	Total
Sales													
Sales													0
Other													0
Total Sales	**0**	**0**	**0**	**0**	**0**	**0**	**0**	**0**	**0**	**0**	**0**	**0**	**0**
Less Cost of Goods Sold													
Materials													0
Labor													0
Overhead													0
Other													0
Total Cost of Goods Sold	**0**	**0**	**0**	**0**	**0**	**0**	**0**	**0**	**0**	**0**	**0**	**0**	**0**
Gross Profit	**0**	**0**	**0**	**0**	**0**	**0**	**0**	**0**	**0**	**0**	**0**	**0**	**0**
Operating Expenses													
Salaries and wages													0
Employee benefits													0
Payroll taxes													0
Rent													0
Utilities													0
Repairs and maintenance													0
Insurance													0
Travel													0
Telephone													0
Postage													0
Office supplies													0
Advertising/Marketing													0
Professional fees													0
Training and development													0
Bank charges													0
Depreciation													0
Miscellaneous													0
Other													0
Total Operating Expenses	**0**	**0**	**0**	**0**	**0**	**0**	**0**	**0**	**0**	**0**	**0**	**0**	**0**
Operating Income	**0**	**0**	**0**	**0**	**0**	**0**	**0**	**0**	**0**	**0**	**0**	**0**	**0**
Interest income (expense)													0
Other income (expense)													0
Total Nonoperating Income (Expense)	**0**	**0**	**0**	**0**	**0**	**0**	**0**	**0**	**0**	**0**	**0**	**0**	**0**
Income (Loss) Before Taxes	**0**	**0**	**0**	**0**	**0**	**0**	**0**	**0**	**0**	**0**	**0**	**0**	**0**
Income Taxes	**0**	**0**	**0**	**0**	**0**	**0**	**0**	**0**	**0**	**0**	**0**	**0**	**0**
Net Income (Loss)	**0**	**0**	**0**	**0**	**0**	**0**	**0**	**0**	**0**	**0**	**0**	**0**	**0**
Cumulative Net Income (Loss)	**0**	**0**	**0**	**0**	**0**	**0**	**0**	**0**	**0**	**0**	**0**	**0**	**0**

Note: This form is available on the accompanying CD as an Excel template.

144. Income Statement–Quarterly

Period/Quarter:	Quarter 1	Quarter 2	Quarter 3	Quarter 4	Total
Sales					
Sales					0
Other					0
Total Sales	**0**	**0**	**0**	**0**	**0**
Less Cost of Goods Sold					
Materials					0
Labor					0
Overhead					0
Other					0
Total Cost of Goods Sold	**0**	**0**	**0**	**0**	**0**
Gross Profit	**0**	**0**	**0**	**0**	**0**
Operating Expenses					
Salaries and wages					0
Employee benefits					0
Payroll taxes					0
Rent					0
Utilities					0
Repairs and maintenance					0
Insurance					0
Travel					0
Telephone					0
Postage					0
Office supplies					0
Advertising/Marketing					0
Professional fees					0
Training and development					0
Bank charges					0
Depreciation					0
Miscellaneous					0
Other					0
Total Operating Expenses	**0**	**0**	**0**	**0**	**0**
Opeating Income	**0**	**0**	**0**	**0**	**0**
Interest income (expense)					**0**
Other income (expense)					**0**
Total Nonoperating Income (Expense)	**0**	**0**	**0**	**0**	**0**
Income (Loss) Before Taxes	**0**	**0**	**0**	**0**	**0**
Income Taxes					**0**
Net Income (Loss)	**0**	**0**	**0**	**0**	**0**
Cumulative Net Income (Loss)	**0**	**0**	**0**	**0**	**0**

Note: This form is available on the accompanying CD as an Excel template.

145. Quarterly Balance Sheet

	Quarter 1	Quarter 2	Quarter 3	Quarter 4
ASSETS				
Current Assets				
Cash				
Marketable securities				
Accounts receivable, net				
Inventory				
Prepaid expenses				
Other				
Total Current Assets	**0**	**0**	**0**	**0**
Long-Term Assets				
Property, plant, and equipment				
Less accumulated depreciation				
Net property, plant, and equipment	0	0	0	0
Goodwill				
Other long-term assets				
Total Long-Term Assets	**0**	**0**	**0**	**0**
Total Assets	**0**	**0**	**0**	**0**
LIABILITIES AND SHAREHOLDERS' EQUITY				
Current Liabilities				
Short-term debt				
Current maturities of long-term debt				
Accounts payable				
Income taxes payable				
Accrued liabilities				
Other				
Total Current Liabilities	**0**	**0**	**0**	**0**
Long-Term Liabilities				
Long-term debt less current maturities				
Deferred income taxes				
Other long-term liabilities				
Total Long-Term Liabilities	**0**	**0**	**0**	**0**
Shareholders' Equity				
Common stock				
Additional paid-in capital				
Retained earnings				
Other				
Total Shareholders' Equity	**0**	**0**	**0**	**0**
Total Liabilities and Shareholders' Equity	**0**	**0**	**0**	**0**

Note: This form is available on the accompanying CD as an Excel template.

146. Year-End Balance Sheet

	Year Ending 20___
ASSETS	
Current Assets	
Cash	
Marketable securities	
Accounts receivable, net	
Inventory	
Prepaid expenses	
Other	
Total Current Assets	**0**
Long-Term Assets	
Property, plant, and equipment	
Less accumulated depreciation	
Net property, plant, and equipment	0
Goodwill	
Other long-term assets	
Total Long-Term Assets	**0**
Total Assets	**0**
LIABILITIES AND SHAREHOLDERS' EQUITY	
Current Liabilities	
Short-term debt	
Current maturities of long-term debt	
Accounts payable	
Income taxes payable	
Accrued liabilities	
Other	
Total Current Liabilities	**0**
Long-Term Liabilities	
Long-term debt less current maturities	
Deferred income taxes	
Other long-term liabilities	
Total Long-Term Liabilities	**0**
Shareholders' Equity	
Common stock	
Additional paid-in capital	
Retained earnings	
Other	
Total Shareholders' Equity	**0**
Total Liabilities and Shareholders' Equity	**0**

Note: This form is available on the accompanying CD as an Excel template.

CHAPTER 15

Miscellaneous Forms

This section offers a mix of useful forms that do not fit any of the preceding 14 sections. Use the *Trademark Infringement Cease and Desist Letter* when you feel that a party is using a trademark or service mark for which you have priority rights.

We have included a familiar *Fax Cover Sheet*, but we have added a confidentiality warning to protect your correspondence in the event of wrongful delivery. The *Message Notes* will also be familiar.

The *Web Site Terms of Service* is a strongly worded legal disclaimer for any business that operates a Web site.

Finally, we have included two sample letters to use in regard to the Digital Millennium Copyright Act of 1998, which updates U.S. copyright law for the Internet. The Act protects online service providers from civil and criminal liability for copyright infringement under some circumstances. If a copyright holder discovers that his or her content appears on the Internet without proper authorization, the holder may take advantage of the Act's "notification and take-down" provisions to have the content removed from the Web site where it appears. Those provisions govern the process of notification by copyright holders and the rights and responsibilities of online service providers once they receive notice of infringing material. The copyright owner would deliver to the online service provider the *Notification of Infringement Letter Under the Digital Millennium Copyright Act.* A subscriber who feels his or her material is not infringing then may deliver a *Counter-Notification Letter Under the Digital Millennium Copyright Act* to respond to the notice.

147. Trademark Infringement Cease and Desist Letter

From:

____

____

____

____

To:

____

____

____

____

Re: Evolution Trademark

To whom it may concern,

This matter requires your immediate attention.

We are the owners of a U.S. trademark registration for the trademark ___________________ for the following services: ____.

We have used our trademark consistently for _________ years.

Your company is currently using a similar mark, specifically, ______________________. A comparison of your mark to our trademark reveals that you are in violation of state unfair competition laws and several provisions of the Federal Trademark Act (15 U.S.C. § 1125 et seq.).

We ask that you immediately cease the manufacture and distribution of any products and/or undertaking any services bearing the trademark ___________________________. Your failure to notify me by ____________, 20______, that you have taken these steps will result in the prompt initiation of legal proceedings against your company. I eagerly await your response, and as a courtesy to you, I will temporarily abstain from contacting any retail establishments in which the offending mark is offered.

Be advised that this matter is of the gravest concern to us and that the protection of our trademark is one of our highest priorities. However, if you agree to cease the manufacture and distribution of products and undertaking any services bearing the infringing mark, we will consider the matter resolved. We sincerely hope that you will take this opportunity to avoid a legal dispute.

Please contact my office if you require any further information.

Yours truly,

148. Fax Cover Sheet

To:	From:
Fax:	Date:
Phone:	Pages:
Re:	CC:

❑ Urgent ❑ For Review ❑ Please Comment ❑ Please Reply ❑ Please Recycle

THIS MESSAGE IS INTENDED ONLY FOR THE USE OF THE INDIVIDUAL OR ENTITY TO WHOM OR WHICH IT IS ADDRESSED AND MAY CONTAIN INFORMATION THAT IS PRIVILEGED, CONFIDENTIAL, AND EXEMPT FROM DISCLOSURE. If the reader of this message is not the intended recipient or an employee or agent responsible for delivering the message to the intended recipient, you are hereby notified that any dissemination, distribution, or copying of this communication is strictly prohibited. If you have received this communication in error, please notify us immediately by telephone and return the original message to us by mail. Thank you.

149. Message Notes

IMPORTANT MESSAGE		
For:		
Date:	Time:	❑ AM ❑ PM
Mr./Ms.		
of		
Phone:		
Fax:		
Mobile:		
❑ Telephoned ❑ Came to see you ❑ Wants to see you ❑ Returned your call	❑ Please call ❑ Will call you again ❑ Rush ❑ Will fax you	
Message: ______		
Taken by:		

IMPORTANT MESSAGE		
For:		
Date:	Time:	❑ AM ❑ PM
Mr./Ms.		
of		
Phone:		
Fax:		
Mobile:		
❑ Telephoned ❑ Came to see you ❑ Wants to see you ❑ Returned your call	❑ Please call ❑ Will call you again ❑ Rush ❑ Will fax you	
Message: ______		
Taken by:		

IMPORTANT MESSAGE		
For:		
Date:	Time:	❑ AM ❑ PM
Mr./Ms.		
of		
Phone:		
Fax:		
Mobile:		
❑ Telephoned ❑ Came to see you ❑ Wants to see you ❑ Returned your call	❑ Please call ❑ Will call you again ❑ Rush ❑ Will fax you	
Message: ______		
Taken by:		

IMPORTANT MESSAGE		
For:		
Date:	Time:	❑ AM ❑ PM
Mr./Ms.		
of		
Phone:		
Fax:		
Mobile:		
❑ Telephoned ❑ Came to see you ❑ Wants to see you ❑ Returned your call	❑ Please call ❑ Will call you again ❑ Rush ❑ Will fax you	
Message: ______		
Taken by:		

150. Web Site Terms of Service

Terms of Service

Some or all of the information on this Web site(s) is provided by ___________________________ ("Company") on one or more Company Web sites. The Company Web sites include the following Web sites: ____. Company provides this service to you, subject to the following Terms of Service ("TOS"), which may be updated by us anytime without notice to you. When using particular Company services, you shall be subject to any posted guidelines or rules applicable to such services that may be posted from time to time. All such guidelines or rules are hereby incorporated by reference into the TOS. For specific services, Company also may put forth specific Terms of Service that differ from this TOS. It is your responsibility to periodically review the TOS. If you do not agree with or understand the TOS, do not use a Company site.

The TOS apply to both "Affiliates" (persons or entities that receive the Service, as defined below, for redistribution and/or republication on a non-Company Web site) and "Users" (all persons, including Affiliates, that make any use whatsoever of any Service, as defined below). Company currently provides Affiliates and Users with several resources, including news feeds, message boards, financial calculators, articles, and stock quotes (the "Service"). Unless expressly stated otherwise, new resources added to the current Service shall be subject to the TOS. You understand and agree that the Service is provided "as is" and that Company assumes no responsibility for the timeliness, deletion, misdelivery, or failure to store any user communications or personalization settings.

In consideration of your use of the Service, you agree to (a) provide true, accurate, current, and complete information about yourself as prompted by the Service's registration form (such information being the "Registration Data") and (b) maintain and promptly update the Registration Data to keep it truthful, accurate, current, and complete. If you provide any information that is untrue, inaccurate, not current, or incomplete, or Company has reasonable grounds to suspect that such information is untrue, inaccurate, not current, or incomplete, Company has the right to suspend or terminate your account and refuse any and all current or future use of the Service (or any portion thereof). You will receive a password and account designation upon completing the registration process for the use of some Services. You are responsible for maintaining the confidentiality of the password and account and are fully responsible for all activities that occur under your password or account. You agree to (a) immediately notify Company of any unauthorized use of your password or account or any other breach of security and (b) ensure that you exit from your account at the end of each session. Company cannot and will not be liable for any loss or damage arising from your failure to comply with this Paragraph.

You understand that all information, data, text, software, music, sound, photographs, graphics, video, messages, or other materials ("Content"), whether publicly posted or privately transmitted, are the sole responsibility of the person from which such Content originated. This means that you, and not Company, are entirely responsible for all Content that you upload, post, e-mail, or otherwise transmit via the Service. Company does not control the Content posted via the Service and thus does not guarantee its accuracy, integrity, or quality. By using the Service, you may be exposed to Content that is offensive, indecent, or objectionable. Under no circumstances will Company be liable in any way for any Content, including, but not limited to, for any errors or omissions in any Content, or for any loss or damage of any kind incurred as a result of the use of any Content posted, e-mailed, or otherwise transmitted via the Service.

You agree to not use the Service to:

i. upload, post, e-mail, or otherwise transmit any Content that is unlawful, harmful, threatening, abusive, harassing, defamatory, vulgar, obscene, libelous, invasive of another's privacy, hateful, or racially, ethnically, or otherwise objectionable;

ii. impersonate any person or entity or falsely state or otherwise misrepresent your affiliation with a person or entity;

iii. forge headers or otherwise manipulate identifiers in order to disguise the origin of any Content transmitted through the Service;

iv. upload, post, e-mail, or otherwise transmit any Content that you do not have a right to transmit under any law or under contractual or fiduciary relationships;

v. upload, post, e-mail, or otherwise transmit any Content that infringes on any patent, trademark, trade secret, copyright, or other proprietary rights ("Rights") of any party;

vi. upload, post, e-mail, or otherwise transmit any unsolicited or unauthorized advertising, promotional materials, "junk mail," "spam," "chain letters," "pyramid schemes," or any other form of solicitation, except in areas designated for such purpose;

vii. upload, post, e-mail, or otherwise transmit any material that contains software viruses or any other computer code, files, or programs designed to interrupt, destroy, or limit the functionality of any computer software or hardware or telecommunications equipment;

viii. interfere with or disrupt the Service or servers or networks connected to the Service, or disobey any requirements, procedures, policies, or regulations of networks connected to the Service;

ix. intentionally or unintentionally violate any applicable local, state, national, or international law, including, but not limited to, regulations promulgated by the U.S. Securities and Exchange Commission, any rules of any national or other securities exchange, including, without limitation, the New York Stock Exchange, the American Stock Exchange, or the NASDAQ, and any regulations having the force of law; or

x. "stalk" or otherwise harass another or collect or store personal data about other Users.

You acknowledge that Company does not pre-screen Content, but that Company and its designees shall have the right (but not the obligation) in their sole discretion to refuse or move any Content that is available via the Service. Without limiting the foregoing, Company and its designees shall have the right to remove any Content that violates the TOS or is otherwise objectionable. You agree that you must evaluate, and bear all risks associated with, the use of any Content, including any reliance on the accuracy, completeness, or usefulness of such Content. In this regard, you acknowledge that you may not rely on any Content created by Company or submitted to Company, including without limitation information in Company Message Boards and in all other parts of the Service.

You acknowledge and agree that Company may preserve Content and may also disclose Content if required to do so by law or in the good faith belief that such preservation or disclosure is reasonably necessary to (a) comply with legal process; (b) enforce the TOS; (c) respond to claims that any Content violates the rights of third parties; or (d) protect the rights, property, or personal safety of Company, its Users, and the public.

You understand that the technical processing and transmission of the Service, including your Content, may involve (a) transmissions over various networks and (b) changes to conform and adapt to technical requirements of connecting networks or devices.

Recognizing the global nature of the Internet, you agree to comply with all local rules regarding online conduct and acceptable Content. Specifically, you agree to comply with all applicable laws regarding the transmission of technical data exported from the United States or the country in which you reside.

With respect to all Content you elect to post to other publicly accessible areas of the Service, you grant Company the royalty-free, perpetual, irrevocable, non-exclusive, and fully sublicensable right and license to use, reproduce, modify, adapt, publish, translate, create derivative works from, distribute, perform, and display such Content (in whole or part) worldwide and/or to incorporate it in other works in any form, media, or technology now known or later developed.

You agree to indemnify and hold Company and its subsidiaries, Affiliates, officers, agents, co-branders or other partners, and employees harmless from any claim or demand, including reasonable attorneys' fees, made by any third party due to or arising out of Content you submit, post to, or transmit through the Service, your use of the Service, your connection to the Service, your violation of the TOS, or your violation of any rights of another.

You agree not to reproduce, duplicate, copy, sell, resell, or exploit for any commercial purposes any portion of the Service, use of the Service, or access to the Service, except in accordance with the TOS.

You acknowledge that Company may establish general practices and limits concerning use of the Service, including without limitation the maximum number of days Content will be retained by the Service, the maximum number of messages that may be sent from or received by an account on the Service, the maximum size of any message that may be sent from or received by an account on the Service, the maximum disk space that will be allotted on Company's servers on your behalf, and the maximum number of times and the maximum duration for which you may access the Service in a given period of time. You agree that Company has no responsibility or liability for the deletion or failure to store any messages and other communications or other Content maintained or transmitted by the Service. You acknowledge that Company reserves the right to log off accounts that are inactive for an extended period of time. You further acknowledge that Company reserves the right to change these general practices and limits at any time, in its sole discretion, with or without notice.

Company reserves the right at any time and from time to time to modify or discontinue, temporarily or permanently, the Service (or any part thereof), with or without notice. You agree that Company shall not be liable to you or to any third party for any modification, suspension, or discontinuance of the Service.

You agree that Company, in its sole discretion, may terminate your password, account (or any part thereof), or use of the Service and remove and discard any Content within the Service for any reason. Company may also, in its sole discretion and at any time, discontinue providing the Service, or any part thereof, or may change the price for the Service, all with or without notice. You agree that any termination of your access to the Service under any provision of this TOS may be affected without prior notice, and acknowledge and agree that Company may immediately deactivate or delete your account and all related information and files in your account and/or bar any further access to such files or the Service. Further, you agree that Company shall not be liable to you or any third party for any termination of your access to the Service.

Your correspondence or business dealings with, or participation in promotions of, advertisers found on or through the Service, including payment and delivery of related goods or services, and any other terms, conditions, warranties, or representations associated with such dealings, are solely between you and such advertiser. You agree that Company shall not be responsible or liable for any loss or damage of any sort incurred as the result of any such dealings or as the result of the presence of such advertisers on the Service.

The Service or third parties may provide links to other World Wide Web sites or resources. Because Company has no control over such sites and resources, you acknowledge and agree that Company is not responsible for the availability of such external sites or resources and does not endorse and is not responsible or liable for any Content, advertising, products, or other materials on or available from such sites or resources. You further acknowledge and agree that Company shall not be responsible or liable, directly or indirectly, for any damage or loss caused or alleged to be caused by or in connection with use of or reliance on any such Content, goods, or services available on or through any such site or resource.

You acknowledge and agree that the Service and any necessary software used in connection with the Service (the "Software") contain proprietary and confidential information that is protected by applicable intellectual property and other laws. You further acknowledge and agree that Content contained in sponsor advertisements or information presented to you through the Service or advertisers is protected by copyrights, trademarks, service marks, patents, or other proprietary rights and laws. Except as expressly authorized by Company or advertisers, you agree not to modify, rent, lease, loan, sell, distribute, or create derivative works based on the Service or the Software, in whole or in part.

Company grants you a personal, non-transferable, and non-exclusive right and license to use the object code of its Software on a single computer, provided that you do not (and do not allow any third party to) copy, modify, create a derivative work of, reverse engineer, reverse assemble, or otherwise attempt to discover any source code, sell, assign, sublicense, grant a security interest in, or otherwise transfer any right in the Software. You agree not to modify the Software in any manner or form or to use modified versions of the Software, including (without limitation) for the purpose of obtaining unauthorized access to the Service. You agree not to access the Service by any means other than through the interface that is provided by Company for use in accessing the Service.

YOU EXPRESSLY UNDERSTAND AND AGREE THAT:

a. YOUR USE OF THE SERVICE IS AT YOUR SOLE RISK. THE SERVICE IS PROVIDED ON AN "AS IS" AND "AS AVAILABLE" BASIS. COMPANY EXPRESSLY DISCLAIMS ALL WARRANTIES OF ANY KIND, WHETHER EXPRESSED OR IMPLIED, INCLUDING, BUT NOT LIMITED TO, THE IMPLIED WARRANTIES OF MERCHANTABILITY, FITNESS FOR A PARTICULAR PURPOSE, AND NON-INFRINGEMENT.

b. COMPANY MAKES NO WARRANTY THAT (i) THE SERVICE WILL MEET YOUR REQUIREMENTS, (ii) THE SERVICE WILL BE UNINTERRUPTED, TIMELY, SECURE, OR ERROR-FREE, (iii) THE RESULTS THAT MAY BE OBTAINED FROM THE USE OF THE SERVICE WILL BE ACCURATE OR RELIABLE, (iv) THE QUALITY OF ANY PRODUCTS, SERVICES, INFORMATION, OR OTHER MATERIAL PURCHASED OR OBTAINED BY YOU THROUGH THE SERVICE WILL MEET YOUR EXPECTATIONS, AND (V) ANY ERRORS IN THE SOFTWARE WILL BE CORRECTED.

c. ANY MATERIAL DOWNLOADED OR OTHERWISE OBTAINED THROUGH THE USE OF THE SERVICE IS DONE AT YOUR OWN DISCRETION AND RISK AND THAT YOU WILL BE SOLELY RESPONSIBLE FOR ANY DAMAGE TO YOUR COMPUTER SYSTEM OR LOSS OF DATA THAT RESULTS FROM THE DOWNLOAD OF ANY SUCH MATERIAL.

d. NO ADVICE OR INFORMATION, WHETHER ORAL OR WRITTEN, OBTAINED BY YOU FROM COMPANY OR THROUGH OR FROM THE SERVICE, SHALL CREATE ANY WARRANTY NOT EXPRESSLY STATED IN THE TOS.

YOU EXPRESSLY UNDERSTAND AND AGREE THAT COMPANY SHALL NOT BE LIABLE FOR ANY DIRECT, INDIRECT, INCIDENTAL, SPECIAL, CONSEQUENTIAL, OR EXEMPLARY DAMAGES, INCLUDING BUT NOT LIMITED TO DAMAGES FOR LOSS OF PROFITS, GOODWILL, USE, DATA, OR OTHER INTANGIBLE LOSSES (EVEN IF COMPANY HAS BEEN ADVISED OF THE POSSIBILITY OF SUCH DAMAGES) RESULTING FROM (i) THE USE OR THE INABILITY TO USE THE SERVICE; (ii) THE COST OF PROCUREMENT OF SUBSTITUTE GOODS AND SERVICES RESULTING FROM ANY GOODS, DATA, INFORMATION, OR SERVICES PURCHASED OR OBTAINED OR MESSAGES RECEIVED OR TRANSACTIONS ENTERED INTO THROUGH OR FROM THE SERVICE; (iii) UNAUTHORIZED ACCESS TO OR ALTERATION OF YOUR TRANSMISSIONS OR DATA; (iv) STATEMENTS OR CONDUCT OF ANY THIRD PARTY ON THE SERVICE; OR (v) ANY OTHER MATTER RELATING TO THE SERVICE.

SOME JURISDICTIONS DO NOT ALLOW THE EXCLUSION OF CERTAIN WARRANTIES OR THE LIMITATION OR EXCLUSION OF LIABILITY FOR INCIDENTAL OR CONSEQUENTIAL DAMAGES. ACCORDINGLY, SOME OF THE ABOVE LIMITATIONS OF LIABILITY MAY NOT APPLY TO YOU.

THE SERVICE IS PROVIDED FOR INFORMATIONAL PURPOSES ONLY AND NO CONTENT INCLUDED IN THE SERVICE IS INTENDED FOR TRADING OR INVESTING PURPOSES. COMPANY SHALL NOT BE RESPONSIBLE OR LIABLE FOR THE ACCURACY, USEFULNESS, OR AVAILABILITY OF ANY INFORMATION TRANSMITTED VIA THE SERVICE AND SHALL NOT BE RESPONSIBLE OR LIABLE FOR ANY TRADING OR INVESTMENT DECISIONS MADE BASED ON SUCH INFORMATION.

Company respects the intellectual property of others and we ask our Users to do the same. If you believe that your work has been copied in a way that constitutes copyright infringement, please contact Company:

____

____

____

The TOS constitute the entire agreement between you and Company and govern your use of the Service, superseding any prior agreements between you and Company. You also may be subject to additional terms and conditions that may apply when you use affiliate services, third-party content, or third-party software. The TOS and the relationship between you and Company shall be governed by the laws of the State of California without regard to its conflict of law provisions. You and Company agree to submit to the personal and exclusive jurisdiction of the courts located within the county of ______________, ______________. The failure of Company to exercise or enforce any right or provision of the TOS shall not constitute a waiver of such right or provision. If any provision of the TOS is found by a court of competent jurisdiction to be invalid, the parties nevertheless agree that the court should endeavor to give effect to the parties' intentions as reflected in the provision and that the other provisions of the TOS remain in full force and effect. You agree that, regardless of any statute or law to the contrary, any claim or cause of action arising out of or related to use of the Service or the TOS must be filed within one (1) year after such claim or cause of action arose or be forever barred.

151. Notification of Infringement Letter Under the Digital Millennium Copyright Act

Date ____________________

To:

____

____

____

____

To Whom It May Concern:

I am writing to you to avail myself of my rights under the Digital Millennium Copyright Act (DMCA). This letter is a Notice of Infringement as authorized in § 512(c) of the U.S. Copyright Law. I wish to report an instance or what I feel in good faith is an instance of copyright infringement. The infringing material appears on a service for which you are the designated agent.

You are registered with the U.S. Copyright Office as the Designated Service Provider Agent to receive notifications of alleged Copyright infringement with respect to users of the Service for which you are the Designated Agent.

1. The material that I contend belongs to me and that appears illegally on the service is the following: (describe the infringing material: e.g., "a song entitled "Legal Battle Blues" and a song entitled "A Little Litigation," both performed by Lawyers in Love).
2. The material appears at the Web site address: (provide the full Web site address and a link to the page on which the material appears).
3. My contact information is as follows: (provide your name, address, telephone number, and e-mail address).
4. I have a good-faith belief that the use of the material that appears on the service is not authorized by the copyright owner, by its agent, or by operation of law.
5. The information in this notice is accurate and I am either the copyright owner or authorized to act on behalf of the copyright owner.

I declare under the perjury laws of the United States of America that this notification is true and correct.

____

Signature

____

Printed Name

152. Counter-Notification Letter Under the Digital Millennium Copyright Act

Date: ____________________

To:

____

____

____

____

To Whom It May Concern:

I am writing to you to avail myself of my rights under the Digital Millennium Copyright Act (DMCA). You recently provided me with a copy of Notice of Infringement from (Name the party who submitted the Notice of Infringement). This letter is a Counter-Notification as authorized in § 512(g) of the U.S. Copyright Law. I have a good-faith belief that the material that was removed or disabled as a result of the Notice of Infringement as a result of mistake or misidentification of the material. I therefore request that the material be replaced and/or no longer disabled.

You are registered with the U.S. Copyright Office as the Designated Service Provider Agent to receive notifications of alleged copyright infringement with respect to users of the Service for which you are the Designated Agent.

1. The material in question formerly appeared at the Web site address: (provide the full Web site address and a link to the page on which the material appears).
2. My contact information is as follows: (provide your name, address, telephone number, and e-mail address).
3. I consent to the jurisdiction of the Federal District Court for the judicial district in which my address is located (solely for the purposes of the resolution of this dispute) and I agree to accept service of process from the person who provided the Notice of Infringement.
4. I have a good-faith belief that the material removed or disabled following the Notice of Infringement was removed or disabled because of mistake or misidentification of the material. I therefore request that the material be replaced and/or no longer disabled.

I declare under the perjury laws of the United States of America that this notification is true and correct.

____

Signature

____

Printed Name

CHAPTER 16

Partnership Forms

If you operate a partnership, you might consider the following sample forms useful. If you are seeking further information on this topic, you might consider purchasing *Entrepreneur Magazine*'s *Ultimate Book on Forming Corporations, LLC's, Sole Proprietorships, and Partnerships* by Michael Spadaccini. That book includes the forms found in this section, as well as step-by-step instructions to the formation of business entities.

The *Delaware Certificate of Limited Partnership* is the charter document used by a limited partnership that is organized in the State of Delaware; this form is included as a sample, and each state will use its own form. The *Sample General Partnership Agreement* is a simple, standard agreement between the owners of a partnership.

A *Partner Ledger* is a written table showing the owners of a partnership and should be kept with the partnership agreement. The ledger must also indicate the percentage held by each partner. As new partners join the partnership through the sale of additional partnership interest (and a new partner's corresponding capital contribution), the new ownership is recorded on the ledger. The partnership ledger should also show transfers of partners' ownership interests, as when a partner passes away and transfers his or her interest through his or her will. Of course, your partnership ledger may never change—partners may simply not come and go from your partnership. Your ledger may simply reflect the initial partners and their initial contributions and percentage interests.

While partnerships enjoy far fewer formalities than corporation owners, a partnership should still maintain records of its meetings. When a partnership calls a meeting of the partners to formally vote on any matter, the results of that vote should be committed to written minutes entitled *Minutes of Partnership Meeting.*

In the real world, most small company votes are taken by written consent rather than by notice and meeting and an in-person vote. Use the *Action by Written Consent of Partners* when you wish to take a partnership action in writing, rather than by a noticed meeting. Written consents are important company records and should be maintained in the records book. Compare this consent form to the minutes in the form just previous to this one. You'll note that it is often far simpler to take votes by written consent.

153. Delaware Certificate of Limited Partnership

STATE OF DELAWARE
CERTIFICATE OF LIMITED PARTNERSHIP

The Undersigned, desiring to form a limited partnership pursuant to the Delaware Revised Uniform Limited Partnership Act, 6 Delaware Code, Chapter 17, do hereby certify as follows:

First: The name of the limited partnership is ______________________________.

Second: The address of its registered office in the State of Delaware is ______________________ in the city of ________________________.

The name of the Registered Agent at such address is ______________________________.

Third: The name and mailing address of each general partner is as follows:

______________________________ ______________________________

______________________________ ______________________________

______________________________ ______________________________

In Witness Whereof, the undersigned has executed this Certificate of Limited

Partnership of ______________________________ as of ______________________________.

By ______________________________
General Partner

Name ______________________________
(type or print name)

154. Sample General Partnership Agreement

GENERAL PARTNERSHIP AGREEMENT
Between
ANDREW LELAND and
DONALD LELAND

This general partnership agreement is made and entered into as of January 1, 2004, by and among Andrew Leland and Donald Leland (all of whom are hereinafter collectively sometimes referred to as "partners").

The parties hereto desire to form a general partnership (hereinafter referred to as the "Partnership"), under the laws of the State of __________________ for the term and upon the conditions set forth in this agreement, and the Partners agree as follows:

1.1. FORMATION OF PARTNERSHIP. The parties hereby form a general partnership, and the name of the partnership shall be __________________________. This agreement shall supersede any previous partnership agreements between the parties to this agreement.

1.2. DEFINITIONS.

"Act" means the laws governing partnerships in the State of organization .

"Bankruptcy" shall be deemed to have occurred with respect to any Partner 60 days after the happening of any of the following: (1) the filing of an application by a Partner for, or a consent to, the appointment of a trustee of the Partner's assets; (2) the filing by a Partner of a voluntary petition in bankruptcy of the filing of a pleading in any court of record admitting in writing the Partner's inability to pay the Partner's debts as they become due; (3) the making by a Partner of a general assignment for the benefit of creditors; (4) the filing by a Partner of an answer admitting the material allegations of, or consenting to or defaulting in answering a bankruptcy petition filed against the Partner in any bankruptcy proceeding; or (5) the entry of an order, judgment, or decree by any court of competent jurisdiction adjudicating a Partner a bankrupt or appointing a trustee of the Partner's assets, and that order, judgment, or decree continuing unstayed and in effect for a period of 60 days.

"Capital Account" means with respect to each Partner, the account established on the books and records of the Partnership for each Partner under Section 2.1. Each Partner's Capital Account shall initially equal the cash and the agreed value of property (net of liabilities assumed or to which the property is subject) contributed by the Partner to the Partnership, and during the term of the Partnership shall be (1) increased by the amount of (a) Taxable Income allocated to the Partner, other than Taxable Income attributable to the difference between the agreed value and adjusted basis of the property at contribution, and (b) any money and the agreed value of property (net of any liabilities assumed or to which the property is subject) subsequently contributed to the Partnership, and (2) decreased by the amount of (a) Tax Losses allocated to the Partner, except (i) Tax Losses attributable to depreciation of contributed property, which shall decrease Capital Accounts only to the extent of depreciation computed as if the property were purchased by the Partnership at its agreed value, and (ii) Tax Losses attributable to the difference between the agreed value and adjusted basis of property of property at contribution (which shall not decrease the contributing Partner's Capital Account), and (b) all cash and the agreed value of property (net of liabilities assumed or to which the property is subject) distributed to such Partner, and shall otherwise be kept in accordance with applicable Treasury Regulations.

"Contract Price" shall be equal to the fair market value of the selling Partner's Interest as of the date of the event triggering the sale. The fair market value shall be determined within 60 days by a valuation of the selling Partner's Interest as if the net assets of the Partnership were sold for cash and the cash distributed in accordance with Section 9.1.

"Incapacity" or "Incapacitated" means the incompetence, insanity, interdiction, death, disability, or incapacity, as the case may be, of any Partner.

"Interest" means the entire ownership interest of a Partner in the Partnership.

"Managing Partner" means Donald Leland but in the event that he is at any time no longer a Partner, or is replaced by vote of the Partners, the term shall mean the party or parties then acting in that capacity.

"Net Income" with respect to any fiscal period means all cash revenues of the Partnership during that period (including interest or other earning on the funds of the Partnership), less the sum of the following to the extent made from those cash revenues:

(a) All principal and interest payments on any indebtedness of the Partnership.

(b) All cash expenses incurred incident to the operations of the Partnership's business.

(c) Funds set aside as reserves for contingencies, working capital, debt service, taxes, insurance, or other costs or expenses incident to the conduct of the Partnership's business, which the Partners deem reasonably necessary or appropriate.

"Partnership Percentage" means the following percentages:

Name	Percentage
Donald Leland	50%
Andrew Leland	50%

Distributions or allocations made in proportion to or in accordance with the Partnership Percentages of the Partners shall be based upon relative Partnership Percentages as of the record date for distributions and in accordance with Section 706(c) and (d) of the Internal Revenue Code (IRC) for allocations.

"Operating Partner" means Andrew Leland but in the event that he is at any time no longer a Partner, or is replaced by vote of the Partners, the term shall mean the party or parties then acting in that capacity.

"Taxable Income" and "Tax Losses" respectively, shall mean the net income or net losses of the Partnership as determined for federal income tax purposes, and all items required to be separately stated by Section 702 of the IRC and the Regulations thereunder.

1.3. BUSINESS OF THE PARTNERSHIP. The business purpose for which this Partnership is organized is ____________________. Any modification of the business purpose outlined in this section shall not void this agreement.

1.4. NAMES AND ADDRESSES OF PARTNERS. The names and addresses of the Partners are:

Donald Leland, ______________________________; and

Andrew Leland, ______________________________.

1.5. TERM. The term of the Partnership shall begin on ____________ and shall continue until the earlier of December 31, 2050, or until dissolved by an act or event specified in the Agreement or by the law as one effecting dissolution.

1.6. BUSINESS OFFICES. The principal place of business of the Partnership shall be ____________________. The Partners may, from time to time, change the principal place of business of the Partnership. The Partners may in their discretion establish additional places of business of the Partnership.

2.1 INITIAL CAPITAL CONTRIBUTIONS. The Partner's initial Capital Contributions are deemed made as of this Agreement. The Partners shall initially make Capital Contributions as follows:

(a) Donald Leland shall contribute the following property: ____________________; and

(b) Andrew Leland shall contribute the following property: ____________________.

2.2. PARTNER'S ASSESSMENTS. In addition to the Capital Contributions required by Section 2.1, each Partner shall be obligated to make additional Capital Contributions, as needed to maintain the profitability of the Partnership. All additional Capital Contributions shall be made in accordance with the Partnership Percentages and within 30 days after the Partners have received notice thereof from the Managing Partner. The Managing Partner shall call these assessments based upon his estimate of all costs, expenses, or charges with respect to operation of the Partnership, less the expected revenues from such operations. Any increases in the Capital Contributions of the Partners pursuant to this Section shall be noted on Annex A attached hereto and incorporated by reference.

2.3. INTEREST ON CAPITAL CONTRIBUTIONS. No Partner shall be paid interest on any Capital Contribution.

2.4. WITHDRAWAL AND RETURN OF CAPITAL CONTRIBUTIONS. No Partner shall be entitled to withdraw any part of his Capital Contribution, or to receive any distributions from the Partnership except as provided by this Agreement.

2.5. LOANS BY PARTNER. The Partners may (but shall not be obligated to) loan or advance to the Partnership such funds as are necessary for the Partnership's operations, provided, however, that interest on those loans or advances shall not be in excess of five percent.

3.1. DISTRIBUTIONS. Net Income shall be distributed among the Partners in proportion to their Partnership Percentages.

3.2. ALLOCATION OF PROFITS AND LOSSES FOR TAX PURPOSES. The Taxable Income to be allocated among the Partners shall be allocated among them in accordance with the previous section concerning distributions. Tax Losses to allocated among the Partners shall be allocated among them in accordance with their respective Partnership Percentages.

4.1. BOOKS OF ACCOUNT, RECORDS, AND REPORTS. Proper and complete records and books of account shall be kept by the Operating Partner in which shall be entered fully and accurately all transactions and other matters relative to the Partnership's business as are usually entered into records and books of account maintained by persons engaged in businesses of a like character, including a Capital Account for each Partner. The Partnership books and records shall be prepared in accordance with generally accepted accounting practices, consistently applied, and shall be kept on a cash basis except in circumstances in which the Managing Partner determines that another bases of accounting will be in the best interests of the Partnership. The books and records shall at all times be maintained at the principal place of business of the Partnership and shall be open to the inspection and examination of the Partners or their duly authorized representatives during reasonable business hours.

4.2. REPORTS TO PARTNERS. As soon as practicable in the particular case, the Operating Partner shall deliver to every other Partner:

(a) Such information concerning the Partnership after the end of each fiscal year as shall be necessary for the preparation by such a Partner of his income or other tax returns.

(b) An unaudited statement prepared by the Operating Partner setting forth, as of the end of and for each fiscal year, a profit and loss statement and a balance sheet of the Partnership and a statement showing the amounts allocated to or against each Interest during that year.

4.3. FISCAL YEAR. The fiscal year of the Partnership shall end on the thirty-first day of December in each year.

4.4. PARTNERSHIP FUNDS. The funds of the Partnership shall be deposited in such bank account or accounts, or invested in such interest-bearing or non interest-bearing investments, as shall be designated by the Managing Partner. All withdrawals from any such bank accounts shall be made by the duly authorized agent or agents of any Partner. Partnership funds shall be held in the name of the Partnership and shall not be commingled with those of any other person.

5.1. INCAPACITATION. Within 90 days after a Partner becomes Incapacitated, his executor, administrator, committee, or analogous fiduciary (the "Representative") shall sell that Interest to the remaining Partners. The Representative shall notify the other Partners in writing within the 90 day period and the other Partners must purchase the Incapacitated Partner's Interest. The purchase price of an Interest sold pursuant to this Section shall be the Contract Price, and payment for the Interest shall be made in the manner set forth in Section 5.5.

5.2. BANKRUPTCY. At the Bankruptcy of any Partner, that Partner (an "Inactive Partner") or his representative shall cease to have any voice in the conduct of the affairs of the partnership and all acts, consents, and decisions with respect to the Partnership shall thereafter be made by the other Partners. The Inactive Partner shall, nonetheless, remain liable for his share of any losses of the Partnership or contributions to the Partnership as provided herein, and shall be entitled to receive his share of Taxable Income, Tax Losses, and Net Income. For six months from and after the date of the Bankruptcy of any Partner, the other Partners shall have the irrevocable option to purchase the Inactive Partner's Interest in the Partnership. That purchase shall be made in proportion to the respective Partnership Percentages of the other Partners at the time or in such other proportion as they may mutually agree. Should the other Partners exercise their option to purchase the Inactive Partner's Interest, they shall notify the Inactive Partner or his representative of their intention to do so within this six-month period. The purchase price of any Interest purchased pursuant to this Section shall be the Contract Price, and shall be payable at the time and in the manner specified in Section 5.5. Should the other Partners not exercise the option to purchase the Inactive Partner's Interest, the Inactive Partner shall remain such in accordance with the provisions set forth above.

5.3. SALE OF PARTNERSHIP INTEREST. If a Partner desires to offer for sale his Interest in the Partnership, such Partner (the "Selling Partner") shall give written notice to the other Partners (the "Buying Partner[s]"). Within 30 days after receipt of the notice, the Buying Partner(s) shall notify the Selling Partner of their intent to purchase the Interest of the Selling Partner. The purchase price of an Interest sold pursuant to this Section shall be the Contract Price, and payment for the Interest shall be made in the manner set forth in Section 5.5. If the Buying Partners fail to notify the Selling Partner that they intend to purchase his or her interest within the 30-day period, the Selling Partner shall have the right to withdraw from the Partnership. If a Partner withdraws, the Partner shall be entitled to a payment from the Partnership equal to the Contract Price and payable at the time and in the manner set forth in Section 5.5. Any amounts received pursuant to this Section shall constitute complete and full discharge of all amounts owing to the withdrawing Partner on account of his Interest as a Partner in the Partnership.

5.4. ASSIGNMENT. A Partner may not assign any part of his Interest in the Partnership.

5.5. PAYMENT; TIME AND MANNER.

(a) Any Interest transferred to other Partners or the Partnership pursuant to this Agreement shall be paid for, at the purchaser's option, either (1) all in cash at the time of transfer of the Interest, or (2) by a down payment computed in accordance with paragraph (b) below and delivery of a promissory note signed by the purchaser(s).

(b) If the purchaser(s) elects the second option in paragraph (a) above, (s)he shall pay as a down payment 33 percent. The remaining portion shall be represented by a promissory note of the purchasers, and providing for four equal annual installments of the remaining unpaid portion of the Contract Price, each installment due on the anniversary of the transfer of the interest. The promissory note shall provide that interest at an annual rate of 5 percent (compounded semi-annually) shall be paid with each payment of principal (or such higher interest rate as shall be necessary to avoid the imputation of interest pursuant to Section 483 of the IRC), from the date of acquisition of the Interest on the portion of the note remaining unpaid from time to time.

6.1. ADJUSTMENT OF PARTNERSHIP PERCENTAGES. If a Partner withdraws pursuant to Section 5.3, the Partnership Percentages of the remaining Partners shall immediately be recalculated so that each Partner's Partnership Percentage is equal to (1) his Capital Contribution, divided by (2) the aggregate Capital Contributions of all remaining Partners. If the Partners purchase an Interest pursuant to Sections 5.1, 5.2, or 5.3, the Partnership Percentage of the selling Partner shall be added to that of the purchasing Partners, pro rata.

6.2. VOTING. All decisions or actions required by the Partners pursuant to this Agreement (including amendment hereof) shall be made or taken by the affirmative vote (at a meeting or, in lieu thereof, by written consent of the required percentage in Interest) of Partners having 100 percent of the aggregate Partnership Percentages.

7.1. MANAGEMENT AND ADMINISTRATION OF BUSINESS. Except as otherwise provided in this agreement, all Partners shall have the authority to manage the day-to-day operations and affairs of the Partnership and to make decisions regarding the business of the Partnership. Any action taken by any Partner shall constitute the act of and serve to bind the Partnership.

7.2. ACTS REQUIRING UNANIMOUS CONSENT. The following acts may be done only with the unanimous consent of the partners: (a) Borrowing money in the Partnership's name, other than in the ordinary course of the Partnership's business; (b) Capital expenditures in excess of $500.00; and (c) Amendment of this agreement.

8.1. LIABILITY AND INDEMNIFICATION. No Partner shall be liable, responsible, or accountable in damages or otherwise to the Partnership or any Partner for any action taken or failure to act on behalf of the Partnership within the scope of the authority conferred on any Partner by this Agreement or by law unless the act or omission was performed or omitted fraudulently or in bad faith or constituted negligence. The Partnership shall indemnify and hold harmless the Partners from and against any loss, expense, damage, or injury suffered or sustained by them by reason of any acts, omissions arising out of their activities on behalf of the Partnership or in furtherance of the interests of the Partnership, including but not limited to any judgment, award, settlement, reasonable attorneys' fees, and other costs or expenses incurred in connection with the defense of any actual or threatened action, proceeding, or claim, if the acts, omissions, or alleged acts or omissions upon which the actual or threatened action, proceeding, or claims are based were for a purpose reasonably believed to be in the best interests of the Partnership and were not performed or omitted fraudulently or in bad faith or as a result of negligence by a Partner and were not in violation of the Partner's fiduciary obligation to the Partnership. Any such indemnification shall be first from the assets of the Partnership, and then from all Partners and borne among them in accordance with their Partnership Percentages.

8.2. LIMITS ON PARTNERS' POWERS. Anything in this Agreement to the contrary notwithstanding, no Partner shall cause the Partnership to (a) Commingle the Partnership's funds with those of any other person, or employ or permit another to employ those funds or assets in any manner except for the exclusive benefit of the Partnership (except to the extent that funds are temporarily retained by agents of the Partnership), or (b) Reimburse any Partner for expenses incurred by any Partner except for the actual cost to the Partner of goods, materials, or services (including reasonable travel and entertainment expenses) used for or by the Partnership.

9.1. DISSOLUTION OF THE PARTNERSHIP. The happening of any one of the following events shall work an immediate dissolution of the Partnership:

(a) The sale or other disposition of all or substantially all of the assets of the Partnership.

(b) The affirmative vote for dissolution of the Partnership by Partners having at least 34 percent of the aggregate Partnership Percentages.

(c) The Bankruptcy or Incapacity of any Partner; provided that the remaining Partners shall continue the business of the Partnership unless the Partnership is dissolved under subparagraph (b) above.

(d) The expiration of the term of the Partnership.

9.2. WINDING UP. If the Partnership is dissolved and its business is not continued under Section 9.1, the Managing

Partner or his/her successor shall commence to wind up the affairs of the Partnership and to liquidate the Partnership's assets. The Partners shall continue to share profits and losses during the period of liquidation in accordance with Sections 3.1 and 3.2. Following the occurrence of any of the events set forth in Section 9.1, the Partners shall determine whether the assets of the Partnership are to be sold or whether the assets are to be distributed to the Partners. If assets are distributed to the Partners, all such assets shall be valued at their then fair market value as determined by the Partners and the difference, if any, of the fair market value over (or under) the adjusted basis of such property to the Partnership shall be credited (or charged) to the Capital Accounts of the Partners in accordance with the provisions of Section 1.2. Such fair market value shall be used for purposes of determining the amount of any distribution to a Partner pursuant to Section 9.3. If the Partners are unable to agree on the fair market value of any asset of the Partnership, the fair market value shall be the average of two appraisals, one prepared by a qualified appraiser selected by Partners having 50 percent or more of the aggregate Partnership Percentages, and the other selected by the remaining Partners.

9.3. DISTRIBUTIONS UPON DISSOLUTION. Subject to the right of the Partners to set up such cash reserves as may be deemed reasonably necessary for any contingent or unforeseen liabilities or obligations of the Partnership, the proceeds of the liquidation and any other funds of the Partnership shall be distributed.

(a) To creditors, in the order of priority as provided by law except those liabilities to Partners in their capacities as Partners.

(b) To the Partners for loans, if any, made by them to the Partnership, or reimbursement for Partnership expenses paid by them.

(c) To the Partners in proportion to their respective Capital Accounts until they have received an amount equal to their Capital Accounts immediately prior to such distribution, but after adjustment for gain or loss with respect to the disposition of the Partnership's assets incident to the dissolution of the Partnership and the winding up of its affairs, whether or not the disposition occurs prior to the dissolution of the Partnership.

(d) To the Partners in accordance with their Partnership Percentages.

9.4. DEFICIT CAPITAL ACCOUNT RESTORATION. If, upon the dissolution and liquidation of the Partnership, after crediting all income upon sale of the Partnership's assets that have been sold and after making the allocations provided for in Section 9.3, any Partner has a negative Capital Account, then the Partner shall be obligated to contribute to the Partnership an amount equal to the negative Capital Account for distribution to creditors, or to Partners with positive Capital Account balances, in accordance with this Section.

10.1. FINAL REPORTS. Within a reasonable time following the completion of the liquidation of the Partnership's properties, the Managing Partner shall supply to each of the other Partners a statement that shall set forth the assets and liabilities of the Partnership as of the date of complete liquidation, and each Partner's portion of distributions pursuant to Section 9.3.

10.2. RIGHTS OF PARTNERS. Each Partner shall look solely to the assets of the Partnership for all distributions with respect to the Partnership and his Capital Contribution (including the return thereof), and share of profits, and shall have no recourse therefor (upon dissolution or otherwise) against any other Partner except as otherwise provided in this agreement.

10.3. TERMINATION. Upon the completion of the liquidation of the Partnership and the distribution of all Partnership funds, the Partnership shall terminate.

10.4. NOTICES. All notices and demands required or permitted under this Agreement shall be in writing and may be sent by certified or registered mail or similar delivery service, postage prepaid, to the Partners at their addresses as shown from time to time on the records of the Partnership, and shall be deemed given when mailed or delivered to the service. Any Partner may specify a different address by notifying the Managing Partner in writing of the different address.

10.5. SEVERABILITY. If any portion of this agreement be deemed by a competent court to be void or unenforceable, the remaining portions shall remain in full force and effect.

10.6. ENTIRE AGREEMENT. This is the entire agreement of the parties. Any oral representations or modifications concerning this instrument shall be of no force or effect unless contained in a subsequent written modification signed by the party to be charged.

IN WITNESS WHEREOF, the undersigned have executed this Agreement as of this date: ___________________.

____

Andrew Leland

____

Donald Leland

Table A: Name, address and initial capital contribution of the Partners

Name and Address of Partner	Value of Initial Capital Contribution	Nature of Partner's Initial Capital Contribution, i.e., cash, services, property	Percentage Interest of Partner

155. Partner Ledger

Date of Original Issue	Partner Name	Percentage Interest	Disposition of Shares (transferred or surrendered stock certificate)

156. Minutes of Partnership Meeting

Note: While partnerships enjoy far fewer formalities than corporation owners, a partnership should still maintain records of its meetings. When a partnership calls a meeting of the partners to formally vote on any matter, the results of that vote should be committed to written minutes.

MINUTES OF MEETING OF THE PARTNERS OF PALOS VERDES PARTNERS

The members of PALOS VERDES PARTNERS, held a meeting on _________ (date), at ______________(time), at___________________(place). The meeting was called by John Miller, and the company managers mailed notice to all members that the meeting would take place.

The following members were present at the meeting, in person or by proxy, representing membership interests as indicated:

John Jones, 50%
Judy Smith, 30%
John Miller, 20%

Also present were Michael Spadaccini, attorney to the company, and Lisa Johnson, the company's sales manager.

John Miller called the meeting to order.

John Miller noted that the meeting was called to decide whether to admit a new partner, Lisa Johnson. It was proposed that Lisa Johnson make a contribution of $10,000 in cash to the partnership, that she be admitted as a 10% owner, thereafter sharing 10% of the profits (or losses) of the partnership.

It was noted that the adjusted partnership percentages would have to be adjusted to accommodate the new partner, so the new partnership percentages would be as follows:

John Jones, 45%
Judy Smith, 27%
John Miller, 18%
Lisa Johnson, 10%

The three current partners all voted in favor of admitting Lisa Johnson.

There being no further business to come before the meeting, on motion duly made, seconded, and adopted, the meeting was adjourned.

____

John Smith, Manager

157. Action by Written Consent of Partners

Note: In the real world, most small company votes are taken by written consent rather than by notice and meeting and an in-person vote. Use the following form when you wish to take a company action in writing, rather than by a noticed meeting. Keep in mind, however, that your operating agreement and articles may require more than a simple majority to pass certain actions. Written consents are important company records and should be maintained in the record books. Compare this consent form to the minutes in the form just previous to this one. You'll note that it is often far simpler to take votes by written consent.

ACTION BY WRITTEN CONSENT OF PARTNERS OF PALOS VERDES PARTNERS

The undersigned members of Palos Verdes Partners, owning the following number of shares:

John Jones, 50%
Judy Smith, 30%
John Miller, 20%

hereby consent(s) to the following company actions.

1. Lisa Johnson is hereby admitted as a partner to the partnership, and her capital contribution of $10,000 in cash is accepted.
2. The partnership percentages are hereby adjusted to accommodate the new partner; the new partnership percentages would be as follows, effective immediately after this resolution is adopted:

   John Jones, 45%
   Judy Smith, 27%
   John Miller, 18%
   Lisa Johnson, 10%

The three current partners all voted in favor of admitting Lisa Johnson.

John Smith and John Miller, both also members, are hereby elected to serve as company managers until the next meeting of members.

Dated ____________________

____
John Smith
Percentage Owned ________

Dated ____________________

____
John Miller
Percentage Owned ________

Dated ____________________

____
Judy Smith
Percentage Owned ________

CHAPTER 17

Limited Liability Company (LLC) Forms

If you operate an LLC, you might consider the following sample forms useful. If you are seeking further information on this topic, you might consider purchasing *Entrepreneur Magazine's Ultimate Book on Forming Corporations, LLC's, Sole Proprietorships, and Partnerships* by Michael Spadaccini. That book includes the forms found in this section, as well as step-by-step instructions to the formation of business entities.

The *LLC-1, California LLC Articles of Organization* is simply the form required in the State of California to organize and register a Limited Liability Company. Each state will require a different form. The *Sample Letter to Secretary of State Accompanying Articles of Organization* is a simple cover letter that you should include when submitting Limited Liability Company papers to the Secretary of State.

A registered agent is a person or entity that is authorized and obligated to receive legal papers on behalf of an LLC. The *Sample Letter to Registered Agent Accompanying Articles of Organization* is a simple cover letter that you should deliver to your registered agent upon the organization of your LLC. Keep in mind that your state of organization may use a different term than registered agent. Typical equivalents include "agent for service of process," "local agent," and "registered agent."

The next group of forms are differing types of *LLC Operating Agreements* and deserve some comment. LLCs are managed in one of two ways, either "member-managed" or "manager-managed." Member-managed LLCs are governed by the LLC's owners (members) equally, just like a standard partnership. Manager-managed LLCs are governed by one or more appointed managers who often need not be members of the LLC. This manner of management by appointment is called "representative management." Manager-managed LLCs are managed much like corporations—with an appointed body of persons other than the company's ownership. The body of managers that undertakes governing responsibilities can come in the form of a board of managers or a committee of managers.

Thus, the *Short-Form Operating Agreement for Member-Managed LLC* and the *Long-Form Agreement for Member-Managed LLC* are both short and long versions of operating agreements for member-managed LLCs. Similarly the *Short-Form Operating Agreement for Manager-Managed LLC* and the *Long-Form Operating Agreement for Manager-Managed LLC* are both short and long versions of operating agreements for manager-managed LLCs.

The *Membership Ledger* is a written table showing the owners of an LLC. The ledger must also indicate the percentage held by each owner. As new members are added to the LLC through the sale of membership interests, their ownership is recorded on the ledger. The membership ledger should also show transfers of members' ownership interest, as when a member passes away and transfers his or her interest through his or her will. The importance of the membership ledger cannot be overstated, and it should be diligently maintained. The membership ledger is akin to the deed on a piece of real estate. The ledger is the primary evidence of ownership in an LLC, and carries a great degree of weight when presented in court. LLC owners should insist upon receiving updated copies of the membership ledger periodically.

Each member admitted to the LLC should execute the *Investment Representation Letter.* The investment representation letter offers some measure of protection to the entity because the member being admitted to the LLC makes certain representations regarding his qualifications and fitness to serve as a member of the LLC. Also, in the investment representation letter the member makes certain representations regarding his or her investment objectives, which are necessary representations in order to comply with state and federal securities laws.

The *Appointment of Proxy for Member's Meeting* is an authorization by one member giving another person the right to vote the owner's shares in a company, in this case an LLC. The term Proxy also refers to the document granting such authority. Proxy rules are typically outlined in state law and an LLC's operating agreement. Often proxies are granted when members do not wish to attend member meetings, but they want their vote to be counted. They can therefore grant their proxy to another person to attend the meeting and vote their shares on their behalf.

The *Call for Meeting of Members* is an instruction by LLC members to the managers that the members want to call a meeting of members. This serves as official notice to the managers that the members wish to call a meeting. This call is only required by manager-managed LLCs; if a member in a member-managed LLC wants to call a meeting of members, he or she would skip the call, and simply send a notice of meeting of members to all other members. The next form in this volume is a notice of meeting of members.

The *Notice of Meeting of LLC Members* is simply an LLC's announcement to its members that a meeting of members has been called.

While LLC members and managers enjoy far fewer corporate formalities than corporation owners, an LLC must still maintain records of its meetings. When an LLC's members meet to formally vote on any matter, the results of that vote should be committed to written minutes called the *Minutes of Meeting of LLC Members.*

In the real world, most LLC votes are taken by written consent in a document called a *Action by Written Consent of LLC Members* rather than by notice and meeting and an in-person vote. Use the written consent form when you wish to take a company action in writing, rather than by a noticed meeting. Keep in mind, however, that your operating agreement and articles may require more than a simple majority to pass certain actions. Written consents are important company records and should be maintained in the record books.

The *Written Consent of Members Approving a Certificate of Amendment of Articles of Organization Changing an LLC's Name* is a specific example of a written consent. In this case, the written consent authorizes a change to the LLC's charter to change the LLC's legal name.

158. LLC-1, California LLC Articles of Organization

ATTENTION: LIMITED LIABILITY COMPANY FILERS

Pursuant to California Revenue and Taxation Code section 17941, every Limited Liability Company (LLC) that is doing business in California or that has Articles of Organization accepted or a Certificate of Registration issued by the Secretary of State's office (pursuant to California Corporations Code section 17050 or 17451) *and* is not taxed as a corporation is subject to the annual LLC minimum tax of $800 (as well as the appropriate fee pursuant to Revenue and Taxation Code section 17942). The tax is paid to the California Franchise Tax Board, is due for the taxable year of organization/registration, and must be paid for each taxable year, or part thereof, until a Certificate of Cancellation of Registration or Certificate of Cancellation of Articles of Organization (pursuant to Corporations Code section 17356 or 17455) is filed with the Secretary of State's office. For further information regarding the payment of this tax, please contact the Franchise Tax Board at:

From within the United States (toll-free)
(800) 852-5711

From outside the United States (not toll-free)
(916) 845-6500

Automated toll-free phone service
(800) 338-0505

California Secretary of State
Business Programs Division
Business Filings Section
(916) 657-5448

State of California
Kevin Shelley
Secretary of State

File # ______________________

LIMITED LIABILITY COMPANY ARTICLES OF ORGANIZATION

A $70.00 filing fee must accompany this form.

IMPORTANT – Read instructions before completing this form.

This Space For Filing Use Only

1. **NAME OF THE LIMITED LIABILITY COMPANY** (END THE NAME WITH THE WORDS "LIMITED LIABILITY COMPANY," "LTD. LIABILITY CO.,"OR THE ABBREVIATIONS "LLC" OR "L.L.C.")

2. **THE PURPOSE OF THE LIMITED LIABILITY COMPANY IS TO ENGAGE IN ANY LAWFUL ACT OR ACTIVITY FOR WHICH A LIMITED LIABILITY COMPANY MAY BE ORGANIZED UNDER THE BEVERLY-KILLEA LIMITED LIABILITY COMPANY ACT.**

3. **CHECK THE APPROPRIATE PROVISION BELOW AND NAME THE AGENT FOR SERVICE OF PROCESS.**

   [ ] AN INDIVIDUAL RESIDING IN CALIFORNIA. PROCEED TO ITEM 4.

   [ ] A CORPORATION WHICH HAS FILED A CERTIFICATE PURSUANT TO SECTION 1505. PROCEED TO ITEM 5.

   AGENT'S NAME: ______________________________________

4. **ADDRESS OF THE AGENT FOR SERVICE OF PROCESS IN CALIFORNIA, IF AN INDIVIDUAL:**

   ADDRESS

   CITY STATE **CA** ZIP CODE

5. **THE LIMITED LIABILITY COMPANY WILL BE MANAGED BY: (CHECK ONE)**

   [ ] ONE MANAGER
   [ ] MORE THAN ONE MANAGER
   [ ] ALL LIMITED LIABILITY COMPANY MEMBER(S)

6. **OTHER MATTERS TO BE INCLUDED IN THIS CERTIFICATE MAY BE SET FORTH ON SEPARATE ATTACHED PAGES AND ARE MADE A PART OF THIS CERTIFICATE. OTHER MATTERS MAY INCLUDE THE LATEST DATE ON WHICH THE LIMITED LIABILITY COMPANY IS TO DISSOLVE.**

7. **NUMBER OF PAGES ATTACHED, IF ANY:**

8. **TYPE OF BUSINESS OF THE LIMITED LIABILITY COMPANY. (FOR INFORMATIONAL PURPOSES ONLY)**

9. **IT IS HEREBY DECLARED THAT I AM THE PERSON WHO EXECUTED THIS INSTRUMENT, WHICH EXECUTION IS MY ACT AND DEED.**

   ______________________________ SIGNATURE OF ORGANIZER

   ______________________________ DATE

   ______________________________ TYPE OR PRINT NAME OF ORGANIZER

10. **RETURN TO:**

   NAME
   FIRM
   ADDRESS
   CITY/STATE
   ZIP CODE

SEC/STATE FORM LLC-1 (Rev. 12/2003) – FILING FEE $70.00

APPROVED BY SECRETARY OF STATE

INSTRUCTIONS FOR COMPLETING THE ARTICLES OF ORGANIZATION (LLC-1)

For easier completion, this form is available in a "fillable" version online at the Secretary of State's website at http://www.ss.ca.gov/business/business.htm. The form can be filled in on your computer, printed and mailed to the Secretary of State, Document Filing Support Unit, P O Box 944228, Sacramento, CA 94244-2280 or can be delivered in person to the Sacramento office, 1500 11th Street, 3rd Floor, Sacramento, CA 95814. If you are not completing this form online, please type or legibly print in black or blue ink.

FILING FEE: The filing fee is $70.00. Make the check(s) payable to the Secretary of State and send the executed document and filing fee to the address stated above.

Statutory filing provisions can be found in California Corporations Code section **17051**. All statutory references are to the California Corporations Code, unless otherwise stated.

Pursuant to California Corporation Code section **17375**, nothing in this title shall be construed to permit a domestic or foreign limited liability company to render professional services, as defined in subdivision (a) of Section **13401**, in this state.

Complete the Articles of Organization (Form LLC-1) as follows:

Item 1. Enter the name of the limited liability company. The name shall contain the words "Limited Liability Company," or the abbreviations "LLC" or "L.L.C." The words "Limited" and "Company" may be abbreviated to "Ltd." and "Co." The name of the limited liability company may not contain the words "bank," "trust," "trustee," incorporated," "inc.," "corporation," or "corp.," and shall not contain the words "insurer" or "insurance company" or any other words suggesting that it is in the business of issuing policies of insurance and assuming insurance risks. (Section **17052**.)

Item 2. Execution of this document confirms the following statement which has been preprinted on the form and may not be altered: "The purpose of the limited liability company is to engage in any lawful act or activity for which a limited liability company may be organized under the Beverly-Killea Limited Liability Company Act." Provisions limiting or restricting the business of the limited liability company may be included as an attachment.

Item 3. Enter the name of the agent for service of process. Check the appropriate provision indicating whether the agent is an individual residing in California or a corporation which has filed a certificate pursuant to Section **1505** of the California Corporations Code. If an individual is designated as agent, proceed to item 4. If a corporation is designated, proceed to item 5.

Item 4. If an individual is designated as the initial agent for service of process, enter an address in California. Do not enter "in care of" (c/o) or abbreviate the name of the city. DO NOT enter an address if a corporation is designated as the agent for service of process.

Item 5. Check the appropriate provision indicating whether the limited liability company is to be managed by one manager, more than one manager or all limited liability company member(s). (Section **17051(a)(5)**.)

Item 6. The Articles of Organization (LLC-1) may include other matters that the person filing the Articles of Organization determines to include. Other matters may include the latest date on which the limited liability company is to dissolve. If other matters are to be included, attach one or more pages setting forth the other matters.

Item 7. Enter the number of pages attached, if any. All attachments should be 8½" x 11", one-sided and legible.

Item 8. Briefly describe the type of business that constitutes the principal business activity of the limited liability company. Note restrictions in the rendering of professional services by Limited Liability Companies. Professional services are defined in California Corporations Code, Section **13401(a)** as: "Any type of professional services that may be lawfully rendered only pursuant to a license, certification, or registration authorized by the Business and Professions Code or the Chiropractic Act."

Item 9. The Articles of Organization (LLC-1) shall be executed with an original signature of the organizer.

The person executing the Articles of Organization (LLC-1) need not be a member or manager of the limited liability company.

If an entity is signing the Articles of Organization (LLC-1), the person who signs for the entity must note the exact entity name, his/her name, and his/her position/title.

If an attorney-in-fact is signing the Articles of Organization (LLC-1), the signature must be followed by the words "Attorney-in-fact for (name of person)."

If a trust is signing the Articles of Organization (LLC-1), the articles must be signed by a trustee as follows: ________________, trustee for ____________ trust (including the date of the trust, if applicable). Example: Mary Todd, trustee of the Lincoln Family Trust (U/T/A 5-1-94).

Item 10. Enter the name and the address of the person or firm to whom a copy of the filing should be returned.

- For further information contact the Business Filings Section at (916) 657-5448.

159. Sample Letter to Secretary of State Accompanying Articles of Organization

Note: This letter is a version appropriate for use in Delaware, but can be modified for use in any state.

Michael Spadaccini
123 Elm Street
San Francisco, CA 94107
415-555-1212

(Date) ____________________

State of Delaware
Division of Corporations
401 Federal Street, Suite 4
Dover, DE 19901

To whom it may concern:

Enclosed you will find articles of organization for 17 Reasons, LLC. Please file the enclosed articles.

I have enclosed five copies of the filing and a check for $______ to cover filing fees. Please return any necessary papers in the envelope that I have provided.

Yours truly,

Michael Spadaccini

160. Sample Letter to Registered Agent Accompanying Articles of Organization

Michael Spadaccini
123 Elm Street
San Francisco, CA 94107
415-555-1212

(Date) ____________________

Harvard Business Services, Inc.
25 Greystone Manor
Lewes, DE 19958

To whom it may concern:

I have enclosed a copy of articles of incorporation I am filing today. As you can see, I have used you as our registered agents in the state of Delaware.

Please use the following contact information:

17 Reasons, LLC
c/o Michael Spadaccini
123 Elm Street
San Francisco, CA 94107

I have enclosed a check for $50.00 to cover the first year's services.

Yours truly,

Michael Spadaccini

161. Short-Form Operating Agreement for Member-Managed LLC

OPERATING AGREEMENT OF (nsert full name of LLC)

THIS OPERATING AGREEMENT (the "Agreement") is hereby entered into by the undersigned, who are owners and shall be referred to as Member or Members.

RECITALS

The Members desire to form (insert full name of LLC), a limited liability company (the "Company"), for the purposes set forth herein, and, accordingly, desire to enter into this Agreement in order to set forth the terms and conditions of the business and affairs of the Company and to determine the rights and obligations of its Members.

NOW, THEREFORE, the Members, intending to be legally bound by this Agreement, hereby agree that the limited liability company operating agreement of the Company shall be as follows:

ARTICLE I. DEFINITIONS

When used in this Agreement, the following terms shall have the meanings set forth below.

1.1 "Act" means the Limited Liability Company Law of the State in which the Company is organized or chartered, including any amendments or the corresponding provision(s) of any succeeding law.

1.2 "Capital Contribution(s)" means the amount of cash and the agreed value of property, services rendered, or a promissory note or other obligation to contribute cash or property or to perform services contributed by the Members for such Members' Interest in the Company, equal to the sum of the Members' initial Capital Contributions plus the Members' additional Capital Contributions, if any, made pursuant to Sections 4.1 and 4.2, respectively, less payments or distributions made pursuant to Section 5.1.

1.3 "Code" means the Internal Revenue Code of 1986 and the regulations promulgated thereunder, as amended from time to time (or any corresponding provision or provisions of succeeding law).

1.4 "Interest" or "Interests" means the ownership Interest, expressed as a number, percentage, or fraction, set forth in Table A, of a Member in the Company.

1.5 "Person" means any natural individual, partnership, firm, corporation, limited liability company, joint-stock company, trust, or other entity.

1.6 "Secretary of State" means the Office of the Secretary of State or the office charged with accepting articles of organization in the Company's state of organization.

ARTICLE II. FORMATION

2.1 Organization. The Members hereby organize the Company as a limited liability company pursuant to the provisions of the Act.

2.2 Effective Date. The Company shall come into being on, and this Agreement shall take effect from, the date the Articles of Organization of the Company are filed with the Secretary of State in the state of organization or charter.

2.3 Agreement: Invalid Provisions and Saving Clause. The Members, by executing this Agreement, hereby agree to the terms and conditions of this Agreement. To the extent any provision of this Agreement is prohibited or ineffective under the Act, this Agreement shall be deemed to be amended to the least extent necessary in order to make this Agreement effective under the Act. In the event the Act is subsequently amended or interpreted in such a way to validate any provision of this Agreement that was formerly invalid, such provision shall be considered to be valid from the effective date of such amendment or interpretation.

ARTICLE III. PURPOSE; NATURE OF BUSINESS

3.1 Purpose; Nature of Business. The purpose of the Company shall be to engage in any lawful business that may be engaged in by a limited liability company organized under the Act, as such business activities may be determined by the Member or Members from time to time.

3.2 Powers. The Company shall have all powers of a limited liability company under the Act and the power to do all things necessary or convenient to accomplish its purpose and operate its business as described in Section 3.1 here.

ARTICLE IV. MEMBERS AND CAPITAL CONTRIBUTIONS

4.1 Members and Initial Capital Contribution. The name, address, Interest, and value of the initial Capital Contribution of the Members shall be set forth on Table A attached hereto.

4.2 Additional Capital Contributions. The Members shall have no obligation to make any additional Capital Contributions to the Company. The Members may make additional Capital Contributions to the Company as the Members unanimously determine are necessary, appropriate, or desirable.

ARTICLE V. DISTRIBUTIONS AND ALLOCATIONS

5.1 Distributions and Allocations. All distributions of cash or other assets of the Company shall be made and paid to the Members at such time and in such amounts as the majority of the Members may determine. All items of income, gain, loss, deduction, and credit shall be allocated to the Members in proportion to their Interests.

ARTICLE VI. TAXATION

6.1 Income Tax Reporting. Each Member is aware of the income tax consequences of the allocations made by Article V here and agrees to be bound by the provisions of Article V here in reporting each Member's share of Company income and loss for federal and state income tax purposes.

6.2 Tax Treatment. Notwithstanding anything contained herein to the contrary and only for purposes of federal and, if applicable, state income tax purposes, the Company shall be classified as a partnership for such federal and state income tax purposes unless and until the Members unanimously determine to cause the Company to file an election under the Code to be classified as an association taxable as a corporation.

ARTICLE VII. MANAGEMENT BY MEMBERS

7.1 Management by Members. The Company shall be managed by its Members, who shall have full and exclusive right, power, and authority to manage the affairs of the Company and to bind the Company to contracts and obligations, to make all decisions with respect thereto, and to do or cause to be done any and all acts or things deemed by the Members to be necessary, appropriate, or desirable to carry out or further the business of the Company.

7.2 Voting Power in Proportion to Interest. The Members shall enjoy voting power and authority in proportion to their Interests. Unless expressly provided otherwise in this Agreement or the Articles of Organization, Company decisions shall be made by majority vote.

7.3 Duties of Members. The Members shall manage and administer the day-to-day operations and business of the Company and shall execute any and all reports, forms, instruments, documents, papers, writings, agreements, and contracts, including but not limited to deeds, bills of sale, assignments, leases, promissory notes, mortgages, and security agreements and any other type or form of document by which property or property rights of the Company are transferred or encumbered, or by which debts and obligations of the Company are created, incurred, or evidenced.

ARTICLE VIII. BOOKS AND RECORDS

8.1 Books and Records. The Members shall keep, or cause to be kept, at the principal place of business of the Company true and correct books of account, in which shall be entered fully and accurately each and every transaction of the Company. The Company's taxable and fiscal years shall end on December 31. All Members shall have the right to inspect the Company's books and records at any time, for any reason.

ARTICLE IX. LIMITATION OF LIABILITY; INDEMNIFICATION

9.1 Limited Liability. Except as otherwise required by law, the debts, obligations, and liabilities of the Company, whether arising in contract, tort, or otherwise, shall be solely the debts, obligations, and liabilities of the Company, and the Members shall not be obligated personally for any such debt, obligation, or liability of the Company solely by reason of being Members. The failure of the Company to observe any formalities or requirements relating to the exercise of its powers or the management of its business or affairs under this Agreement or by law shall not be grounds for imposing personal liability on the Members for any debts, liabilities, or obligations of the Company. Except as otherwise expressly required by law, the Members, in such Members' capacity as such, shall have no liability in excess of (a) the amount of such Members' Capital Contributions, (b) such Members' share of any assets and undistributed profits of the Company, and (c) the amount of any distributions required to be returned according to law.

9.2 Indemnification. The Company shall, to the fullest extent provided or allowed by law, indemnify, save harmless, and pay all judgments and claims against the Members, and each of the Company's or Members' agents, affiliates, heirs, legal representatives, successors, and assigns (each, an "Indemnified Party") from, against, and in respect of any and all liability, loss, damage, and expense incurred or sustained by the Indemnified Party in connection with the business of the Company or by reason of any act performed or omitted to be performed in connection with the activities of the Company or in dealing with third parties on behalf of the Company, including costs and attorneys' fees before and at trial and at all appellate levels, whether or not suit is instituted (which attorneys' fees may be paid as incurred), and any amounts expended in the settlement of any claims of liability, loss, or damage, to the fullest extent allowed by law.

9.3. Insurance. The Company shall not pay for any insurance covering liability of the Members or the Company's or Members' agents, affiliates, heirs, legal representatives, successors, and assigns for actions or omissions for which indemnification is not permitted hereunder; provided, however, that nothing contained here shall preclude the Company from purchasing and paying for such types of insurance, including extended coverage liability and casualty and worker's compensation, as would be customary for any Person owning, managing, and/or operating comparable property and engaged in a similar business, or from naming the Members and any of the Company's or Members' agents, affiliates, heirs, legal representatives, successors, or assigns or any Indemnified Party as additional insured parties thereunder.

9.4 Non-Exclusive Right. The provisions of this Article IX shall be in addition to and not in limitation of any other rights of indemnification and reimbursement or limitations of liability to which an Indemnified Party may be entitled under the Act, common law, or otherwise.

ARTICLE X. AMENDMENT

10.1 Amendment. This Agreement may not be altered or modified except by the unanimous written consent or agreement of the Members as evidenced by an amendment hereto whereby this Agreement is amended or amended and restated.

ARTICLE XI. WITHDRAWAL

11.1 Withdrawal of a Member. No Member may withdraw from the Company except by written request of the Member given to each of the other Members and with the unanimous written consent of the other Members (the effective date of withdrawal being the date on which the unanimous written consent of all of the other Members is given) or upon the effective date of any of the following events:

(a) the Member makes an assignment of his or her property for the benefit of creditors;

(b) the Member files a voluntary petition of bankruptcy;

(c) the Member is adjudged bankrupt or insolvent or there is entered against the Member an order for relief in any bankruptcy or insolvency proceeding;

(d) the Member seeks, consents to, or acquiesces in the appointment of a trustee or receiver for, or liquidation of the Member or of all or any substantial part of the Member's property;

(e) the Member files an answer or other pleading admitting or failing to contest the material allegations of a petition filed against the Member in any proceeding described in Subsections 11.1 (a) through (d);

(f) if the Member is a corporation, the dissolution of the corporation or the revocation of its articles of incorporation or charter;

(g) if the Member is an estate, the distribution by the fiduciary of the estate's Interest in the Company;

(h) if the Member is an employee of the Company and he or she resigns, retires, or for any reason ceases to be employed by the Company in any capacity; or

(i) if the other Members owning more than fifty percent (50%) of the Interests vote or request in writing that a Member withdraw and such request is given to the Member (the effective date of withdrawal being the date on which the vote or written request of the other Members is given to the Member).

11.2 Valuation of Interest. The value of the withdrawing Member's Interest in all events shall be equal to the greater of the following: (a) the amount of the Member's Capital Contribution or (b) the amount of the Member's share of the Members' equity in the Company, plus the amount of any unpaid and outstanding loans or advances made by the Member to the Company (plus any due and unpaid interest thereon, if interest on the loan or advance has been agreed to between the Company and the Member), calculated as of the end of the fiscal quarter immediately preceding the effective date of the Member's withdrawal.

11.3 Payment of Value. The value shall be payable as follows: (a) If the value is equal to or less than $500, at closing, and (b) If the value is greater than $500, at the option of the Company, $500 at closing with the balance of the purchase price paid by delivering a promissory note of the Company dated as of the closing date and bearing interest at the prime rate published in *The Wall Street Journal* as of the effective date of withdrawal, with the principal amount being payable in five (5) equal annual installments beginning one (1) year from closing and with the interest on the accrued and unpaid balance being payable at the time of payment of each principal installment.

11.4 Closing. Payment of the value of the departing Member's Interest shall be made at a mutually agreeable time and date on or before thirty (30) days from the effective date of withdrawal. Upon payment of the value of the Interest as calculated in Section 11.3 above: (a) the Member's right to receive any and all further payments or distributions on account of the Member's ownership of the Interest in the Company shall cease; (b) the Member's loans or advances to the Company shall be paid and satisfied in full; and (c) the Member shall no longer be a Member or creditor of the Company on account of the Capital Contribution or the loans or advances.

11.5 Limitation on Payment of Value. If payment of the value of the Interest would be prohibited by any statute or law prohibiting distributions that would

(a) render the Company insolvent; or

(b) be made at a time that the total Company liabilities (other than liabilities to Members on account of their Interests) exceed the value of the Company's total assets;

then the value of the withdrawing Member's Interest in all events shall be $1.00.

ARTICLE XII. MISCELLANEOUS PROVISIONS

12.1 Assignment of Interest and New Members. No Member may assign such person's Interest in the Company in whole or in part except by the vote or written consent of the other Members owning more than fifty percent (50%) of the Interests. No additional Person may be admitted as a Member except by the vote or written consent of the Members owning more than fifty percent (50%) of the Interests.

12.2 Determinations by Members: Except as required by the express provisions of this Agreement or of the Act:

(a) Any transaction, action, or decision which requires or permits the Members to consent to, approve, elect, appoint, adopt, or authorize or to make a determination or decision with respect thereto under this Agreement, the Act, the Code, or otherwise shall be made by the Members owning more than fifty percent (50%) of the Interests.

(b) The Members shall act at a meeting of Members or by consent in writing of the Members. Members may vote or give their consent in person or by proxy.

(c) Meetings of the Members may be held at any time, upon call of any Member or Members owning, in the aggregate, at least ten percent (10%) of the Interests.

(d) Unless waived in writing by the Members owning more than fifty percent (50%) of the Interests (before or after a meeting), at least two (2) business days, prior notice of any meeting shall be given to each Member. Such notice shall state the purpose for which such meeting has been called. No business may be conducted or action taken at such meeting that is not provided for in such notice.

(e) Members may participate in a meeting of Members by means of conference telephone or similar communications equipment by means of which all Persons participating in the meeting can hear each other, and such participation shall constitute presence in person at such meeting.

(f) The Members shall cause to be kept a book of minutes of all meetings of the Members in which there shall be recorded the time and place of such meeting, by whom such meeting was called, the notice thereof given, the names of those present, and the proceedings thereof. Copies of any consents in writing shall also be filed in such minute book.

12.3 Binding Effect. This Agreement shall be binding upon and inure to the benefit of the undersigned Members, their legal representatives, heirs, successors, and assigns. This Agreement and the rights and duties of the Members hereunder shall be governed by, and interpreted and construed in accordance with, the laws of the Company's state of organization or charter, without regard to principles of choice of law.

12.5 Headings. The article and section headings in this Agreement are inserted as a matter of convenience and are for reference only and shall not be construed to define, limit, extend, or describe the scope of this Agreement or the intent of any provision.

12.6 Number and Gender. Whenever required by the context here, the singular shall include the plural, and vice versa, and the masculine gender shall include the feminine and neuter genders, and vice versa.

12.7 Entire Agreement and Binding Effect. This Agreement constitutes the sole operating agreement among the Members and supersedes and cancels any prior agreements, representations, warranties, or communications, whether oral or written, between the Members relating to the affairs of the Company and the conduct of the Company's business. No amendment or modification of this Agreement shall be effective unless approved in writing as provided in Section 10.1. The Articles of Organization and this Agreement are binding upon and shall inure to the benefit of the Members and Agent(s) and shall be binding upon their successors, assigns, affiliates, subsidiaries, heirs, beneficiaries, personal representatives, executors, administrators, and guardians, as applicable and appropriate.

IN WITNESS WHEREOF, this Agreement has been made and executed by the Members effective as of the date first written above.

______________________________ (Member)

______________________________ (Member)

______________________________ (Member)

Table A: Name, Address and Initial Capital Contribution of the Members

Name and Address of Member	Value of Initial Capital Contribution	Nature of Member's Initial Capital Contribution (i.e., cash, services, property)	Percentage Interest of Member

162. Long-Form Operating Agreement for Member-Managed LLC

OPERATING AGREEMENT OF (INSERT NAME), LLC

THIS OPERATING AGREEMENT (the "Agreement") is made and entered into on _______, 20__, and those persons whose names, addresses, and signatures are set forth below, being the Members of (Insert Name), LLC (the "Company"), represent and agree that they have caused or will cause to be filed, on behalf of the Company, Articles of Organization, and that they desire to enter into an operating agreement.

The Members agree as follows:

ARTICLE I. DEFINITIONS

1.1. "Act" means the Limited Liability Company Law of the State in which the Company is organized or chartered, including any amendments or the corresponding provision(s) of any succeeding law.

1.2. "Affiliate" or "Affiliate of a Member" means any Person under the control of, in common control with, or in control of a Member, whether that control is direct or indirect. The term "control," as used herein, means, with respect to a corporation or limited liability company, the ability to exercise more than fifty percent (50%) of the voting rights of the controlled entity, and with respect to an individual, partnership, trust, or other entity or association, the ability, directly or indirectly, to direct the management of policies of the controlled entity or individual.

1.3. "Agreement" means this Operating Agreement, in its original form and as amended from time to time.

1.4. "Articles" means the Articles of Organization or other charter document filed with the Secretary of State in the state of organization forming this limited liability company, as initially filed and as they may be amended from time to time.

1.5. "Capital Account" means the amount of the capital interest of a Member in the Company, consisting of the amount of money and the fair market value, net of liabilities, of any property initially contributed by the Member, as (1) increased by any additional contributions and the Member's share of the Company's profits; and (2) decreased by any distribution to that Member as well as that Member's share of Company losses.

1.6. "Code" means the Internal Revenue Code of 1986, as amended from time to time, the regulations promulgated thereunder, and any corresponding provision of any succeeding revenue law.

1.7. "Company Minimum Gain" shall have the same meaning as set forth for the term "Partnership Minimum Gain" in the Regulations section 1.704-2(d) (26 CFR Section1.704-2(d)).

1.8. "Departing Member" means any Member whose conduct results in a Dissolution Event or who withdraws from or is expelled from the Company in accordance with Section 4.3, where such withdrawal does not result in dissolution of the Company.

1.9. "Dissolution Event" means, with respect to any Member, one or more of the following: the death, resignation, retirement, expulsion, bankruptcy, or dissolution of any Member.

1.10. "Distribution" means the transfer of money or property by the Company to the Members without consideration.

1.11. "Member" means each Person who has been admitted into membership in the Company, executes this Agreement and any subsequent amendments, and has not engaged in conduct resulting in a Dissolution Event or terminated membership for any other reason.

1.12. "Member Nonrecourse Debt" shall have the same meaning as set forth for the term "Partnership Nonrecourse Debt" in the Code.

1.13. "Member Nonrecourse Deductions" means items of Company loss, deduction, or Code Section 705(a)(2)(B) expenditures which are attributable to Member Nonrecourse Debt.

1.14. "Membership Interest" means a Member's rights in the Company, collectively, including the Member's economic interest, right to vote and participate in management, and right to information concerning the business and affairs of the Company provided in this Agreement or under the Act.

1.15. "Net Profits" and "Net Losses" mean the Company's income, loss, and deductions computed at the close of each fiscal year in accordance with the accounting methods used to prepare the Company's information tax return filed for federal income tax purposes.

1.16. "Nonrecourse Liability" has the meaning provided in the Code.

1.17. "Percentage Interest" means the percentage ownership of the Company of each Member as set forth in the column entitled "Member's Percentage Interest" contained in Table A as recalculated from time to time pursuant to this Agreement.

1.18. "Person" means an individual, partnership, limited partnership, corporation, limited liability company, registered limited liability partnership, trust, association, estate, or any other entity.

1.19. "Remaining Members" means, upon the occurrence of a Dissolution Event, those members of the Company whose conduct did not cause its occurrence.

ARTICLE II. FORMATION AND ORGANIZATION

2.1. Initial Date and Initial Parties. This Agreement is deemed entered into upon the date of the filing of the Company's Articles.

2.2. Subsequent Parties. No Person may become a Member of the Company without agreeing to and without becoming a signatory of this Agreement, and any offer or assignment of a Membership Interest is contingent upon the fulfillment of this condition.

2.3. Term. The Company shall commence upon the filing of its Articles and it shall continue in existence until December 31, 2050, unless terminated earlier under the provisions of this Agreement.

2.4. Principal Place of Business. The Company will have its principal place of business at (insert address of principal place of business) or at any other address upon which the Members agree. The Company shall maintain its principal executive offices at its principal place of business, as well as all required records and documents.

2.5. Authorization and Purpose. The purpose of the Company is to engage in any lawful business activity that is permitted by the Act.

ARTICLE III. CAPITAL CONTRIBUTIONS AND ACCOUNTS

3.1. Initial Capital Contributions. The initial capital contribution of each Member is listed in Table A attached hereto. Table A shall be revised to reflect and additional contributions pursuant to Section 3.2.

3.2. Additional Contributions. No Member shall be required to make any additional contributions to the Company. However, upon agreement by the Members that additional capital is desirable or necessary, any Member may, but shall not be required to, contribute additional capital to the Company on a pro rata basis consistent with the Percentage Interest of each of the Members.

3.3. Interest Payments. No Member shall be entitled to receive interest payments in connection with any contribution of capital to the Company, except as expressly provided herein.

3.4. Right to Return of Contributions. No Member shall be entitled to a return of any capital contributed to the Company, except as expressly provided in the Agreement.

3.5. Capital Accounts. A Capital Account shall be created and maintained by the Company for each Member, in conformance with the Code, which shall reflect all Capital Contributions to the Company. Should any Member transfer or assign all or any part of his or her membership interest in accordance with this Agreement, the successor shall receive that portion of the Member's Capital Account attributable to the interest assigned or transferred.

ARTICLE IV. MEMBERS

4.1. Limitation of Liability. No Member shall be personally liable for the debts, obligations, liabilities, or judgments of the Company solely by virtue of his or her Membership in the Company, except as expressly set forth in this Agreement or required by law.

4.2. Additional Members. The Members may admit additional Members to the Company only if approved by a two-thirds majority in interest of the Company Membership. Additional Members shall be permitted to participate in management at the discretion of the existing Members. Likewise, the existing Members shall agree upon an Additional Member's participation in Net Profits, Net Losses, and Distributions, as those terms are defined in this Agreement. Table A shall be amended to include the name, present mailing address, and percentage ownership of any Additional Members.

4.3. Withdrawal or Expulsion from Membership. Any Member may withdraw at any time after sixty (60) days' written notice to the company, without prejudice to the rights of the Company or any Member under any contract to which the withdrawing Member is a party. Such withdrawing Member shall have the rights of a transferee under this Agreement and the remaining Members shall be entitled to purchase the withdrawing Member's Membership Interest in accordance with this Agreement. Any Member may be expelled from the Company upon a vote of two-thirds majority in interest of the Company Membership. Such expelled Member shall have the rights of a transferee under this Agreement and the remaining Members shall be entitled to purchase the expelled Member's Membership Interest in accordance with this Agreement.

4.4. Competing Activities. The Members and their officers, directors, shareholders, partners, managers, agents, employees, and Affiliates are permitted to participate in other business activities which may be in competition, direct or indirect, with those of the Company. The Members further acknowledge that they are under no obligation to present to the Company any business or investment opportunities, even if the opportunities are of such a character as to be appropriate for the Company's undertaking. Each Member hereby waives the right to any claim against any other Member or Affiliate on account of such competing activities.

4.5. Compensation of Members. No Member or Affiliate shall be entitled to compensation for services rendered to the Company, absent agreement by the Members. However, Members and Affiliates shall be entitled to reimbursement for the actual cost of goods and services provided to the Company, including, without limitation, reimbursement for any professional services required to form the Company.

4.6. Transaction with the Company. The Members may permit a Member to lend money to and transact business with the Company, subject to any limitations contained in this Agreement or in the Act. To the extent permitted by applicable laws, such a Member shall be treated like any other Person with respect to transactions with the Company.

4.7. Meetings.

(a) There will be no regular or annual meeting of the Members. However, any Member(s) with an aggregate Percentage Interest of ten percent (10%) or more may call a meeting of the Members at any time. Such meeting shall be held at a place to be agreed upon by the Members.

(b) Minutes of the meeting shall be made and maintained along with the books and records of the Company.

(c) If any action on the part of the Members is to be proposed at the meeting, then written notice of the meeting must be provided to each Member entitled to vote not less than ten (10) days or more than sixty (60) days prior to the meeting. Notice may be given in person, by fax, by first class mail, or by any other written communication, charges prepaid, at the Members' address listed in Table A. The notice shall contain the date, time, and place of the meeting and a statement of the general nature of this business to be transacted there.

4.8. Actions at Meetings.

(a) No action may be taken at a meeting that was not proposed in the notice of the meeting, unless there is unanimous consent among all Members entitled to vote.

(b) No action may be taken at a meeting unless a quorum of Members is present, either in person or by proxy. A quorum of Members shall consist of Members holding a majority of the Percentage Interest in the Company.

(c) A Member may participate in, and is deemed present at, any meeting by clearly audible conference telephone or other similar means of communication.

(d) Any meeting may be adjourned upon the vote of the majority of the Membership Interests represented at the meeting.

(e) Actions taken at any meeting of the Members have full force and effect if each Member who was not present, in person or by proxy, signs a written waiver of notice and consent to the holding of the meeting or approval of the minutes of the meeting. All such waivers and consents shall become Company records.

(f) Presence at a meeting constitutes a waiver of the right to object to notice of a meeting, unless the Member expresses such an objection at the start of the meeting.

4.9. Actions Without Meetings. Any action that may be taken at a meeting of the Members may be taken without a meeting and without prior notice, if written consents to the action are submitted to the Company within sixty (60) days of the record date for the taking of the action, executed by Members holding a sufficient number of votes to authorize the taking of the action at a meeting at which all Members entitled to vote thereon are present and vote. All such consents shall be maintained as Company records.

4.10. Record Date. For the purposes of voting, notices of meetings, distributions, or any other rights under this Agreement, the Articles, or the Act, the Members representing in excess of ten percent (10%) of the Percentage Interests in the Company may fix, in advance, a record date that is not more than sixty (60) or less than ten (10) days prior to the date of such meeting or sixty (60) days prior to any other action. If no record date is fixed, the record date shall be determined in accordance with the Act.

4.11. Voting Rights. Except as expressly set forth in this Agreement, all actions requiring the vote, approval, or consent of the Members may be authorized upon the vote, approval, or consent of those Members holding a majority of the Percentage Interests in the Company. The following actions require the unanimous vote, approval, or consent of all Members who are neither the subjects of a dissolution event nor the transferors of a Membership Interest:

(a) Approval of the purchase by the Company or its nominee of the Membership Interest of a transferor Member;

(b) Approval of the sale, transfer, exchange, assignment, or other disposition of a Member's interest in the Company and admission of the transferee as a Member;

(c) A decision to make any amendment to the Articles or to this Agreement; and

(d) A decision to compromise the obligation of any Member to make a Capital Contribution or return money or property distributed in violation of the Act.

ARTICLE V. MANAGEMENT

5.1. Management by Members. The Company shall be managed by the Members. Each Member has the authority to manage and control the Company and to act on its behalf, except as limited by the Act, the Articles, or this Agreement.

5.2. Limitation on Exposing Members to Personal Liability. Neither the Company nor any Member may take any action that will have the effect of exposing any Member of the Company to personal liability for the obligations of the Company, without first obtaining the consent of the affected Member.

5.3. Limitation on Powers of Members. The Members shall not be authorized to permit the Company to perform the following acts or to engage in the following transactions without first obtaining the affirmative vote or written consent of the Members holding a majority Interest or such greater Percentage Interest as may be indicated below:

(a) The sale or other disposition of all or a substantial part of the Company's assets, whether occurring as a single transaction or a series of transactions over a 12-month period, except if the same is part of the orderly liquidation and winding up of the Company's affairs upon dissolution;

(b) The merger of the Company with any other business entity without the affirmative vote or written consent of all members;

(c) Any alteration of the primary purpose or business of the Company shall require the affirmative vote or written consent of Members holding at least sixty-six percent (66%) of the Percentage Interest in the Company;

(d) The establishment of different classes of Members;

(e) Transactions between the Company and one or more Members or one or more of any Member's Affiliates, or transactions in which one or more Members or Affiliates thereof have a material financial interest;

(f) Without limiting subsection (e) of this section, the lending of money to any Member or Affiliate of the Company;

(g) Any act which would prevent the Company from conducting its duly authorized business;

(h) The confession of a judgment against the Company.

Notwithstanding any other provisions of this Agreement, the written consent of all of the Members is required to permit the Company to incur an indebtedness or obligation greater than one hundred thousand dollars ($100,000.00). All checks, drafts, or other instruments requiring the Company to make payment of an amount less than fifty thousand dollars ($50,000.00) may be signed by any Member, acting alone. Any check, draft, or other instrument requiring the Company to make payment in the amount of fifty thousand dollars ($50,000.00) or more shall require the signature of two (2) Members acting together.

5.4. Fiduciary Duties. The fiduciary duties a Member owes to the Company and to the other Members of the Company are those of a partner to a partnership and to the partners of a partnership.

5.5. Liability for Acts and Omissions. As long as a Member acts in accordance with Section 5.4, no Member shall incur liability to any other Member or to the Company for any act or omission which occurs while in the performance of services for the Company.

ARTICLE VI. ALLOCATION OF PROFIT AND LOSS

6.1. Compliance with the Code. The Company intends to comply with the Code and all applicable Regulations, including without limitation the minimum gain chargeback requirements, and intends that the provisions of this Article be interpreted consistently with that intent.

6.2. Net Profits. Except as specifically provided elsewhere in this Agreement, Distributions of Net Profit shall be made to Members in proportion to their Percentage Interest in the Company.

6.3. Net Losses. Except as specifically provided elsewhere in this Agreement, Net Losses shall be allocated to the Members in proportion to their Percentage Interest in the Company. However, the foregoing will not apply to the extent that it would result in a Negative Capital Account balance for any Member equal to the Company Minimum Gain which would be realized by that Member in the event of a foreclosure of the Company's assets. Any Net Loss which is not allocated in accordance with the foregoing provision shall be allocated to other Members who are unaffected by that provision. When subsequent allocations of profit and loss are calculated, the losses reallocated pursuant to this provision shall be taken into account such that the net amount of the allocation shall be as close as possible to that which would have been allocated to each Member if the reallocation pursuant to this section had not taken place.

6.4. Regulatory Allocations. Notwithstanding the provisions of Section 6.3, the following applies:

(a) Should there be a net decrease in Company Minimum Gain in any taxable year, the Members shall specially allocate to each Member items of income and gain for that year (and, if necessary, for subsequent years) as required by the Code governing minimum gain chargeback requirements.

(b) Should there be a net decrease in Company Minimum Gain based on a Member Nonrecourse Debt in any taxable year, the Members shall first determine the extent of each Member's share of the Company Minimum Gain attributable to Member Nonrecourse Debt in accordance with the Code. The Members shall then specially allocate items of income and gain for that year (and, if necessary, for subsequent years) in accordance with the Code to each Member who has a share of the Company Nonrecourse Debt Minimum Gain.

(c) The Members shall allocate Nonrecourse Deductions for any taxable year to each Member in proportion to his or her Percentage Interest.

(d) The Members shall allocate Member Nonrecourse Deductions for any taxable year to the Member who bears the risk of loss with respect to the Nonrecourse Debt to which the Member Nonrecourse Deduction is attributable, as provided in the Code.

(e) If a Member unexpectedly receives any allocation of loss or deduction, or item thereof, or distributions which result in the Member's having a Negative Capital Account balance at the end of the taxable year greater than the Member's share of Company Minimum Gain, the Company shall specially allocate items of income and gain to that Member in a manner designed to eliminate the excess Negative Capital Account balance as rapidly as possible. Any allocations made in accordance with this provision shall taken into consideration in determining subsequent allocations under Article VI, so that, to the extent possible, the total amount allocated in this and subsequent allocations equals that which would have been allocated had there been no unexpected adjustments, allocations, and distributions and no allocation pursuant to Section 6.4(e).

(f) In accordance with Code Section 704(c) and the Regulations promulgated pursuant thereto, and notwithstanding any other provision in this Article, income, gain, loss, and deductions with respect to any property contributed to the Company shall, solely for tax purposes, be allocated among Members, taking into account any variation between the adjusted basis of the property to the Company for federal income tax purposes and its fair market value on the date of contribution. Allocations pursuant to this subsection are made solely for federal, state, and local taxes and shall not be taken into consideration in determining a Member's Capital Account or share of Net Profits or Net Losses or any other items subject to Distribution under this agreement.

6.5. Distributions. The Members may elect, by unanimous vote, to make a Distribution of assets at any time that would not be prohibited under the Act or under this Agreement. Such a Distribution shall be made in proportion to the unreturned capital contributions of each Member until all contributions have been paid, and thereafter in proportion to each Member's Percentage Interest in the Company. All such Distributions shall be made to those Persons who, according to the books and records of the Company, were the holders of record of Membership Interests on the date of the Distribution. Subject to Section 6.6, neither the Company nor any Members shall be liable for the making of any Distributions in accordance with the provisions of this section.

6.6. Limitations on Distributions.

(a) The Members shall not make any Distribution if, after giving effect to the Distribution, (1) the Company would not be able to pay its debts as they become due in the usual course of business, or (2) the Company's total assets would be less than the sum of its total liabilities plus, unless this Agreement provides otherwise, the amount that would be needed, if the Company were to be dissolved at the time of Distribution, to satisfy the preferential rights of other Members upon dissolution that are superior to the rights of the Member receiving the Distribution.

(b) The Members may base a determination that a Distribution is not prohibited under this section on any of the following: (1) financial statements prepared on the basis of accounting practices and principles that are reasonable under the circumstances, (2) a fair valuation, or (3) any other method that is reasonable under the circumstances.

6.7. Return of Distributions. Members shall return to the Company any Distributions received which are in violation of this Agreement or the Act. Such Distributions shall be returned to the account or accounts of the Company from which they were taken in order to make the Distribution. If a Distribution is made in compliance with the Act and this Agreement, a Member is under no obligation to return it to the Company or to pay the amount of the Distribution for the account of the Company or to any creditor of the Company.

6.8. Members Bound by These Provisions. The Members understand and acknowledge the tax implications of the provisions of this Article of the Agreement and agree to be bound by these provisions in reporting items of income and loss relating to the Company on their federal and state income tax returns.

ARTICLE VII. TRANSFERS AND TERMINATIONS OF MEMBERSHIP INTERESTS

7.1. Restriction on Transferability of Membership Interests. A Member may not transfer, assign, encumber, or convey all or any part of his or her Membership Interest in the Company, except as provided herein. In entering into this Agreement, each of the Members acknowledges the reasonableness of this restriction, which is intended to further the purposes of the Company and the relationships among the Members.

7.2. Permitted Transfers. In order to be permitted, a transfer or assignment of all or any part of a Membership Interest must have the approval of a two-thirds majority of the Members of the Company. Each Member, in his or her sole discretion, may proffer or withhold approval. In addition, the following conditions must be met:

(a) The transferee must provide a written agreement, satisfactory to the Members, to be bound by all of the provisions of this Agreement;

(b) The transferee must provide the Company with his or her taxpayer identification number and initial tax basis in the transferred interest;

(c) The transferee must pay the reasonable expenses incurred in connection with his or her admission to Membership;

(d) The transfer must be in compliance with all federal and state securities laws;

(e) The transfer must not result in the termination of the Company pursuant to Code Section 708.

(f) The transfer must not render the Company subject to the Investment Company Act of 1940, as amended; and

(g) The transferor must comply with the provisions of this Agreement.

7.3. Company's Right to Purchase Transferor's Interest and Valuation of Transferor's Interest. Any Member who wishes to transfer all or any part of his or her interest in the Company shall immediately provide the Company with written notice of his or her intention. The notice shall fully describe the nature of the interest to be transferred. Thereafter, the Company, or its nominee, shall have the option to purchase the transferor's interest at the Repurchase Price (as defined below).

(a) The "Repurchase Price" shall be determined as of the date of the event causing the transfer or dissolution event (the "Effective Date"). The date that the Company receives notice of a Member's intention to transfer his or her interest pursuant to this paragraph shall be deemed to be the Effective Date. The Repurchase Price shall be determined as follows:

i. The Repurchase Price of a Member's Percentage Interest shall be computed by the independent certified public accountant (CPA) regularly used by the Company or, if the Company has no CPA or if the CPA is unavailable, then by a qualified appraiser selected by the Company for this purpose. The Repurchase Price of a Member's Percentage Interest shall be the sum of the Company's total Repurchase Price multiplied by the Transferor's Percentage Interest as of the Effective Date.

ii. The Repurchase Price shall be determined by the book value method, as more further described herein. The book value of the interests shall be determined in accordance with the regular financial statements prepared by the Company and in accordance with generally accepted accounting principles, applied consistently with the accounting principles previously applied by the Company, adjusted to reflect the following:

(1) All inventory, valued at cost.

(2) All real property, leasehold improvements, equipment, and furnishings and fixtures valued at their fair market value.

(3) The face amount of any accounts payable.

(4) Any accrued taxes or assessments, deducted as liabilities.

(5) All usual fiscal year-end accruals and deferrals (including depreciation), prorated over the fiscal year.

(6) The reasonable fair market value of any good will or other intangible assets.

(b) The cost of the assessment shall be borne by the Company.

(c) The option provided to the Company shall be irrevocable and shall remain open for thirty (30) days from the Effective Date, except that if notice is given by regular mail, the option shall remain open for thirty-five (35) days from the Effective Date.

(d) At any time while the option remains open, the Company (or its nominee) may elect to exercise the option and purchase the transferor's interest in the Company. The transferor Member shall not vote on the question of whether the Company should exercise its option.

(e) If the Company chooses to exercise its option to purchase the transferor Member's interest, it shall provide written notice to the transferor within the option period. The notice shall specify a "Closing Date" for the purchase, which shall occur within thirty (30) days of the expiration of the option period.

(f) If the Company declines to exercise its option to purchase the transferor Member's interest, the transferor Member may then transfer his or her interest in accordance with Section 7.2. Any transfer not in compliance with the provisions of Section 7.2 shall be null and void and have no force or effect.

(g) In the event that the Company chooses to exercise its option to purchase the transferor Member's interest, the Company may elect to purchase the Member's interest on the following terms:

i. The Company may elect to pay the Repurchase Price in cash, by making such cash payment to the transferor Member upon the Closing Date.

ii. The Company may elect to pay any portion of the Repurchase Price by delivering to the transferor Member, upon the Closing Date, all of the following:

(1) An amount equal to at least 10% of the Repurchase Price in cash or in an immediately negotiable draft, and

(2) A Promissory Note for the remaining amount of the Repurchase Price, to be paid in 12 successive monthly installments, with such installments beginning 30 days following the Closing Date, and ending one year from the Closing Date, and

(3) A security agreement guaranteeing the payment of the Promissory Note by offering the Transferor's former membership interest as security for the payment of the Promissory Note.

7.4. Occurrence of Dissolution Event. Upon the death, withdrawal, resignation, retirement, expulsion, insanity, bankruptcy, or dissolution of any Member (a Dissolution Event), the Company shall be dissolved, unless all of the Remaining Members elect by a majority in interest within 90 days thereafter to continue the operation of the business. In the event that the Remaining Members to agree, the Company and the Remaining Members shall have the right to purchase the interest of the Member whose actions caused the occurrence of the Dissolution Event. The interest shall be sold in the manner described in Section 7.6.

7.5. Withdrawal from Membership. Notwithstanding Section 7.4, in the event that a Member withdraws in accordance with Section 4.3 and such withdrawal does not result in the dissolution of the Company, the Company and the Remaining Members shall have the right to purchase the interest of the withdrawing Member in the manner described in Section 7.6.

7.6. Purchase of Interest of Departing Member. The purchase price of a Departing Member's interest shall be determined in accordance with the procedure provided in Section 7.3.

(a) Once a value has been determined, each Remaining Member shall be entitled to purchase that portion of the Departing Member's interest that corresponds to his or her percentage ownership of the Percentage Interests of those Members electing to purchase a portion of the Departing Member's interest in the Company.

(b) Each Remaining Member desiring to purchase a share of the Departing Member's interest shall have thirty (30) days to provide written notice to the Company of his or her intention to do so. The failure to provide notice shall be deemed a rejection of the opportunity to purchase the Departing Member's interest.

(c) If any Member elects not to purchase all of the Departing Member's interest to which he or she is entitled, the other Members may purchase that portion of the Departing Member's interest. Any interest which is not purchased by the Remaining Members may be purchased by the Company.

(d) The Members shall assign a closing date within 60 days after the Members' election to purchase is completed. At that time, the Departing Member shall deliver to the Remaining Members an instrument of title, free of any encumbrances and containing warranties of title, duly conveying his or her interest in the Company and, in return, he or she shall be paid the purchase price for his or her interest in cash. The Departing Member and the Remaining Members shall perform all acts reasonably necessary to consummate the transaction in accordance with this agreement.

7.7. No Release of Liability. Any Member or Departing Member whose interest in the Company is sold pursuant to Article VII is not relieved thereby of any liability he or she may owe the Company.

ARTICLE VIII. BOOKS, RECORDS, AND REPORTING

8.1. Books and Records. The Members shall maintain at the Company's principal place of business the following books and records: a current list of the full name and last known business or residence address of each Member together with the Capital Contribution, Capital Account, and Membership Interest of each Member; a copy of the Articles and all amendments thereto; copies of the Company's federal, state; and local income tax or information returns and reports, if any; for the six (6) most recent taxable years; a copy of this Agreement and any amendments to it; copies of the Company's financial statements, if any; the books and records of the Company as they relate to its internal affairs for at least the current and past four (4) fiscal years; and true and correct copies of all relevant documents and records indicating the amount, cost, and value of all the property and assets of the Company.

8.2. Accounting Methods. The books and records of the Company shall be maintained in accordance with the accounting methods utilized for federal income tax purposes.

8.3. Reports. The Members shall cause to be prepared and filed in a timely manner all reports and documents required by any governmental agency. The Members shall cause to be prepared at least annually all information concerning the Company's operations that is required by the Members for the preparation of their federal and state tax returns.

8.4. Inspection Rights. For purposes reasonably related to their interests in the Company, all Members shall have the right to inspect and copy the books and records of the Company during normal business hours, upon reasonable request.

8.5. Bank Accounts. The Members shall maintain all of the funds of the Company in a bank account or accounts in the name of the Company, at a depository institution or institutions to be determined by a majority of the Members. The Members shall not permit the funds of the Company to be commingled in any manner with the funds or accounts of any other Person. The Members shall have the powers enumerated in Section 5.3 with respect to endorsing, signing, and negotiating checks, drafts, or other evidence of indebtedness to the Company or obligating the Company money to a third party.

ARTICLE IX. DISSOLUTION, LIQUIDATION, AND WINDING UP

9.1. Conditions Under Which Dissolution Shall Occur. The Company shall dissolve and its affairs shall be wound up upon the happening of the first of the following: at the time specified in the Articles; upon the happening of a Dissolution Event and the failure of the Remaining Members to elect to continue, in accordance with Section 7.4; upon the vote of all of the Members to dissolve; upon the entry of a decree of judicial dissolution pursuant to the Act; upon the happening of any event specified in the Articles as causing or requiring dissolution; or upon the sale of all or substantially all of the Company's assets.

9.2. Winding Up and Dissolution. If the Company is dissolved, the Members shall wind up its affairs, including the selling of all of the Company's assets and the provision of written notification to all of the Company's creditors of the commencement of dissolution proceedings.

9.3. Order of Payment. After determining that all known debts and liabilities of the Company in the process of winding up have been paid or provided for, including, without limitation, debts and liabilities to Members who are creditors of the Company, the Members shall distribute the remaining assets among the Members in accordance with their Positive Capital Account balances, after taking into consideration the profit and loss allocations made pursuant to Section 6.4. Members shall not be required to restore Negative Capital Account Balances.

ARTICLE X. INDEMNIFICATION

10.1. Indemnification. The Company shall indemnify any Member and may indemnify any Person to the fullest extent permitted by law on the date such indemnification is requested for any judgments, settlements, penalties, fines, or expenses of any kind incurred as a result of the Person's performance in the capacity of Member, officer, employee, or agent of the Company, as long as the Member or Person did not behave in violation of the Act or this Agreement.

ARTICLE XI. MISCELLANEOUS PROVISIONS

11.1. Assurances. Each Member shall execute all documents and certificates and perform all acts deemed appropriate by the Members and the Company or required by this Agreement or the Act in connection with the formation and operation of the Company and the acquisition, holding, or operation of any property by the Company.

11.2. Complete Agreement. This Agreement and the Articles constitute the complete and exclusive statement of the agreement among the Members with respect to the matters discussed herein and therein and they supersede all prior written or oral statements among the Members, including any prior statement, warranty, or representation.

11.3. Section Headings. The section headings which appear throughout this Agreement are provided for convenience only and are not intended to define or limit the scope of this Agreement or the intent of subject matter of its provisions.

11.4. Binding Effect. Subject to the provisions of this Agreement relating to the transferability of Membership Interests, this Agreement is binding upon and shall inure to the benefit of the parties hereto and their respective heirs, administrators, executors, successors, and assigns.

11.5. Interpretation. All pronouns and common nouns shall be deemed to refer to the masculine, feminine, neuter, singular, and plural, as the context may require. In the event that any claim is made by any Member relating to the drafting and interpretation of this Agreement, no presumption, inference, or burden of proof or persuasion shall be created or implied solely by virtue of the fact that this Agreement was drafted by or at the behest of a particular Member or his or her counsel.

11.6. Applicable Law. Each Member agrees that all disputes arising under or in connection with this Agreement and any transactions contemplated by this Agreement shall be governed by the internal law, and not the law of conflicts, of the state of organization.

11.7. Specific Performance. The Members acknowledge and agree that irreparable injury shall result from a breach of this Agreement and that money damages will not adequately compensate the injured party. Accordingly, in the event of a breach or a threatened breach of this Agreement, any party who may be injured shall be entitled, in addition to any other remedy which may be available, to injunctive relief to prevent or to correct the breach.

11.8. Remedies Cumulative. The remedies described in this Agreement are cumulative and shall not eliminate any other remedy to which a Person may be lawfully entitled.

11.9. Notice. Any notice or other writing to be served upon the Company or any Member thereof in connection with this Agreement shall be in writing and shall be deemed completed when delivered to the address specified in Table A, if to a Member, and to the resident agent, if to the Company. Any Member shall have the right to change the address at which notices shall be served upon ten (10) days' written notice to the Company and the other Members.

11.10. Amendments. Any amendments, modifications, or alterations to this Agreement or the Articles must be in writing and signed by all of the Members.

11.11. Severability. Each provision of this Agreement is severable from the other provisions. If, for any reason, any provision of this Agreement is declared invalid or contrary to existing law, the inoperability of that provision shall have no effect on the remaining provisions of the Agreement, which shall continue in full force and effect.

11.12. Counterparts. This Agreement may be executed in counterparts, each of which shall be deemed an original and all of which shall, when taken together, constitute a single document.

IN WITNESS WHEREOF, this Agreement has been made and executed by the Members effective as of the date first written above.

_______________________________ (Member)

_______________________________ (Member)

_______________________________ (Member)

Table A: Name, Address and Initial Capital Contribution of the Members

Name and Address of Member	Value of Initial Capital Contribution	Nature of Member's Initial Capital Contribution (i.e., cash, services, property)	Member's Percentage Interest

163. Short-Form Operating Agreement for Manager-Managed LLC

OPERATING AGREEMENT OF (insert full name of LLC)

THIS OPERATING AGREEMENT (the "Agreement") is hereby entered into by the undersigned, who are owners and shall be referred to as Member or Members.

RECITALS

The Members desire to form (insert full name of LLC), a limited liability company (the "Company"), for the purposes set forth herein, and, accordingly, desire to enter into this Agreement in order to set forth the terms and conditions of the business and affairs of the Company and to determine the rights and obligations of its Members.

NOW, THEREFORE, the Members, intending to be legally bound by this Agreement, hereby agree that the limited liability company operating agreement of the Company shall be as follows:

ARTICLE I. DEFINITIONS

When used in this Agreement, the following terms shall have the meanings set forth below.

1.1 "Act" means the Limited Liability Company Law of the State in which the Company is organized or chartered, including any amendments or the corresponding provision(s) of any succeeding law.

1.2 "Capital Contribution(s)" means the amount of cash and the agreed value of property, services rendered, or a promissory note or other obligation to contribute cash or property or to perform services contributed by the Members for such Members' Interest in the Company, equal to the sum of the Members' initial Capital Contributions plus the Members' additional Capital Contributions, if any, made pursuant to Sections 4.1 and 4.2, respectively, less payments or distributions made pursuant to Section 5.1.

1.3 "Code" means the Internal Revenue Code of 1986 and the regulations promulgated thereunder, as amended from time to time (or any corresponding provision or provisions of succeeding law).

1.4 "Interest" or "Interests" means the ownership Interest, expressed as a number, percentage, or fraction, set forth in Table A, of a Member in the Company.

1.5 "Manager" or "Managers" means the natural person or persons who have authority to govern the Company according to the terms of this Agreement.

1.6 "Person" means any natural individual, partnership, firm, corporation, limited liability company, joint-stock company, trust, or other entity.

1.7 "Secretary of State" means the Office of the Secretary of State or the office charged with accepting articles of organization in the Company's state of organization.

ARTICLE II. FORMATION

2.1 Organization. The Members hereby organize the Company as a limited liability company pursuant to the provisions of the Act.

2.2 Effective Date. The Company shall come into being on, and this Agreement shall take effect from, the date the Articles of Organization of the Company are filed with the Secretary of State in the state of organization or charter.

2.3 Agreement: Invalid Provisions and Saving Clause. The Members, by executing this Agreement, hereby agree to the terms and conditions of this Agreement. To the extent any provision of this Agreement is prohibited or ineffective under the Act, this Agreement shall be deemed to be amended to the least extent necessary in order to make this Agreement effective under the Act. In the event the Act is subsequently amended or interpreted in such a way to validate any provision of this Agreement that was formerly invalid, such provision shall be considered to be valid from the effective date of such amendment or interpretation.

ARTICLE III. PURPOSE; NATURE OF BUSINESS

3.1 Purpose; Nature of Business. The purpose of the Company shall be to engage in any lawful business that may be engaged in by a limited liability company organized under the Act, as such business activities may be determined by the Manager or Managers from time to time.

3.2 Powers. The Company shall have all powers of a limited liability company under the Act and the power to do all things necessary or convenient to accomplish its purpose and operate its business as described in Section 3.1 here.

ARTICLE IV. MEMBERS AND CAPITAL CONTRIBUTIONS

4.1 Members and Initial Capital Contribution. The name, address, Interest, type of property, and value of the initial Capital Contribution of the Members shall be set forth on Table A attached hereto.

4.2 Additional Capital Contributions. The Members shall have no obligation to make any additional Capital Contributions to the Company. The Members may make additional Capital Contributions to the Company as the Members unanimously determine are necessary, appropriate, or desirable.

ARTICLE V. DISTRIBUTIONS AND ALLOCATIONS

5.1 Distributions and Allocations. All distributions of cash or other assets of the Company shall be made and paid to the Members at such time and in such amounts as a majority of the Managers may determine. All items of income, gain, loss, deduction, and credit shall be allocated to the Members in proportion to their Interests.

ARTICLE VI. TAXATION

6.1 Income Tax Reporting. Each Member is aware of the income tax consequences of the allocations made by Article V here and agrees to be bound by the provisions of Article V here in reporting each Member's share of Company income and loss for federal and state income tax purposes.

6.2 Tax Treatment. Notwithstanding anything contained herein to the contrary and only for purposes of federal and, if applicable, state income tax purposes, the Company shall be classified as a partnership for such federal and state income tax purposes unless and until the Members determine to cause the Company to file an election under the Code to be classified as an association taxable as a corporation.

ARTICLE VII. MANAGERS AND AGENTS

7.1 Management by Manager(s). The Members shall elect and appoint the Manager(s), who shall have the full and exclusive right, power, and authority to manage the affairs of the Company and to bind the Company to contracts and obligations, to make all decisions with respect thereto, and to do or cause to be done any and all acts or things deemed by the Members to be necessary, appropriate, or desirable to carry out or further the business of the Company. All decisions and actions of the Manager(s) shall be made by majority vote of the Manager(s) as provided in Section 12.3. No annual meeting shall be required to reappoint Manager(s). Such Person(s) shall serve in such office(s) at the pleasure of the Members and until his, her, or their successors are duly elected and appointed by the Members. Until further action of the Members as provided herein, the Manager(s) whose names appear on Table B below are the Manager(s) of the Company.

7.2 Agents. Without limiting the rights of the Members, the Manager(s), or the Company, the Manager(s) shall appoint the Person(s) who is (are) to act as the agent(s) of the Company to carry out and further the decisions and actions of the Members or the Manager(s), to manage and the administer the day-to-day operations and business of the Company, and to execute any and all reports, forms, instruments, documents, papers, writings, agreements, and contracts, including but not limited to deeds, bills of sale, assignments, leases, promissory notes, mortgages, and security agreements and any other type or form of document by which property or property rights of the Company are transferred or encumbered, or by which debts and obligations of the Company are created, incurred, or evidenced, which are necessary, appropriate, or beneficial to carry out or further such decisions or actions and to manage and administer the day-to-day operations and business.

ARTICLE VIII. BOOKS AND RECORDS

8.1 Books and Records. The Managers shall keep, or cause to be kept, at the principal place of business of the Company true and correct books of account, in which shall be entered fully and accurately each and every transaction of the Company. The Company's taxable and fiscal years shall end on December 31. All Members shall have the right to inspect the Company's books and records at any time, for any reason.

ARTICLE IX. LIMITATION OF LIABILITY; INDEMNIFICATION

9.1 Limited Liability. Except as otherwise required by law, the debts, obligations, and liabilities of the Company, whether arising in contract, tort, or otherwise, shall be solely the debts, obligations, and liabilities of the Company, and the Members shall not be obligated personally for any such debt, obligation, or liability of the Company solely by reason of being Members. The failure of the Company to observe any formalities or requirements relating to the exercise of its powers or the management of its business or affairs under this Agreement or by law shall not be grounds for imposing personal liability on the Members for any debts, liabilities, or obligations of the Company. Except as otherwise expressly required by law, the Members, in such Members' capacity as such, shall have no liability in excess of (a) the amount of such Members' Capital Contributions, (b) such Members' share of any assets and undistributed profits of the Company, and (c) the amount of any distributions required to be returned according to law.

9.2 Indemnification. The Company shall, to the fullest extent provided or allowed by law, indemnify, save harmless, and pay all judgments and claims against the Members or Manager(s), and each of the Company's, Members', or Manager(s)' agents, affiliates, heirs, legal representatives, successors, and assigns (each, an "Indemnified Party") from, against, and in respect of any and all liability, loss, damage, and expense incurred or sustained by the Indemnified Party in connection with the business of the Company or by reason of any act performed or omitted to be performed in connection with the activities of the Company or in dealing with third parties on behalf of the Company, including costs and attorneys' fees before and at trial and at all appellate levels, whether or not suit is instituted (which attorneys' fees may be paid as incurred), and any amounts expended in the settlement of any claims of liability, loss, or damage, to the fullest extent allowed by law.

9.3. Insurance. The Company shall not pay for any insurance covering liability of the Members or the Manager(s) or the Company's, Members', or Manager(s)' agents, affiliates, heirs, legal representatives, successors, and assigns for actions or omissions for which indemnification is not permitted hereunder; provided, however, that nothing contained here shall preclude the Company from purchasing and paying for such types of insurance, including extended coverage liability and casualty and worker's compensation, as would be customary for any Person owning, managing, and/or operating comparable property and engaged in a similar business, or from naming the Members or the Manager(s) and any of the Company's, Members', or Manager(s)' agents, affiliates, heirs, legal representatives, successors, or assigns or any Indemnified Party as additional insured parties thereunder.

9.4 Non-Exclusive Right. The provisions of this Article IX shall be in addition to and not in limitation of any other rights of indemnification and reimbursement or limitations of liability to which an Indemnified Party may be entitled under the Act, common law, or otherwise.

ARTICLE X. AMENDMENT

10.1 Amendment. This Agreement may not be altered or modified except by the unanimous written consent or agreement of the Members as evidenced by an amendment hereto whereby this Agreement is amended or amended and restated.

ARTICLE XI. WITHDRAWAL

11.1 Withdrawal of a Member. No Member may withdraw from the Company except by written request of the Member given to each of the other Members and with the unanimous written consent of the other Members (the effective date of withdrawal being the date on which the unanimous written consent of all of the other Members is given) or upon the effective date of any of the following events:

(a) the Member makes an assignment of his or her property for the benefit of creditors;

(b) the Member files a voluntary petition of bankruptcy;

(c) the Member is adjudged bankrupt or insolvent or there is entered against the Member an order for relief in any bankruptcy or insolvency proceeding;

(d) the Member seeks, consents to, or acquiesces in the appointment of a trustee or receiver for, or liquidation of the Member or of all or any substantial part of the Member's property;

(e) the Member files an answer or other pleading admitting or failing to contest the material allegations of a petition filed against the Member in any proceeding described in Subsections 11.1 (a) through (d);

(f) if the Member is a corporation, the dissolution of the corporation or the revocation of its articles of incorporation or charter;

(g) if the Member is an estate, the distribution by the fiduciary of the estate's Interest in the Company;

(h) if the Member is an employee of the Company and he or she resigns, retires, or for any reason ceases to be employed by the Company in any capacity; or

(i) if the other Members owning more than fifty percent (50%) of the Interests vote or request in writing that a Member withdraw and such request is given to the Member (the effective date of withdrawal being the date on which the vote or written request of the other Members is given to the Member).

11.2 Valuation of Interest. The value of the withdrawing Member's Interest in all events shall be equal to the greater of the following: (a) the amount of the Member's Capital Contribution or (b) the amount of the Member's share of the Members' equity in the Company, plus the amount of any unpaid and outstanding loans or advances made by the Member to the Company (plus any due and unpaid interest thereon, if interest on the loan or advance has been agreed to between the Company and the Member), calculated as of the end of the fiscal quarter immediately preceding the effective date of the Member's withdrawal.

11.3 Payment of Value. The value shall be payable as follows: (a) If the value is equal to or less than $500, at closing, and (b) If the value is greater than $500, at the option of the Company, $500 at closing with the balance of the purchase price paid by delivering a promissory note of the Company dated as of the closing date and bearing interest at the prime rate published in *The Wall Street Journal* as of the effective date of withdrawal, with the principal amount being payable in five (5) equal annual installments beginning one (1) year from closing and with the interest on the accrued and unpaid balance being payable at the time of payment of each principal installment.

11.4 Closing. Payment of the value of the departing Member's Interest shall be made at a mutually agreeable time and date on or before thirty (30) days from the effective date of withdrawal. Upon payment of the value of the Interest as calculated in Section 11.3 above: (a) the Member's right to receive any and all further payments or distributions on account of the Member's ownership of the Interest in the Company shall cease; (b) the Member's loans or advances to the Company shall be paid and satisfied in full; and (c) the Member shall no longer be a Member or creditor of the Company on account of the Capital Contribution or the loans or advances.

11.5 Limitation on Payment of Value. If payment of the value of the Interest would be prohibited by any statute or law prohibiting distributions that would

(a) render the Company insolvent; or

(b) be made at a time that the total Company liabilities (other than liabilities to Members on account of their Interests) exceed the value of the Company's total assets;

then the value of the withdrawing Member's Interest in all events shall be $1.00.

ARTICLE XII. MISCELLANEOUS PROVISIONS

12.1 Assignment of Interest and New Members. No Member may assign such person's Interest in the Company in whole or in part except by the vote or written consent of the other Members owning more than fifty percent (50%) of the Interests. No additional Person may be admitted as a Member except by the vote or written consent of the Members owning more than fifty percent (50%) of the Interests.

12.2 Determinations by Members: Except as required by the express provisions of this Agreement or of the Act:

(a) Any transaction, action, or decision which requires or permits the Members to consent to, approve, elect, appoint, adopt, or authorize or to make a determination or decision with respect thereto under this Agreement, the Act, the Code, or otherwise shall be made by the Members owning more than fifty percent (50%) of the Interests.

(b) The Members shall act at a meeting of Members or by consent in writing of the Members. Members may vote or give their consent in person or by proxy.

(c) Meetings of the Members may be held at any time, upon call of any Manager or a Member or Members owning, in the aggregate, at least ten percent (10%) of the Interests.

(d) Unless waived in writing by the Members owning more than fifty percent (50%) of the Interests (before or after a meeting), at least two (2) business days' prior notice of any meeting shall be given to each Member. Such notice shall state the purpose for which such meeting has been called. No business may be conducted or action taken at such meeting that is not provided for in such notice.

(e) Members may participate in a meeting of Members by means of conference telephone or similar communications equipment by means of which all Persons participating in the meeting can hear each other, and such participation shall constitute presence in person at such meeting.

(f) The Managers shall cause to be kept a book of minutes of all meetings of the Members in which there shall be recorded the time and place of such meeting, by whom such meeting was called, the notice thereof given, the names of those present, and the proceedings thereof. Copies of any consents in writing shall also be filed in such minutes book.

12.3 Determinations by Managers. Except as required by the express provisions of this Agreement or of the Act and if there shall be more than one Manager:

(a) Any transaction, action, or decision which requires or permits the Managers to consent to, approve, elect, appoint, adopt, or authorize or to make a determination or decision with respect thereto under this Agreement, the Act, the Code, or otherwise shall be made by a majority of the Managers.

(b) The Managers shall act only at a meeting of the Managers or by consent in writing of the Managers. Managers may vote or give their consent in person only and not by proxy.

(c) Meetings of the Managers may be held at any time, upon call of any agent of the Company appointed pursuant to Section 7.2 of this Agreement or any Manager.

(d) Notice of any meeting shall be given to a majority of the Managers at any time prior to the meeting, in writing or by verbal communication. Such notice need not state the purpose for which such meeting has been called.

(e) The Managers may participate in a meeting of the Managers by means of conference telephone or similar communications equipment by means of which all Persons participating in the meeting can hear each other, and such participation shall constitute presence in person at such meeting.

(f) The Managers may cause to be kept a book of minutes of all meetings of the Managers in which there shall be recorded the time and place of such meeting, by whom such meeting was called, the notice thereof given, the names of those present, and the proceedings thereof. Copies of any consents in writing shall also be filed in such minute book.

12.4 Binding Effect. This Agreement shall be binding upon and inure to the benefit of the undersigned, their legal representatives, heirs, successors, and assigns. This Agreement and the rights and duties of the Members hereunder shall be governed by, and interpreted and construed in accordance with, the laws of the State of Florida, without regard to principles of choice of law.

12.5 Headings. The article and section headings in this Agreement are inserted as a matter of convenience and are for reference only and shall not be construed to define, limit, extend, or describe the scope of this Agreement or the intent of any provision.

12.6 Number and Gender. Whenever required by the context here, the singular shall include the plural, and vice versa, and the masculine gender shall include the feminine and neuter genders, and vice versa.

12.7 Entire Agreement and Binding Effect. This Agreement constitutes the sole operating agreement among the Members and supersedes and cancels any prior agreements, representations, warranties, or communications, whether oral or written, between the Members relating to the affairs of the Company and the conduct of the Company's business. No amendment or modification of this Agreement shall be effective unless approved in writing as provided in Section 10.1. The Articles of Organization and this Agreement are binding upon and shall inure to the benefit of the Members and Agent(s) and shall be binding upon their successors, assigns, affiliates, subsidiaries, heirs, beneficiaries, personal representatives, executors, administrators, and guardians, as applicable and appropriate.

IN WITNESS WHEREOF, this Agreement has been made and executed by the Members effective as of the date first written above.

______________________________ (Member)

______________________________ (Member)

______________________________ (Member)

Table A: Name, Address, and Initial Capital Contribution of the Members

Name and Address of Member	Value of Initial Capital Contribution	Nature of Member's Initial Capital Contribution (i.e., cash, services, property)	Percentage Interest of Member

Table B: Managers

Name of Manager	Address of Manager

164. Long-Form Operating Agreement for Manager-Managed LLC

OPERATING AGREEMENT OF (insert full name), LLC

THIS OPERATING AGREEMENT (the "Agreement") is made and entered into on _______, 20__, and those persons whose names, addresses and signatures are set forth below, being the Members of (insert name), LLC (the "Company"), represent and agree that they have caused or will cause to be filed, on behalf of the Company, Articles of Organization, and that they desire to enter into an operating agreement.

The Members agree as follows:

ARTICLE I. DEFINITIONS

1.1. "Act" means the Limited Liability Company Law of the State in which the Company is organized or chartered, including any amendments or the corresponding provision(s) of any succeeding law.

1.2. "Affiliate" or "Affiliate of a Member" means any Person under the control of, in common control with, or in control of a Member, whether that control is direct or indirect. The term "control," as used herein, means, with respect to a corporation or limited liability company, the ability to exercise more than fifty percent (50%) of the voting rights of the controlled entity, and with respect to an individual, partnership, trust, or other entity or association, the ability, directly or indirectly, to direct the management of policies of the controlled entity or individual.

1.3. "Agreement" means this Operating Agreement, in its original form and as amended from time to time.

1.4. "Articles" means the Articles of Organization or other charter document filed with the Secretary of State in the state of organization forming this limited liability company, as initially filed and as they may be amended from time to time.

1.5. "Capital Account" means the amount of the capital interest of a Member in the Company, consisting of the amount of money and the fair market value, net of liabilities, of any property initially contributed by the Member, as (1) increased by any additional contributions and the Member's share of the Company's profits; and (2) decreased by any distribution to that Member as well as that Member's share of Company losses.

1.6. "Code" means the Internal Revenue Code of 1986, as amended from time to time, the regulations promulgated thereunder, and any corresponding provision of any succeeding revenue law.

1.7. "Company Minimum Gain" shall have the same meaning as set forth for the term "Partnership Minimum Gain" in the Regulations section 1.704-2(d) (26 CFR Section1.704-2(d)).

1.8. "Departing Member" means any Member whose conduct results in a Dissolution Event or who withdraws from or is expelled from the Company in accordance with Section 4.3, where such withdrawal does not result in dissolution of the Company.

1.9. "Dissolution Event" means, with respect to any Member, one or more of the following: the death, resignation, retirement, expulsion, bankruptcy, or dissolution of any Member.

1.10. "Distribution" means the transfer of money or property by the Company to the Members without consideration.

1.11 "Manager" means each Person who has been appointed to serve as a Manager of the Company in accordance with the Act, the Articles, and this Agreement.

1.12. "Member" means each Person who has been admitted into membership in the Company, executes this Agreement and any subsequent amendments, and has not engaged in conduct resulting in a Dissolution Event or terminated membership for any other reason.

1.13. "Member Nonrecourse Debt" shall have the same meaning as set forth for the term "Partnership Nonrecourse Debt" in the Code.

1.14. "Member Nonrecourse Deductions" means items of Company loss, deduction, or Code Section 705(a)(2)(B) expenditures which are attributable to Member Nonrecourse Debt.

1.15. "Membership Interest" means a Member's rights in the Company, collectively, including the Member's economic interest, right to vote and participate in management, and right to information concerning the business and affairs of the Company provided in this Agreement or under the Act.

1.16. "Net Profits" and "Net Losses" mean the Company's income, loss, and deductions computed at the close of each fiscal year in accordance with the accounting methods used to prepare the Company's information tax return filed for federal income tax purposes.

1.17. "Nonrecourse Liability" has the meaning provided in the Code.

1.18. "Percentage Interest" means the percentage ownership of the Company of each Member as set forth in the column entitled "Member's Percentage Interest" contained in Table A as recalculated from time to time pursuant to this Agreement.

1.19. "Person" means an individual, partnership, limited partnership, corporation, limited liability company, registered limited liability partnership, trust, association, estate, or any other entity.

1.20. "Remaining Members" means, upon the occurrence of a Dissolution Event, those members of the Company whose conduct did not cause its occurrence.

ARTICLE II. FORMATION AND ORGANIZATION

2.1. Initial Date and Initial Parties. This Agreement is deemed entered into upon the date of the filing of the Company's Articles.

2.2. Subsequent Parties. No Person may become a Member of the Company without agreeing to and without becoming a signatory of this Agreement, and any offer or assignment of a Membership Interest is contingent upon the fulfillment of this condition.

2.3. Term. The Company shall commence upon the filing of its Articles and it shall continue in existence until December 31, 2050, unless terminated earlier under the provisions of this Agreement.

2.4. Principal Place of Business. The Company will have its principal place of business at (insert address of principal place of business) or at any other address upon which the Members agree. The Company shall maintain its principal executive offices at its principal place of business, as well as all required records and documents.

2.5. Authorization and Purpose. The purpose of the Company is to engage in any lawful business activity that is permitted by the Act.

ARTICLE III. CAPITAL CONTRIBUTIONS AND ACCOUNTS

3.1. Initial Capital Contributions. The initial capital contribution of each Member is listed in Table A attached hereto. Table A shall be revised to reflect and additional contributions pursuant to Section 3.2.

3.2. Additional Contributions. No Member shall be required to make any additional contributions to the Company. However, upon agreement by the Members that additional capital is desirable or necessary, any Member may, but shall not be required to, contribute additional capital to the Company on a pro rata basis consistent with the Percentage Interest of each of the Members.

3.3. Interest Payments. No Member shall be entitled to receive interest payments in connection with any contribution of capital to the Company, except as expressly provided herein.

3.4. Right to Return of Contributions. No Member shall be entitled to a return of any capital contributed to the Company, except as expressly provided in the Agreement.

3.5. Capital Accounts. A Capital Account shall be created and maintained by the Company for each Member, in conformance with the Code, which shall reflect all Capital Contributions to the Company. Should any Member transfer or assign all or any part of his or her membership interest in accordance with this Agreement, the successor shall receive that portion of the Member's Capital Account attributable to the interest assigned or transferred.

ARTICLE IV. MEMBERS

4.1. Limitation of Liability. No Member shall be personally liable for the debts, obligations, liabilities, or judgments of the Company solely by virtue of his or her Membership in the Company, except as expressly set forth in this Agreement or required by law.

4.2. Additional Members. The Members may admit additional Members to the Company only if approved by a two-thirds majority in interest of the Company Membership. Additional Members shall be permitted to participate in management at the discretion of the existing Members. Likewise, the existing Members shall agree upon an Additional Member's participation in Net Profits, Net Losses, and Distributions, as those terms are defined in this Agreement. Table A shall be amended to include the name, present mailing address, and percentage ownership of any Additional Members.

4.3. Withdrawal or Expulsion from Membership. Any Member may withdraw at any time after sixty (60) days' written notice to the company, without prejudice to the rights of the Company or any Member under any contract to which the withdrawing Member is a party. Such withdrawing Member shall have the rights of a transferee under this Agreement and the remaining Members shall be entitled to purchase the withdrawing Member's Membership Interest in accordance with this Agreement. Any Member may be expelled from the Company upon a vote of two-thirds majority in interest of the Company Membership. Such expelled Member shall have the rights of a transferee under this Agreement and the remaining Members shall be entitled to purchase the expelled Member's Membership Interest in accordance with this Agreement.

4.4. Competing Activities. The Members and their officers, directors, shareholders, partners, managers, agents, employees, and Affiliates are permitted to participate in other business activities which may be in competition, direct or indirect, with those of the Company. The Members further acknowledge that they are under no obligation to present to the Company any business or investment opportunities, even if the opportunities are of such a character as to be appropriate for the Company's undertaking. Each Member hereby waives the right to any claim against any other Member or Affiliate on account of such competing activities.

4.5. Compensation of Members. No Member or Affiliate shall be entitled to compensation for services rendered to the Company, absent agreement by the Members. However, Members and Affiliates shall be entitled to reimbursement for the actual cost of goods and services provided to the Company, including, without limitation, reimbursement for any professional services required to form the Company.

4.6. Transaction with the Company. The Members may permit a Member to lend money to and transact business with the Company, subject to any limitations contained in this Agreement or in the Act. To the extent permitted by applicable laws, such a Member shall be treated like any other Person with respect to transactions with the Company.

4.7. Meetings.

(a) There will be no regular or annual meeting of the Members. However, any Member(s) with an aggregate Percentage Interest of ten percent (10%) or more may call a meeting of the Members at any time. Such meeting shall be held at a place to be agreed upon by the Members.

(b) Minutes of the meeting shall be made and maintained along with the books and records of the Company.

(c) If any action on the part of the Members is to be proposed at the meeting, then written notice of the meeting must be provided to each Member entitled to vote not less than ten (10) days or more than sixty (60) days prior to the meeting. Notice may be given in person, by fax, by first class mail, or by any other written communication, charges prepaid, at the Members' address listed in Table A. The notice shall contain the date, time, and place of the meeting and a statement of the general nature of this business to be transacted there.

4.8. Actions at Meetings.

(a) No action may be taken at a meeting that was not proposed in the notice of the meeting, unless there is unanimous consent among all Members entitled to vote.

(b) No action may be taken at a meeting unless a quorum of Members is present, either in person or by proxy. A quorum of Members shall consist of Members holding a majority of the Percentage Interest in the Company.

(c) A Member may participate in, and is deemed present at, any meeting by clearly audible conference telephone or other similar means of communication.

(d) Any meeting may be adjourned upon the vote of the majority of the Membership Interests represented at the meeting.

(e) Actions taken at any meeting of the Members have full force and effect if each Member who was not present in person or by proxy, signs a written waiver of notice and consent to the holding of the meeting or approval of the minutes of the meeting. All such waivers and consents shall become Company records.

(f) Presence at a meeting constitutes a waiver of the right to object to notice of a meeting, unless the Member expresses such an objection at the start of the meeting.

4.9. Actions Without Meetings. Any action that may be taken at a meeting of the Members may be taken without a meeting and without prior notice, if written consents to the action are submitted to the Company within sixty (60) days of the record date for the taking of the action, executed by Members holding a sufficient number of votes to authorize the taking of the action at a meeting at which all Members entitled to vote thereon are present and vote. All such consents shall be maintained as Company records.

4.10. Record Date. For the purposes of voting, notices of meetings, distributions, or any other rights under this Agreement, the Articles, or the Act, the Members representing in excess of ten percent (10%) of the Percentage Interests in the Company may fix, in advance, a record date that is not more than sixty (60) or less than ten (10) days prior to the date of such meeting or sixty (60) days prior to any other action. If no record date is fixed, the record date shall be determined in accordance with the Act.

4.11. Voting Rights. Except as expressly set forth in this Agreement, all actions requiring the vote, approval, or consent of the Members may be authorized upon the vote, approval, or consent of those Members holding a majority of the Percentage Interests in the Company. The following actions require the unanimous vote, approval, or consent of all Members who are neither the subjects of a dissolution event nor the transferors of a Membership Interest:

(a) Approval of the purchase by the Company or its nominee of the Membership Interest of a transferor Member;

(b) Approval of the sale, transfer, exchange, assignment, or other disposition of a Member's interest in the Company, and admission of the transferee as a Member;

(c) A decision to make any amendment to the Articles or to this Agreement; and

(d) A decision to compromise the obligation to any Member to make a Capital Contribution or return money or property distributed in violation of the Act.

ARTICLE V. MANAGEMENT

5.1. Management by Appointed Managers. The Company shall be managed by one or more appointed Managers. The number of Managers and the identity of each Manager are set forth in Table B, below. The Members shall elect and appoint the Managers (and also determine the number of managers), who shall have the full and exclusive right, power, and authority to manage the affairs of the Company and to bind the Company to contracts and obligations, to make all decisions with respect thereto, and to do or cause to be done any and all acts or things deemed by the Members to be necessary, appropriate, or desirable to carry out or further the business of the Company. All decisions and actions of the Managers shall be made by majority vote of the Managers as provided in this Agreement. There shall be no annual meetings of the Members or Managers; Managers shall serve at the pleasure of the Members and until their successors and are duly elected and appointed by the Members.

5.2. Limitation on Powers of Managers; Member Vote Required for Some Actions. The Mangers shall not be authorized to permit the Company to perform the following acts or to engage in the following transactions without first obtaining the affirmative vote or written consent of the Members holding a majority Interest or such greater Percentage Interest as may be indicated below:

(a) The sale or other disposition of all or a substantial part of the Company's assets, whether occurring as a single transaction or a series of transactions over a 12-month period, except if the same is part of the orderly liquidation and winding up of the Company's affairs upon dissolution;

(b) The merger of the Company with any other business entity without the affirmative vote or written consent of all members;

(c) Any alteration of the primary purpose or business of the Company shall require the affirmative vote or written consent of Members holding at least sixty-six percent (66%) of the Percentage Interest in the Company;

(d) The establishment of different classes of Members;

(e) Transactions between the Company and one or more Members or one or more of any Member's Affiliates, or transactions in which one or more Members or Affiliates thereof have a material financial interest;

(f) Without limiting subsection (e) of this section, the lending of money to any Member or Affiliate of the Company;

(g) Any act which would prevent the Company from conducting its duly authorized business;

(h) The confession of a judgment against the Company.

Notwithstanding any other provisions of this Agreement, the written consent of all of the Members is required to permit the Company to incur an indebtedness or obligation greater than one hundred thousand dollars ($100,000.00). All checks, drafts, or other instruments requiring the Company to make payment of an amount less than fifty thousand dollars ($50,000.00) may be signed by any Member, acting alone. Any check, draft, or other instrument requiring the Company to make payment in the amount of fifty thousand dollars ($50,000.00) or more shall require the signature of two (2) Members acting together.

5.3. Fiduciary Duties. The fiduciary duties a Member owes to the Company and to the other Members of the Company are those of a partner to a partnership and to the partners of a partnership.

5.4. Liability for Acts and Omissions. As long as a Member acts in accordance with Section 5.3, no Member shall incur liability to any other Member or to the Company for any act or omission which occurs while in the performance of services for the Company.

ARTICLE VI. ALLOCATION OF PROFIT AND LOSS

6.1. Compliance with the Code. The Company intends to comply with the Code and all applicable Regulations, including without limitation the minimum gain chargeback requirements, and intends that the provisions of this Article be interpreted consistently with that intent.

6.2. Net Profits. Except as specifically provided elsewhere in this Agreement, Distributions of Net Profit shall be made to Members in proportion to their Percentage Interest in the Company.

6.3. Net Losses. Except as specifically provided elsewhere in this Agreement, Net Losses shall be allocated to the Members in proportion to their Percentage Interest in the Company. However, the foregoing will not apply to the extent that it would result in a Negative Capital Account balance for any Member equal to the Company Minimum Gain which would be realized by that Member in the event of a foreclosure of the Company's assets. Any Net Loss which is not allocated in accordance with the foregoing provision shall be allocated to other Members who are unaffected by that provision. When subsequent allocations of profit and loss are calculated, the losses reallocated pursuant to this provision shall be taken into account such that the net amount of the allocation shall be as close as possible to that which would have been allocated to each Member if the reallocation pursuant to this section had not taken place.

6.4. Regulatory Allocations. Notwithstanding the provisions of Section 6.3, the following applies:

(a) Should there be a net decrease in Company Minimum Gain in any taxable year, the Members shall specially allocate to each Member items of income and gain for that year (and, if necessary, for subsequent years) as required by the Code governing minimum gain chargeback requirements.

(b) Should there be a net decrease in Company Minimum Gain based on a Member Nonrecourse Debt in any taxable year, the Members shall first determine the extent of each Member's share of the Company Minimum Gain attributable to Member Nonrecourse Debt in accordance with the Code. The Members shall then specially allocate items of income and gain for that year (and, if necessary, for subsequent years) in accordance with the Code to each Member who has a share of the Company Nonrecourse Debt Minimum Gain.

(c) The Members shall allocate Nonrecourse Deductions for any taxable year to each Member in proportion to his or her Percentage Interest.

(d) The Members shall allocate Member Nonrecourse Deductions for any taxable year to the Member who bears the risk of loss with respect to the Nonrecourse Debt to which the Member Nonrecourse Deduction is attributable, as provided in the Code.

(e) If a Member unexpectedly receives any allocation of loss or deduction, or item thereof, or distributions which result in the Member's having a Negative Capital Account balance at the end of the taxable year greater than the Member's share of Company Minimum Gain, the Company shall specially allocate items of income and gain to that Member in a manner designed to eliminate the excess Negative Capital Account balance as rapidly as possible. Any allocations made in accordance with this provision shall taken into consideration in determining subsequent allocations under Article VI, so that, to the extent possible, the total amount allocated in this and subsequent allocations equals that which would have been allocated had there been no unexpected adjustments, allocations, and distributions and no allocation pursuant to Section 6.4(e).

(f) In accordance with Code Section 704(c) and the Regulations promulgated pursuant thereto, and notwithstanding any other provision in this Article, income, gain, loss, and deductions with respect to any property contributed to the Company shall, solely for tax purposes, be allocated among Members, taking into account any variation between the adjusted basis of the property to the Company for federal income tax purposes and its fair market value on the date of contribution. Allocations pursuant to this subsection are made solely for federal, state, and local taxes and shall not be taken into consideration in determining a Member's Capital Account or share of Net Profits or Net Losses or any other items subject to Distribution under this agreement.

6.5. Distributions. The Members may elect, by unanimous vote, to make a Distribution of assets at any time that would not be prohibited under the Act or under this Agreement. Such a Distribution shall be made in proportion to the unreturned capital contributions of each Member until all contributions have been paid, and thereafter in proportion to each Member's Percentage Interest in the Company. All such Distributions shall be made to those Persons who, according to the books and records of the Company, were the holders of record of Membership Interests on the date of the Distribution. Subject to Section 6.6, neither the Company nor any Members shall be liable for the making of any Distributions in accordance with the provisions of this section.

6.6. Limitations on Distributions.

(a) The Members shall not make any Distribution if, after giving effect to the distribution, (1) the Company would not be able to pay its debts as they become due in the usual course of business, or (2) the Company's total assets would be less than the sum of its total liabilities plus, unless this Agreement provides otherwise, the amount that would be needed, if the Company were to be dissolved at the time of Distribution, to satisfy the preferential rights of other Members upon dissolution that are superior to the rights of the Member receiving the Distribution.

(b) The Members may base a determination that a Distribution is not prohibited under this section on any of the following: (1) financial statements prepared on the basis of accounting practices and principles that are reasonable under the circumstances, (2) a fair valuation, or (3) any other method that is reasonable under the circumstances.

6.7. Return of Distributions. Members shall return to the Company any Distributions received which are in violation of this Agreement or the Act. Such Distributions shall be returned to the account or accounts of the Company from which they were taken in order to make the Distribution. If a Distribution is made in compliance with the Act and this Agreement, a Member is under no obligation to return it to the Company or to pay the amount of the Distribution for the account of the Company or to any creditor of the Company.

6.8. Members Bound by These Provisions. The Members understand and acknowledge the tax implications of the provisions of this Article of the Agreement and agree to be bound by these provisions in reporting items of income and loss relating to the Company on their federal and state income tax returns.

ARTICLE VII. TRANSFERS AND TERMINATIONS OF MEMBERSHIP INTERESTS

7.1. Restriction on Transferability of Membership Interests. A Member may not transfer, assign, encumber, or convey all or any part of his or her Membership Interest in the Company, except as provided herein. In entering into this Agreement, each of the Members acknowledges the reasonableness of this restriction, which is intended to further the purposes of the Company and the relationships among the Members.

7.2. Permitted Transfers. In order to be permitted, a transfer or assignment of all or any part of a Membership interest must have the approval of a two-thirds majority of the Members of the Company. Each Member, in his or her sole discretion, may proffer or withhold approval. In addition, the following conditions must be met:

(a) The transferee must provide a written agreement, satisfactory to the Members, to be bound by all of the provisions of this Agreement;

(b) The transferee must provide the Company with his or her taxpayer identification number and initial tax basis in the transferred interest;

(c) The transferee must pay the reasonable expenses incurred in connection with his or her admission to Membership;

(d) The transfer must be in compliance with all federal and state securities laws;

(e) The transfer must not result in the termination of the Company pursuant to Code Section 708.

(f) The transfer must not render the Company subject to the Investment Company Act of 1940, as amended; and

(g) The transferor must comply with the provisions of this Agreement.

7.3. Company's Right to Purchase Transferor's Interest and Valuation of Transferor's Interest. Any Member who wishes to transfer all or any part of his or her interest in the Company shall immediately provide the Company with written notice of his or her intention. The notice shall fully describe the nature of the interest to be transferred. Thereafter, the Company, or its nominee, shall have the option to purchase the transferor's interest at the Repurchase Price (as defined below).

(a) The "Repurchase Price" shall be determined as of the date of the event causing the transfer or dissolution event (the "Effective Date"). The date that the Company receives notice of a Member's intention to transfer his or her interest pursuant to this paragraph shall be deemed to be the Effective Date. The Repurchase Price shall be determined as follows:

i. The Repurchase Price of a Member's Percentage Interest shall be computed by the independent certified public accountant (CPA) regularly used by the Company or, if the Company has no CPA or if the CPA is unavailable, then by a qualified appraiser selected by the Company for this purpose. The Repurchase Price of a Member's Percentage Interest shall be the sum of the Company's total Repurchase Price multiplied by the Transferor's Percentage Interest as of the Effective Date.

ii. The Repurchase Price shall be determined by the book value method, as more further described herein. The book value of the interests shall be determined in accordance with the regular financial statements prepared by the Company and in accordance with generally accepted accounting principles, applied consistently with the accounting principles previously applied by the Company, adjusted to reflect the following:

(1) All inventory, valued at cost.

(2) All real property, leasehold improvements, equipment, and furnishings and fixtures valued at their fair market value.

(3) The face amount of any accounts payable.

(4) Any accrued taxes or assessments, deducted as liabilities.

(5) All usual fiscal year-end accruals and deferrals (including depreciation), prorated over the fiscal year.

(6) The reasonable fair market value of any good will or other intangible assets.

The cost of the assessment shall be borne by the Company.

(b) The option provided to the Company shall be irrevocable and shall remain open for thirty (30) days from the Effective Date, except that if notice is given by regular mail, the option shall remain open for thirty-five (35) days from the Effective Date.

(c) At any time while the option remains open, the Company (or its nominee) may elect to exercise the option and purchase the transferor's interest in the Company. The transferor Member shall not vote on the question of whether the Company should exercise its option.

(d) If the Company chooses to exercise its option to purchase the transferor Member's interest, it shall provide written notice to the transferor within the option period. The notice shall specify a "Closing Date" for the purchase, which shall occur within thirty (30) days of the expiration of the option period.

(e) If the Company declines to exercise its option to purchase the transferor Member's interest, the transferor Member may then transfer his or her interest in accordance with Section 7.2. Any transfer not in compliance with the provisions of Section 7.2 shall be null and void and have no force or effect.

(f) In the event that the Company chooses to exercise its option to purchase the transferor Member's interest, the Company may elect to purchase the Member's interest on the following terms:

i. The Company may elect to pay the Repurchase Price in cash, by making such cash payment to the transferor Member upon the Closing Date.

ii. The Company may elect to pay any portion of the Repurchase Price by delivering to the transferor Member, upon the Closing Date, all of the following:

(1) An amount equal to at least 10% of the Repurchase Price in cash or in an immediately negotiable draft, and

(2) A Promissory Note for the remaining amount of the Repurchase Price, to be paid in 12 successive month-

ly installments, with such installments beginning 30 days following the Closing Date, and ending one year from the Closing Date, and

(3) A security agreement guaranteeing the payment of the Promissory Note by offering the Transferor's former membership interest as security for the payment of the Promissory Note.

7.4. Occurrence of Dissolution Event. Upon the death, withdrawal, resignation, retirement, expulsion, insanity, bankruptcy, or dissolution of any Member (a Dissolution Event), the Company shall be dissolved, unless all of the Remaining Members elect by a majority in interest within 90 days thereafter to continue the operation of the business. In the event that the Remaining Members to agree, the Company and the Remaining Members shall have the right to purchase the interest of the Member whose actions caused the occurrence of the Dissolution Event. The interest shall be sold in the manner described in Section 7.6.

7.5. Withdrawal from Membership. Notwithstanding Section 7.4, in the event that a Member withdraws in accordance with Section 4.3 and such withdrawal does not result in the dissolution of the Company, the Company and the Remaining Members shall have the right to purchase the interest of the withdrawing Member in the manner described in Section 7.6.

7.6. Purchase of Interest of Departing Member. The purchase price of a Departing Member's interest shall be determined in accordance with the procedure provided in Section 7.3.

(a) Once a value has been determined, each Remaining Member shall be entitled to purchase that portion of the Departing Member's interest that corresponds to his or her percentage ownership of the Percentage Interests of those Members electing to purchase a portion of the Departing Member's interest in the Company.

(b) Each Remaining Member desiring to purchase a share of the Departing Member's interest shall have thirty (30) days to provide written notice to the Company of his or her intention to do so. The failure to provide notice shall be deemed a rejection of the opportunity to purchase the Departing Member's interest.

(c) If any Member elects not to purchase all of the Departing Member's interest to which he or she is entitled, the other Members may purchase that portion of the Departing Member's interest. Any interest which is not purchased by the Remaining Members may be purchased by the Company.

(d) The Members shall assign a closing date within 60 days after the Members' election to purchase is completed. At that time, the Departing Member shall deliver to the Remaining Members an instrument of title, free of any encumbrances and containing warranties of title, duly conveying his or her interest in the Company and, in return, he or she shall be paid the purchase price for his or her interest in cash. The Departing Member and the Remaining Members shall perform all acts reasonably necessary to consummate the transaction in accordance with this agreement.

7.7. No Release of Liability. Any Member or Departing Member whose interest in the Company is sold pursuant to Article VII is not relieved thereby of any liability he or she may owe the Company.

ARTICLE VIII. BOOKS, RECORDS, AND REPORTING

8.1. Books and Records. The Members shall maintain at the Company's principal place of business the following books and records: a current list of the full name and last known business or residence address of each Member, together with the Capital Contribution, Capital Account, and Membership Interest of each Member; a copy of the Articles and all amendments thereto; copies of the Company's federal, state, and local income tax or information returns and reports, if any, for the six (6) most recent taxable years; a copy of this Agreement and any amendments to it; copies of the Company's financial statements, if any; the books and records of the Company as they relate to its internal affairs for at least the current and past four (4) fiscal years; and true and correct copies of all relevant documents and records indicating the amount, cost, and value of all the property and assets of the Company.

8.2. Accounting Methods. The books and records of the Company shall be maintained in accordance with the accounting methods utilized for federal income tax purposes.

8.3. Reports. The Members shall cause to be prepared and filed in a timely manner all reports and documents required by any governmental agency. The Members shall cause to be prepared at least annually all information concerning the Company's operations that is required by the Members for the preparation of their federal and state tax returns.

8.4. Inspection Rights. For purposes reasonably related to their interests in the Company, all Members shall have the right to inspect and copy the books and records of the Company during normal business hours, upon reasonable request.

8.5. Bank Accounts. The Managers shall maintain all of the funds of the Company in a bank account or accounts in the name of the Company, at a depository institution or institutions to be determined by a majority of the Members. The Managers shall not permit the funds of the Company to be commingled in any manner with the funds or accounts of any other Person. The Managers shall have the powers enumerated in Section 5.2 with respect to endorsing, signing, and negotiating checks, drafts, or other evidence of indebtedness to the Company or obligating the Company money to a third party.

ARTICLE IX. DISSOLUTION, LIQUIDATION, AND WINDING UP

9.1. Conditions Under Which Dissolution Shall Occur. The Company shall dissolve and its affairs shall be wound up upon the happening the first of the following: at the time specified in the Articles; upon the happening of a Dissolution Event; and the failure of the Remaining Members to elect to continue, in accordance with Section 7.4; upon the vote of all of the Members to dissolve; upon the entry of a decree of judicial dissolution pursuant to the Act; upon the happening of any event specified in the Articles as causing or requiring dissolution; or upon the sale of all or substantially all of the Company's assets.

9.2. Winding Up and Dissolution. If the Company is dissolved, the Members shall wind up its affairs, including the selling of all of the Company's assets and the provision of written notification to all of the Company's creditors of the commencement of dissolution proceedings.

9.3. Order of Payment. After determining that all known debts and liabilities of the Company in the process of winding up have been paid or provided for, including, without limitation, debts and liabilities to Members who are creditors of the Company, the Members shall distribute the remaining assets among the Members in accordance with their Positive Capital Account balances, after taking into consideration the profit and loss allocations made pursuant to Section 6.4. Members shall not be required to restore Negative Capital Account Balances.

ARTICLE X. INDEMNIFICATION

10.1. Indemnification. The Company shall indemnify any Member and may indemnify any Person to the fullest extent permitted by law on the date such indemnification is requested for any judgments, settlements, penalties, fines, or expenses of any kind incurred as a result of the Person's performance in the capacity of Member, officer, employee, or agent of the Company, as long as the Member, or Person did not behave in violation of the Act or this Agreement.

ARTICLE XI. MISCELLANEOUS PROVISIONS

11.1. Assurances. Each Member shall execute all documents and certificates and perform all acts deemed appropriate by the Members and the Company or required by this Agreement or the Act in connection with the formation and operation of the Company and the acquisition, holding, or operation of any property by the Company.

11.2. Complete Agreement. This Agreement and the Articles constitute the complete and exclusive statement of the agreement among the Members with respect to the matters discussed herein and therein and they supersede all prior written or oral statements among the Members, including any prior statement, warranty, or representation.

11.3. Section Headings. The section headings which appear throughout this Agreement are provided for convenience only and are not intended to define or limit the scope of this Agreement or the intent of subject matter of its provisions.

11.4. Binding Effect. Subject to the provisions of this Agreement relating to the transferability of Membership Interests, this Agreement is binding upon and shall inure to the benefit of the parties hereto and their respective heirs, administrators, executors, successors, and assigns.

11.5. Interpretation. All pronouns and common nouns shall be deemed to refer to the masculine, feminine, neuter, singular, and plural, as the context may require. In the event that any claim is made by any Member relating to the drafting and interpretation of this Agreement, no presumption, inference, or burden of proof or persuasion shall be created or implied solely by virtue of the fact that this Agreement was drafted by or at the behest of a particular Member or his or her counsel.

11.6. Applicable Law. Each Member agrees that all disputes arising under or in connection with this Agreement and any transactions contemplated by this Agreement shall be governed by the internal law, and not the law of conflicts, of the state of organization.

11.7. Specific Performance. The Members acknowledge and agree that irreparable injury shall result from a breach of this Agreement and that money damages will not adequately compensate the injured party. Accordingly, in the event of a breach or a threatened breach of this Agreement, any party who may be injured shall be entitled, in addition to any other remedy which may be available, to injunctive relief to prevent or to correct the breach.

11.8. Remedies Cumulative. The remedies described in this Agreement are cumulative and shall not eliminate any other remedy to which a Person may be lawfully entitled.

11.9. Notice. Any notice or other writing to be served upon the Company or any Member thereof in connection with this Agreement shall be in writing and shall be deemed completed when delivered to the address specified in Table A, if to a Member, and to the resident agent, if to the Company. Any Member shall have the right to change the address at which notices shall be served upon ten (10) days' written notice to the Company and the other Members.

11.10. Amendments. Any amendments, modifications, or alterations to this Agreement or the Articles must be in writing and signed by all of the Members.

11.11. Severability. Each provision of this Agreement is severable from the other provisions. If, for any reason, any provision of this Agreement is declared invalid or contrary to existing law, the inoperability of that provision shall have no effect on the remaining provisions of the Agreement, which shall continue in full force and effect.

11.12. Counterparts. This Agreement may be executed in counterparts, each of which shall be deemed an original and all of which shall, when taken together, constitute a single document.

IN WITNESS WHEREOF, this Agreement has been made and executed by the Members effective as of the date first written above.

________________________________ (Member)

________________________________ (Member)

________________________________ (Member)

Table A. Name, Address, and Initial Capital Contribution of the Members

Name and Address of Member	Value of Initial Capital Contribution	Nature of Member's Initial Capital Contribution (i.e., cash, services, property)	Member's Percentage Interest

Table B: Managers

Name of Manager	Address of Manager

165. Membership Ledger

Date of Original Issue	Member Name	Percentage Interest	Disposition of Shares (transferred or surrendered stock certificate)

166. Investment Representation Letter

Note: The following Investment Representation Letter should be executed by each LLC member and delivered to the company. The Representation Letter seeks to ensure company compliance with securities laws, by asking owners to certify that they are joining the LLC as an investment, and not to trade shares in the LLC.

(insert date)

To whom it may concern,

I am delivering this letter to Olde Craft, LLC in connection with my purchase of a 25% interest in Olde Craft, Inc. for a total sum of $75,000.00. I represent the following:

I am purchasing the shares in my own name and for my own account, for investment and not with an intent to sell or for sale in connection with any distribution of such stock; and no other person has any interest in or right with respect to the shares; nor have I agreed to give any person any such interest or right in the future.

I recognize that the shares have not been registered under the Federal Securities Act of 1933, as amended, or qualified under any state securities law, and that any sale or transfer of the shares is subject to restrictions imposed by federal and state law.

I also recognize that I cannot dispose of the shares absent registration and qualification or an available exemption from registration and qualification. I understand that no federal or state securities commission or other government body has approved of the fairness of the shares offered by the corporation and that the Commissioner has not and will not recommend or endorse the shares.

I have not seen or received any advertisement or general solicitation with respect to the sale of the shares.

I have a preexisting personal or business relationship with the Company or one or more of its officers, directors, or controlling persons and I am aware of its character and general financial and business circumstances.

I acknowledge that during the course of this transaction and before purchasing the shares I have been provided with financial and other written information about the Company. I have been given the opportunity by the Company to obtain any information and ask questions concerning the Company, the shares, and my investment that I felt necessary; and to the extent I availed myself of that opportunity, I have received satisfactory information and answers.

In reaching the decision to invest in the shares, I have carefully evaluated my financial resources and investment position and the risks associated with this investment, and I acknowledge that I am able to bear the economic risks of this investment.

____

John Miller

167. Appointment of Proxy for Member's Meeting

Note: Use the following form when a Member wants to give his or her vote to another person at a meeting of an LLC's membership.

APPOINTMENT OF PROXY FOR (Annual/Special) MEETING

MadHatter, LLC

SHAREHOLDER: John Miller

PERCENTAGE INTEREST HELD BY SHAREHOLDER: 32%

I, the undersigned, as record holder of a 32% interest in MadHatter, LLC, revoke any previous proxies and appoint the person whose name appears just below this paragraph as my proxy to attend the member's meeting on ________________ and any adjournment of that meeting.

The person I want to appoint as my proxy is ________________________

The proxy holder is entitled to cast a total number of votes equal to, but not exceeding the number of shares which I would be entitled to cast if I were personally present.

I authorize my proxy holder to vote and otherwise represent me with regard to any business that may come before this meeting in the same manner and with the same effect as if I were personally present.

I may revoke this proxy at any time. This proxy will lapse three months after the date of its execution.

If you are signing for a business entity, state your title:

Date (*important*):________________

____

Name

____

Title

Note: All proxies must be signed. Sign exactly as your name appears on your stock certificate. Joint shareholders must each sign this proxy. If signed by an attorney in fact, the Power of Attorney must be attached.

168. Call for Meeting of Members

Note: This "call" is an instruction by LLC members to the managers that the members want to call a meeting of members. This serves as official notice. This call is required only in manager-managed LLCs; if a member in a member-managed LLC wants to call a meeting of members, he or she would skip the call and simply send a notice of meeting of members to all other members. The next form is a notice of meeting of members.

CALL FOR MEETING OF LLC MEMBERS

TO: The Managers of MadHatter, LLC

(insert date)

The party or parties whose name appears below are members of MadHatter, LLC, and own percentage interests entitled to cast not less than 10 percent of MadHatter's votes. We hereby call a meeting of the members of MadHatter to be held ________________ (date), at ________________ (time), for the purpose of considering and acting upon the following matters:

(Insert matters to be considered, such as "A proposal that John Jones be removed as a manager of MadHatter.")

You are directed to give notice of this meeting of the members, in the manner prescribed by MadHatter's operating agreement and by law, to all members entitled to receive notice of the meeting.

Date ________________________

____

____

____

169. Notice of Meeting of LLC Members

Note: This form is an LLC's announcement to its members that a meeting of members has been called.

NOTICE OF MEETING OF MEMBERS OF OLDECRAFT, LLC

Certain members of OldeCraft, LLC, have called a meeting of the members of OldeCraft pursuant to OldeCraft's operating agreement.

Therefore, this is your official notice as an OldeCraft member that a meeting of members of OldeCraft, LLC, will be held on __________ (date), at ______________ (time), at _________________________ (address), to consider and act on the following matters:

(insert matters to be considered, such as "A proposal that John Jones be removed from the board of directors.")

If you do not expect to be present at the meeting and wish your shares to be voted, you may complete the attached form of proxy and mail it in the enclosed addressed envelope.

Date______________________

____

John Wilson, Manager

170. Minutes of Meeting of LLC Members

Note: While LLC members and managers enjoy far fewer corporate formalities than corporation owners, an LLC must still maintain records of its meetings. When an LLC's members meet to formally vote on any matter, the results of that vote should be committed to written minutes.

MINUTES OF MEETING OF MEMBERS OF OLDECRAFT, LLC

The members of OLDECRAFT, LLC, held a meeting on __________ (date), at _______________(time), at __________________(place). The meeting was called by John Miller and the company managers mailed notice to all members that the meeting would take place.

The following members were present at the meeting, in person or by proxy, representing membership interests as indicated:

John Jones, 50%
John Smith, 30%
John Miller, 20%

Also present were Michael Spadaccini, attorney to the company, and Lisa Jones, wife of John Jones, and the company's president and sole manager.

The company's president called the meeting to order and announced that she would chair the meeting, that a quorum was present, and that the meeting was held pursuant to a written notice of meeting given to all members of the company. A copy of the notice was ordered inserted in the minute book immediately preceding the minutes of this meeting.

The minutes of the previous meeting of shareholders were then read and approved.

The chairperson then announced that the election of a manager was in order. Lisa Jones stated that she could no longer serve as manager of the company. John Smith was then elected to serve until the next meeting of members, and until the manager's successor was duly elected and qualified, as follows:

(Include agreement for selecting new manager here.)

There being no further business to come before the meeting, on motion duly made, seconded, and adopted, the meeting was adjourned.

____

John Smith, Manager

171. Action by Written Consent of LLC Members

Note: Most company votes are taken by written consent rather than by notice and meeting and an in-person vote. Use the following form when you wish to take a company action in writing, rather than by a noticed meeting. Keep in mind, however, that your operating agreement and articles may require more than a simple majority to pass certain actions. Written consents are important company records and should be maintained in the record books.

ACTION BY WRITTEN CONSENT OF SHAREHOLDERS OF OLDECRAFT, LLC

The undersigned members of OldeCraft, LLC, owning of record the number of shares entitled to vote as set forth, hereby consent to the following company actions. The vote was unanimous. (For actions where a unanimous vote is not required: "A vote of 66% was required to take the actions listed below, and 80% of the membership interest in the company have given their consent."):

1. Pete Wilson is hereby removed as manager of the company.

2. The number of managers of the company is increased from one to two.

John Smith and John Miller, both also members, are hereby elected to serve as company managers until the next meeting of members.

DATED: ____________________

____

John Smith

Percentage Owned: ___________

DATED: ________________

____

John Miller

Percentage Owned:______

172. Written Consent of Members Approving a Certificate of Amendment of Articles of Organization Changing an LLC's Name

ACTION OF MEMBERS BY WRITTEN CONSENT TO APPROVE AN AMENDMENT TO ARTICLES OF ORGANIZATION CHANGING LLC NAME

The undersigned, who comprise all the members of PLASTICWORLD, LLC, agree unanimously to the following:

RESOLVED, that the Certificate of Amendment of Articles of Organization presented to the undersigned members, specifically changing the name of the company to PLASTICUNIVERSE, LLC is approved.

Date ________________

____
Scott Bess

____
Brian Bess

CHAPTER 18

Corporation Forms

If you operate a Corporation, you might consider the following sample forms useful. If you are seeking further information on this topic, you might consider purchasing *Entrepreneur Magazine's Ultimate Book on Forming Corporations, LLC's, Sole Proprietorships, and Partnerships* by Michael Spadaccini. That book includes the forms found in this section, as well as step-by-step instructions to the formation of business entities.

The *Sample California Articles of Incorporation* are suitable articles of incorporation for a basic California corporation. Similarly, the *Sample Delaware Certificate of Incorporation* is a suitable certificate of incorporation for a basic Delaware corporation. The *Sample Nevada Articles of Incorporation (Long Form, with Full Indemnity Provisions)* are suitable articles of incorporation for a Nevada corporation; this sample is a long form, with provisions that indemnify officers and directors from lawsuits and claims made against them as a result of their duties to the corporation.

The *Optional Provisions for Inclusion in Articles of Incorporation* are a set of optional provisions that one can include in articles of incorporation that authorize two separate classes of stock. The *Sample Letter to Secretary of State Accompanying Articles of Incorporation* is a sample letter that one can include when presenting corporation paperwork for filing with a Secretary of State.

A registered agent is a person or entity that is authorized and obligated to receive legal papers on behalf of a corporation. The *Sample Letter to Registered Agent* (which is intended to accompany articles of incorporation) is a simple cover letter that you should deliver to your registered agent upon the organization of your corporation. Keep in mind that your state of organization may use a different term than registered agent. Typical equivalents include "agent for service of process," "local agent," and "registered agent."

An incorporator is the person or entity that organizes a corporation and files its articles of incorporation. The incorporator enjoys certain powers: he or she can take corporate actions before directors and officers are appointed. For example, an incorporator can amend articles of incorporation, approve bylaws, and appoint directors. Typically, an incorporator's power is quite broad. The *Sample Action by Incorporator Appointing Directors and Approving Bylaws* is a written resolution undertaken by the incorporator that appoints directors and approves bylaws for governance of the corporation.

Bylaws are the internal operating rules of a corporation. Bylaws govern such matters as holding meetings, voting, quorums, elections, and the powers of directors and officers. The *Sample Corporate Bylaws* are simple, universal bylaws usable in any state. Consider, however, that these simple bylaws may not take advantage of favorable laws in your particular state of incorporation.

To finalize your incorporation, you must have an organizational meeting of the board of directors. You must also prepare minutes of this meeting. Because the format of the meeting is relatively standard, the minutes are nearly always drafted beforehand, and followed like a script. The *Sample Minutes of Organizational Meeting of the Board of Directors* is such a document.

The *Shareholder's Agreement* is an agreement between the shareholders of a corporation that covers various matters such as a commitment to vote particular persons as directors and allowing other shareholders to have a right of first refusal to purchase the shares of departing shareholders. Shareholder's agreements are complex documents best handled by an attorney, but this sample should give you some insight into the devices available in such a document.

The *Share Transfer Ledger* is a ledger indicating the owners of a corporation and their proportion of ownership, as well as transfers of such ownership. All corporations should begin the ledger upon the formation of the corporation and should diligently update the ledger when shares are transferred, gifted, sold, repurchased by the corporation, or when new shares are issued.

Each member admitted to the corporation should execute the *Investment Representation Letter*. The investment representation letter offers some measure of protection to the entity because the member being admitted to the corporation makes certain representations regarding his qualifications and fitness to serve as a member of the corporation. Also, in the investment representation letter, the member makes certain representations regarding his or her investment objectives, which are necessary representations to comply with state and federal securities laws.

A proxy is an authorization by one member giving another person the right to vote the member's shares. Proxy also refers to the document granting such authority. We have included several proxy forms here: The *Appointment of Proxy for Annual or Special Shareholders' Meeting* a simple proxy form in which shareholder's grant their proxy for a shareholder's meeting and the *Long-Form Appointment of Proxy for Annual or Special Shareholders' Meeting*, which serves the same purpose but is a more thorough and complex document.

A "call" is an instruction by a corporation's shareholders to the corporation's officers and managers that the shareholders want to call a meeting of shareholders. This *Call for Special Meeting of Shareholders* serves as official notice to the managers that the members wish to call a meeting. The *Notice of Special Meeting of Shareholders* is simply a notice to shareholders of a corporation that a meeting has been called.

Annual and special meetings of shareholders and of directors must be recorded. The written record of the actions taken at such meetings are called minutes. Minutes are very simple to prepare and are often quite short. We have included several sample minutes here. The *Minutes of Annual or Special Meeting of Shareholders* is appropriate for documenting a shareholder meeting. As an alternative to a formally called meeting, subject to certain restrictions, shareholders or directors may take an action without a meeting if their action is memorialized in a "written consent." A written consent is simply a formal written document that sets forth a corporate action or resolution to be taken or made, and it is signed by the shareholders or directors consenting to the action. The *Action by Written Consent of Shareholder(s)* is such a document.

The *Call for Special Meeting of Directors* serves as official notice to the directors that either an officer or director wishes to call a meeting of a corporation's board of directors. The *Minutes of Annual Meeting of Directors* is a sample document memorializing the actions taken at an annual meeting of directors. The *Minutes of Special Meeting of Directors* memorializes the actions taken at a special meeting of directors.

A corporation's directors, like shareholders, can vote by written consent in lieu of a formally noticed and held meeting. The *Action of Directors by Written Consent* allows directors to take such action. Note, however, that most bylaws require the unanimous vote of directors to utilize a written consent. A more specific use of the written consent form is the *Written Consent of Directors Approving a Certificate of Amendment of Articles of Incorporation Changing*

Corporation's Name in which the directors unanimously vote to amend the corporation's charter to change the corporation's name.

The *Certificate of Amendment of Articles of Incorporation Changing Corporation's Name* is the formal and official document that a corporation would file with a Secretary of State in its state of incorporation that formally amends its articles of incorporation to change its name, while the *Certificate of Amendment of Articles of Incorporation Electing Close Corporation Status* formally effects a change to the corporation's status from regular corporation to close corporation. A close corporation, generally speaking, is a smaller corporation that elects close corporation status, and is therefore entitled to operate without the strict formalities normally required in the operation of standard corporations. Many small business owners find this benefit invaluable. In essence, a close corporation is a corporation whose shareholders and directors are entitled to operate much like a partnership.

Internal Revenue Service Tax Form SS-4 is the form by which a business entity obtains its Federal Tax ID Number. The *Internal Revenue Service Tax Form 2553* is the tax form under which a corporation elects "S" corporation status. (**Note:** these forms not included here, but they are on the CD and available online at www.irs.gov.) Subchapter S of the Internal Revenue Code permits eligible smaller corporations to avoid double taxation and be taxed as partnerships. Corporations that make such an election are known as "S" corporations. An S corporation differs from a standard C corporation solely with respect to its taxation.

A Corporation must meet certain conditions to be eligible for a subchapter S election. First, the corporation must have no more than 75 shareholders. In calculating the 75 shareholder limit, a husband and wife count as one shareholder. Also, only the following entities may be shareholders: individuals, estates, certain trusts, certain partnerships, tax-exempt charitable organizations, and other S corporations (but only if the other S corporation is the sole shareholder).

S corporations may only have one class of stock. A Corporation must make the subchapter S election no later than two months and fifteen days after the first day of the taxable year—it cannot wait until the end of the taxable year to elect. Subchapter S election requires the consent of all shareholders.

The states treat S corporations differently. Some states disregard subchapter S status entirely, offering no tax break at all. Other states honor the federal election automatically. Finally, some states require the filing of a state-specific form to complete subchapter S election.

173. Sample California Articles of Incorporation

ARTICLES OF INCORPORATION
OF
(CORPORATION NAME)

1. The name of this corporation is (Corporation Name).

2. The purpose of the corporation is to engage in any lawful act or activity for which a corporation may be organized under the General Corporation Law of California other than the banking business, the trust company business, or the practice of a profession permitted to be incorporated by the California Corporations Code.

3. The name and address in the State of California of this corporation's initial agent for service of process is (insert name and address of initial agent for service of process).

4. This corporation is authorized to issue only one class of shares of stock; and the total number of shares which this corporation is authorized to issue is one million (1,000,000) shares.

5. The liability of the directors of the corporation for monetary damages shall be eliminated to the fullest extent permissible under California law.

Dated:

____
Donald Leland, Incorporator

174. Sample Delaware Certificate of Incorporation

CERTIFICATE OF INCORPORATION OF
(CORPORATION NAME)

FIRST: The name of the corporation is (Corporation Name).

SECOND: Its registered office in the State of Delaware is located at (registered office address here). The registered agent in charge thereof is (insert name of registered agent). (**Note:** Delaware corporations must have a registered agent in Delaware.)

THIRD: The purpose of the corporation is to engage in any lawful activity for which corporations may be organized under the General Corporation Law of Delaware.

FOURTH: The total number of shares of stock that the corporation is authorized to issue is 3,000 shares having a par value of $0.0001 per share. (**Note:** Delaware corporations with more than 3,000 authorized shares pay their annual franchise tax fees according to a complex formula. Such fees are not terribly expensive, but see the Delaware Division of Corporations Web site for information before authorizing more than 3,000 shares.)

FIFTH: The business and affairs of the corporation shall be managed by or under the direction of the board of directors, and the directors need not be elected by ballot unless required by the bylaws of the corporation.

SIXTH: The corporation shall be perpetual unless otherwise decided by a majority of the board of directors.

SEVENTH: In furtherance and not in limitation of the powers conferred by the laws of Delaware, the board of directors is authorized to amend or repeal the bylaws.

EIGHTH: The corporation reserves the right to amend or repeal any provision in this Certificate of Incorporation in the manner prescribed by the laws of Delaware.

NINTH: The incorporator is (insert name of Incorporator). The powers of the incorporator are to file this certificate of incorporation, approve the bylaws of the corporation, and elect the initial directors.

TENTH: To the fullest extent permitted by the Delaware General Corporation Law, a director of this corporation shall not be liable to the corporation or its stockholders for monetary damages for breach of fiduciary duty as a director.

I, (insert name of incorporator), for the purpose of forming a corporation under the laws of the State of Delaware do make and file this certificate, and do certify that the facts herein stated are true, and have accordingly signed below, on (date).

Signed and attested to by:

____

Andrew Leland, Incorporator

175. Sample Nevada Articles of Incorporation (Long-Form, with Full Indemnity Provisions)

ARTICLES OF INCORPORATION
OF
(COMPANY NAME) COMPANY,
a Nevada Corporation

I, the undersigned, being the original incorporator herein named, for the purpose of forming a Corporation under the General Corporation Laws of the State of Nevada, to do business both within and without the State of Nevada, do make and file these Articles of Incorporation, hereby declaring that the facts herein stated are true:

ARTICLE I. NAME

The name of the Corporation is (COMPANY NAME) COMPANY.

ARTICLE II. RESIDENT AGENT and REGISTERED OFFICE

Section 2.01. Resident Agent. The name and address of the resident agent for service of process is Resident Agents of Nevada, Inc., 711 South Carson Street, Carson City, NV 89701.

Section 2.02. Registered Office. The address of its registered Office is 711 South Carson Street, Carson City, NV 89701.

Section 2.03. Other Offices. The Corporation may also maintain offices for the transaction of any business at such other places within or without the State of Nevada as it may from time to time determine. Corporate business of every kind and nature may be conducted and meetings of Directors and Stockholders held outside the State of Nevada with the same effect as if in the State of Nevada.

ARTICLE III. PURPOSE

The Corporation is organized for the purpose of engaging in any lawful activity, within or without the State of Nevada.

ARTICLE IV. SHARES OF STOCK

Section 4.01 Number and Class. The total number of voting common stock authorized that may be issued by the Corporation is seventy-five million (75,000,000) shares of stock @ $.001 par value. Said common shares may be issued by the Corporation from time to time for such considerations as may be fixed by the Board of Directors.

Notwithstanding the foregoing these Articles hereby vest the Board of Directors of the Corporation with the following authority: Preferred Stock may also be issued by the Corporation from time to time in one or more series and in such amounts as may be determined by the Board of Directors. The designations, voting rights, amounts of preference upon distribution of assets, rates of dividends, premiums of redemption, conversion rights and other variations, if any, the qualifications, limitations, or restrictions, if any, of the Preferred Stock, and of each series thereof, shall be such as are fixed by the Board of Directors, authority so to do being hereby expressly granted, and as are stated and expressed in a resolution or resolutions adopted by the Board of Directors providing for the issue of such series of Preferred Stock.

Section 4.02. No Preemptive Rights. Unless otherwise determined by the Board of Directors, holders of the Stock of the Corporation shall not have any preference, preemptive right, or right of subscription to acquire any shares of the Corporation authorized, issued, or sold or to be authorized, issued, or sold, and convertible into shares of the Corporation, nor to any right of subscription thereto.

Section 4.03. Non-Assessability of Shares. The Shares of the Corporation, after the amount of the subscription price has been paid, in money, property, or services, as the Directors shall determine, shall not be subject to assessment to pay the debts of the Corporation, nor for any other purpose, and no Stock issued as fully paid shall ever be assessable or assessed, and the Articles of Incorporation shall not be amended in the particular.

ARTICLE V. DIRECTORS

Section 5.01. Governing Board. The members of the governing Board of the Corporation shall be styled as Directors.

Section 5.0. Initial Board of Directors. The initial Board of Directors shall consist on not less than one (1) and not more than seven (7) members. The name and address of an initial member of the Board of Directors is as follows:

NAME	ADDRESS
Michael Spadaccini	731 9th Ave., Suite E, San Diego, CA 92101

This individual shall serve as Director until the first annual meeting of the Stockholders or until his successor(s) shall have been elected and qualified.

Section 5.03. Change in Number of Directors. The number of Directors may be increased or decreased by a duly adopted amendment to the Bylaws of the Corporation.

ARTICLE VI. INCORPORATOR

The name and address of the incorporator is Michael Spadaccini, 731 9th Ave., Suite E, San Diego, CA 92101.

ARTICLE VII. PERIOD OF DURATION

The Corporation is to have a perpetual existence.

ARTICLE VIII. DIRECTORS' AND OFFICERS' LIABILITY

A Director or Officer of the Corporation shall not be personally liable to this Corporation or its Stockholders for damages for breach of fiduciary duty as a Director or Officer, but this Article shall not eliminate or limit the liability of a Director or Officer for (i) acts or omissions which involve intentional misconduct, fraud, or a knowing violation of law or (ii) the unlawful payment of distributions. Any repeal or modification of the Article by the Stockholders of the Corporation shall be prospective only, and shall not adversely affect any limitation on the personal liability of a Director or Officer of the Corporation for acts or omissions prior to such repeal or modification.

ARTICLE IX. INDEMNITY

Every person who was or is a party to, or is threatened to be made a party to, or is involved in any action, suit, or proceeding, whether civil, criminal, administrative, or investigative, by reason of the fact that he, or a person of whom he is the legal representative, is or was a Director or Officer of the Corporation, or is or was serving at the request of the Corporation as a Director or Officer of another Corporation, or as its representative in a partnership, joint venture, trust, or other enterprise, shall be indemnified and held harmless to the fullest extent legally permissible under the laws of the State of Nevada from time to time against all expenses, liability, and loss (including attorneys' fees, judgments, fines, and amounts paid or to be paid in settlement) reasonably incurred or suffered by him in connection therewith. Such right of indemnification shall be a contract right which may be enforced in any manner desired by such person. The expenses of Officers and Directors incurred in defending a civil or criminal action, suit, or proceeding must be paid by the Corporation as they are incurred and in advance of the final disposition of the action, suit, or proceeding, upon receipt of an undertaking by or on behalf of the Director of Officer to repay the amount if it is ultimately determined by a court of competent jurisdiction that he is not entitled to be indemnified by the Corporation. Such right of indemnification shall not be exclusive of any other right which such Directors, Officers, or representatives may have or hereafter acquire, and, without limiting the generality of such statement, they shall be entitled to their respective rights of indemnification under any bylaw, agreement, vote of Stockholders, provision of law, or otherwise, as well as their rights under this Article. Without limiting the application of the foregoing, the Stockholders or Board of Directors may adopt bylaws from time to time with respect to indemnification, to provide at all times the fullest indemnification permitted by the laws of the State of Nevada, and may cause the Corporation to purchase and maintain insurance on behalf of any person who is or was a Director of Officer of the Corporation, or is or was serving at the request of the Corporation as a Director or Officer of another Corporation, or as its repre-

sentative in a partnership, joint venture, trust, or other enterprise against any liability asserted against such person and incurred in any such capacity or arising out of such status, whether or not the Corporation would have the power to indemnify such person. The indemnification provided in this Article shall continue as to a person who has ceased to be a Director, Officer, Employee, or Agent, and shall inure to the benefit of the heirs, executors, and administrators of such person.

ARTICLE X. AMENDMENTS

Subject at all times to the express provisions of Section 4.03 which cannot by amended, this Corporation reserves the right to amend, alter, change, or repeal any provision contained in these Articles of Incorporation or its bylaws, in the manner now or hereafter prescribed by statute or by these Articles of Incorporation or said bylaws, and all rights conferred upon the Stockholders are granted subject to this reservation.

ARTICLE XI. POWERS OF DIRECTORS

In furtherance and not in limitation of the powers conferred by statute, the Board of Directors is expressly authorized: (1) subject to the bylaws, if any, adopted by the stockholders, to make, alter or repeal the bylaws of the Corporation; (2) to authorize and cause to be executed mortgages and liens, with or without limit as to amount, upon the real and personal property of the Corporation; (3) to authorize the guaranty by the Corporation of securities, evidences of indebtedness, and obligations of other persons, Corporation, and business entities; (4) to set apart out of any of the funds of the Corporation available for distributions a reserve or reserves for any proper purpose and to abolish any such reserve; (5) by resolution, to designate one or more committees, each committee to consist of at least one Director of the Corporation, which to the extent provided in the resolution or in the bylaws of the Corporation shall have and may exercise the powers of the Board of Directors in the management of the business and affairs of the Corporation, and may authorize the seal of the Corporation to be affixed to all papers which may acquire it. Such committee or committees shall have such name or names as may be stated in the bylaws of the Corporation or as may be determined from time to time by resolution adopted by the Board of Directors; and (6) to authorize the Corporation by its Officers or Agents to exercise all such powers and to do all such acts and things as may be exercised or done by the Corporation, except and to the extent that any such statute shall require action by the Stockholders of the Corporation with regard to the exercising of any such power or the doing of any such act or thing.

In addition to the powers and authorities hereinbefore or by statute expressly conferred upon them, the Board of Directors may exercise all such powers and do all such acts and things as may be exercised or done by the Corporation, except as otherwise provided herein and by law.

IN WITNESS WHEREOF, I, Michael Spadaccini, Incorporator of this Corporation, have hereunto set my hand this ___ day of __________, 20__, hereby declaring and certifying that the facts stated hereinabove are true.

____

Michael Spadaccini, Incorporator

I, ______________________________, hereby accept as Resident Agent for the previously named

Corporation on this _____ day of _____________, 20__.

____

Resident Agent

176. Optional Provisions for Inclusion in Articles of Incorporation

a. Clause establishing a class of voting common stock and a class of non-voting common stock:

This corporation is authorized to issue two classes of shares: "Class A Common Stock" and "Class B Common Stock." This corporation may issue 1,000,000 shares of Class A Common Stock and 500,000 shares of Class B Common Stock. The Class B Common Stock has no voting rights. The Class A Common Stock has exclusive voting rights except as otherwise provided by law.

b. Clause establishing a class of voting common stock and a class of preferred stock:

This corporation is authorized to issue two classes of shares: "Common Stock" and "Preferred Stock." This corporation may issue 1,000,000 shares of Common Stock and 500,000 shares of Preferred Stock. The Common Stock has voting rights. The Preferred Stock has no voting rights except as otherwise provided by law.

The Preferred Stock has a liquidation preference. Upon the liquidation or dissolution of the corporation, holders of the Preferred Stock are entitled to receive out of the assets available for distribution to shareholders, before any payment to the holders of the Common Stock, the sum of $______ per share. If the assets of the corporation are insufficient to pay this liquidation preference to the Preferred Stock, all of the entire remaining assets shall be paid to holders of the Preferred Stock and holders of the Common Stock shall receive nothing. After the liquidation preference has been paid or set apart for holders of the Preferred Stock, the remaining assets shall be paid to holders of the Common Stock.

The Preferred Stock has a dividend preference. Holders of the Preferred Stock are entitled to receive dividends on a noncumulative basis at the rate of $______ per share, as and when declared by the board of directors from funds legally available for dividends and distributions. The holders of the Common Stock may not receive dividends or other distributions during any fiscal year of the corporation until dividends on the Preferred Stock in the total amount of $______ per share during that fiscal year have been declared and paid or set apart for payment. The payment of such dividends is discretionary, and the holders of the Preferred Stock shall not enjoy a right to dividends if such dividends are not declared, even if the corporation has sufficient funds to lawfully pay such dividends.

177. Sample Letter to Secretary of State Accompanying Articles of Incorporation

Note: This letter is a version appropriate for use in Delaware, but can be modified for use in any state.

Michael Spadaccini
123 Elm Street
San Francisco, CA 94107
415-555-1212

September 28, 2004

State of Delaware
Division of Corporations
401 Federal Street, Suite 4
Dover, DE 19901

To whom it may concern:

Enclosed you will find articles of incorporation for Banquo Acquisition Corporation, a corporation that I wish to file in Delaware.

I have enclosed a filing fee of $74.00. Please return any necessary papers in the envelope that I have provided.

Yours truly,

Michael Spadaccini

178. Sample Letter to Registered Agent

Michael Spadaccini
123 Elm Street
San Francisco, CA 94107
415-555-1212

September 28, 2004

Harvard Business Services, Inc.
25 Greystone Manor
Lewes, DE 19958

To whom it may concern:

I have enclosed a copy of articles of incorporation I am filing today. As you can see, I have used you as our registered agents in the state of Delaware.

Please use the following contact information:

Banquo Acquisition Corporation
c/o Michael Spadaccini
801 Minnesota Street, Suite 7
San Francisco, CA 94107
Phone: (415) 282-7901

I have enclosed a check for $50.00 to cover the first year's services.

Yours truly,

Michael Spadaccini

179. Sample Action by Incorporator Appointing Directors and Approving Bylaws

MINUTES OF ACTION OF INCORPORATOR TAKEN WITHOUT A MEETING BY WRITTEN CONSENT

The following action is taken by the incorporator of OLDE CRAFT, INC., by written consent, without a meeting on the date specified below.

The following resolution approving a form of bylaws for the governance of this corporation is adopted:

RESOLVED, that the bylaws presented to the incorporator be adopted as the bylaws of this corporation, and that a copy of those bylaws shall be inserted in the minute book of this corporation.

The following resolution electing the directors of the corporation is adopted:

RESOLVED, that pursuant to the foregoing bylaws, authorizing *three* directors, the following persons are hereby appointed as directors of this corporation for the ensuing year and until their successor(s) have been elected and qualified.

John Jones
John Smith
John Miller

The undersigned, the incorporator of this corporation, consents to the foregoing action.

Dated: _______________

____
Michael Spadaccini, Incorporator

180. Sample Corporate Bylaws

BYLAWS OF (CORPORATION NAME)

Part A. Board of Directors

1. Subject to state law and the articles of incorporation, the business and affairs of this corporation shall be managed by and all corporate powers shall be exercised by or under the direction of the board of directors.

2. Each director shall exercise such powers and otherwise perform such duties in good faith and in the manner provided for by law.

3. This corporation shall have (insert number of directors) directors. This number may be changed by amendment of the bylaws, adopted by the vote or written consent of a majority of shareholders entitled to vote. The term "board of directors" as used in these bylaws means the number of directors authorized in this paragraph, even if that number is one.

4. Directors shall be elected at each annual meeting of the shareholders to hold office until the next annual meeting, subject to any rights of shareholders outlined in any shareholder's agreement. Each director, including a director elected to fill a vacancy, shall hold office until expiration of the term for which elected and until a successor has been elected and qualified.

5. Vacancies in the board of directors may be filled by a majority of the remaining directors, though less than a quorum, or by a sole remaining director. Each director so elected shall hold office until the next annual meeting of the shareholders and until a successor has been elected and qualified.

6. A vacancy in the board of directors shall be deemed to exist in the event of the death, resignation, or removal of any director, or if the shareholders fail, at any meeting of the shareholders at which any directors are elected, to elect the full number of authorized directors. The shareholders may elect a director or directors to fill any vacancy or vacancies not filled by the directors, but any such election by written consent shall require a consent of a majority of the outstanding shares entitled to vote. Any director may resign effective upon giving written notice to the President or the Secretary, unless the notice specifies a later time for that resignation to become effective. If the resignation of a director is effective at a future time, the shareholders may elect a successor to take office when the resignation becomes effective. No reduction of the authorized number of directors shall have the effect of removing any director before the director's term of office expires.

7. The entire board of directors or any individual director named may be removed from office as provided by state law. In such a case, the shareholder(s) may elect a successor director to fill such vacancy for the remaining unexpired term of the director so removed.

8. Regular meetings of the board of directors shall be held at any place within or without the state that has been designated from time to time by resolution of the board. In the absence of such resolution, regular meetings shall be held at the principal executive office of the corporation. Special meetings of the board shall be held at any place within or without the state that has been designated in the notice of the meeting or, if not stated in the notice or there is no notice, at the principal executive office of the corporation. Any meeting, regular or special, may be held by conference telephone or similar communication equipment, so long as all directors participating in such meeting can hear one another, and all such directors shall be deemed to have been present in person at such meeting.

9. Immediately following each annual meeting of shareholders, the board of directors shall hold a regular meeting for the purpose of organization, the election of officers, and the transaction of other business. Notice of this meeting shall not be required. Minutes of any meeting of the board, or any committee of the board, shall be maintained by the Secretary or other officer designated for that purpose.

10. Other regular meetings of the board of directors shall be held without call at such time as shall from time to time be fixed by the board of directors. Such regular meetings may be held without notice, provided the time and place

of such meetings has been fixed by the board of directors, and further provided the notice of any change in the time of such meeting shall be given to all the directors. Notice of a change in the determination of the time shall be given to each director in the same manner as notice for special meetings of the board of directors. If said day falls upon a holiday, such meetings shall be held on the next succeeding day thereafter.

11. Special meetings of the board of directors for any purpose or purposes may be called at any time by the Chairman of the Board or the President or any Vice President or the Secretary or any two directors.

12. Notice of the time and place for special meetings shall be delivered personally or by telephone to each director or sent by first class mail or telegram, charges prepaid, addressed to each director at his or her address as it is shown in the records of the corporation. In case such notice is mailed, it shall be deposited in the United States mail at least ten (10) days prior to the time of holding of the meeting. In case such notice is delivered personally or by telephone or telegram, it shall be delivered personally or by telephone or to the telegram company at least forty-eight (48) hours prior to the time of the holding of the meeting. Any oral notice given personally or by telephone may be communicated either to the director or to a person at the office of the director who the person giving the notice has reason to believe will promptly communicate it to the director. The notice need not specify the purpose of the meeting nor the place, if the meeting is to be held at the principal executive of the corporation.

13. The transactions of any meeting of the board of directors, however called, noticed, or wherever held, shall be as valid as though had at a meeting duly held after the regular call and notice if a quorum be present and if, either before or after the meeting, each of the directors not present signs a written waiver of notice, a consent to holding the meeting, or an approval of the minutes thereof. Waiver of notices or consents need not specify the purpose of the meeting. All such waivers, consents, and approvals shall be filed with the corporate records or made part of the minutes of the meeting. Notice of a meeting shall also be deemed given to any director who attends the meeting without protesting, prior thereto or at its commencement, the lack of notice to such director. A majority of the authorized number of directors shall constitute a quorum for the transaction of business, except to adjourn as otherwise provided in these bylaws. Every act or decision done or made by a majority of the directors present at a meeting duly held at which a quorum was present shall be regarded as the act of the board of directors.

14. A majority of the directors present, whether or not constituting a quorum, may adjourn any meeting to another time and place.

15. Notice of the time and place of the holding of an adjourned meeting need not be given, unless the meeting is adjourned for more than twenty-four (24) hours, in which case notice of such time and place shall be given prior to the time of the adjourned meeting to the directors who were not present at the time of the adjournment.

16. Any action required or permitted to be taken by the board of directors may be taken without a meeting with the same force and effect as if taken by unanimous vote of directors, if authorized by a consent in writing signed individually or collectively by all members of the board. Such consent shall be filed with the regular minutes of the board.

17. Directors and members of a directors' committee may receive such compensation and such reimbursement of expenses as may be fixed or determined by resolution of the board of directors. Nothing herein contained shall be construed to preclude any director from serving the corporation in any other capacity as an officer, employee, or otherwise and receiving compensation for such services.

18. Committees of the board may be appointed by resolution passed by a majority of the whole board. Committees shall be composed of two (2) or more members of the board and shall have such powers of the board as may be expressly delegated to them by resolution of the board of directors. The board may designate one (1) or more directors as alternate members of any committee, who may replace any absent member at any meeting of the committee. Committees shall have such powers of the board of directors as may be expressly delegated to it by resolution of the board of directors.

19. The board of directors from time to time may elect one (1) or more persons to be advisory directors, who shall not by such appointment be members of the board of directors. Advisory directors shall be available from time to time to perform special assignments specified by the President, to attend meetings of the board of directors upon invitation and to furnish consultation to the board. The period during which the title shall be held may be prescribed by the board of directors. If no period is prescribed, the title shall be held at the pleasure of the board.

Part B. Officers

20. The principal officers of the corporation shall be a President, a Secretary, and a Chief Financial Officer who may also be called Treasurer. The corporation may also have, at the discretion of the board of directors, one or more Vice Presidents, one or more Assistant Secretaries, and such other officers as may be appointed in accordance with paragraph 22 of these bylaws. One person may hold two or more offices.

21. The principal officers of the corporation, except such officers as may be appointed in accordance with paragraph 22 of these bylaws, shall be chosen by the board of directors, and each shall serve at the pleasure of the board of directors, subject to the rights, if any, of an officer under any contract of employment.

22. The board of directors may empower the President to appoint and remove such officers (other than the principal officers) as the business of the corporation may require, each of whom shall hold office for such period, have such authority, and perform such duties as are provided in the bylaws or as the board of directors may from time to time determine.

23. Subject to the rights, if any, of an officer under any contract of employment, any officer may be removed, either with or without cause, by a majority of the directors at that time in office, at any regular or special meeting of the board or, excepting the case of an officer chosen by the board of directors, by any officer upon whom such power of removal may be conferred by the board of directors.

24. A vacancy in any office because of death, resignation, removal, disqualification, or any other cause shall be filled in the manner prescribed in these bylaws for regular appointments to such office.

25. The Chairman of the Board, if an officer be elected, shall, if present, preside at all meetings of the board of directors and exercise and perform such other powers and duties as may from time to time be assigned to him by the board of directors or prescribed by the bylaws. If there is no President, the Chairman of the Board shall in addition be the Chief Executive Officer of the corporation and shall have the powers and duties prescribed in paragraph 26 of these bylaws.

26. Subject to such supervisory powers, if any, as may be given by the board of directors to the Chairman of the Board, if there be such an officer, the President shall be the Chief Executive Officer of the corporation and shall, subject to the control of the board of directors, have general supervision, direction, and control of the business and the officers of the corporation. He or she shall preside at all the meetings of the shareholders and, in the absence of the Chairman of the Board, or if there be none, at all meetings of shareholders and, in the absence of the Chairman of the Board, or if there be none, at all meetings of the board of directors. He or she shall have the general powers and duties of management usually vested in the office of President of a corporation, shall be ex officio a member of all the standing committees, including the executive committee, if any, and shall have such other powers and duties as may be described by the board of directors or the bylaws.

27. In the absence or disability of the President, the Vice Presidents, if any, in order of their rank as fixed by the board of directors, shall perform all the duties of the President, and so acting shall have all the powers of, and be subject to the restriction upon, the President. The Vice Presidents shall have such other powers and perform such other duties as from time to time may be prescribed for them respectively by the board of directors or the bylaws, the President, or the Chairman of the Board.

28. The Secretary shall keep or cause to be kept at the principal executive office or such other place as the board of directors may order, a book of minutes of all meetings of directors, committees of directors, and shareholders, with

the time and place of holding, whether regular or special, and, if special, how authorized, the notice thereof given, the names of those present at directors and committee meetings, the number of shares present or represented at shareholders' meetings, and the proceedings thereof. The Secretary shall keep or cause to be kept at the principal office or at the office of the corporation's transfer agent, a share register, or duplicate share register, showing the names of the shareholders and their addresses; the number of classes of shares held by each; the number and date of certificates issued for the same; and the number and date of cancellation of every certificate surrendered for cancellation. The Secretary shall give or cause to be given notice of all meetings of the shareholders and of the board of directors required by the bylaws or by law to be given, shall keep the seal of the corporation in safe custody, and shall have such other powers and perform such other duties as may be prescribed by the board of directors or by the bylaws.

29. The Chief Financial Officer shall keep and maintain, or cause to be kept and maintained, adequate and correct books and records of accounts of the properties and business transactions of the corporation, including accounts of its assets, liabilities, receipts, disbursements, gains, losses, capital, retained earnings, and shares. The books of account shall at all reasonable times be open to inspection by any director. The Chief Financial Officer shall deposit all moneys and other valuables in the name and to the credit of the corporation with such depositories as may be designated by the board of directors. He or she shall disburse the funds of the corporation as may be ordered by the board of directors, shall render to the President and directors, whenever they request it, an account of all of his or her transactions as Chief Financial Officer and of the financial condition of the corporation, and shall have other powers and perform such other duties as may be prescribed by the board of directors or the bylaws.

Part C. Shareholders

30. Meetings of shareholders shall be held at any place designated by the board of directors. In the absence of any such designation, shareholders' meetings shall be held at the principal executive office of the corporation.

31. The annual meeting of the shareholders shall be held on March 1. If this day be a legal holiday, then the meeting shall be held on the next succeeding business day, at the same time. At the annual meeting, the shareholders shall elect a board of directors, report the affairs of the corporation, and transact such other business as may properly be brought before the meeting. If the above date is inconvenient, the annual meeting of shareholders shall be held each year on a date and at a time designated by the board of directors within twenty (20) days of the above date upon proper notice to all shareholders.

32. A special meeting of the shareholders, for any purpose or purposes whatsoever, may be called at any time by the board of directors, or by the Chairman of the board of directors, or by the President, or by one or more shareholders holding shares in the aggregate entitled to cast not less than 10% of the votes at any such meeting. If a special meeting is called by any person or persons other than the board of directors, the request shall be in writing, specifying the time of such meeting and the general nature of the business proposed to be transacted, and shall be delivered personally or sent by registered mail or by telegraphic or other facsimile transmission to the Chairman of the board, the President, any Vice President, or the Secretary of the corporation. The officer receiving such request shall forthwith cause notice to be given to the shareholders entitled to vote, in accordance with the provisions of paragraphs 33 and 34 of these bylaws, that a meeting will be held at the time requested by the person or persons calling the meeting, not less than thirty-five (35) nor more than sixty (60) days after the receipt of the request. If the notice is not given within twenty (20) days after receipt of the request, the person or persons requesting the meeting may give the notice in the manner provided in these bylaws. Nothing contained in this paragraph shall be construed as limiting, fixing, or affecting the time when a meeting of shareholders called by action of the board of directors may be held.

33. Notice of meetings, annual or special, shall be given in writing not less than ten (10) nor more than sixty (60) days before the date of the meeting, to shareholders entitled to vote thereat by the Secretary or the Assistant Secretary, or if there be no such officer, or in the case of his or her neglect or refusal, by any director or shareholder. Such notices or any reports shall be given personally or by mail or by other means of communication as provided by state law, and shall be sent to each shareholder's address appearing on the books of the corporation or supplied by him or her

to the corporation for the purposes of notice. Notice of any meeting of shareholders shall specify the place, date, and hour of the meeting and (i) in the case of a special meeting, the general nature of the business to be transacted, and no other business may be transacted, or (ii) in the case of an annual meeting, those matters which the board of directors, at the date of the mailing of notice, intends to present for action by the shareholders. At any meetings where directors are elected, notice shall include the names of the nominees, if any, intended at the date of notice to be presented by the management for election.

34. The presence in person or by proxy of the holders of a majority of the shares entitled to vote at any meeting of shareholders shall constitute a quorum for the transaction of business. The shareholders present at a duly called or held meeting at which a quorum is present may continue to do business until adjournment, notwithstanding the withdrawal of enough shareholders to leave less than a quorum, if any action taken (other than adjournment) is approved by at least a majority of the shares required to constitute a quorum.

35. Any shareholders' meeting, annual or special, whether or not a quorum is present, may be adjourned from time to time by the vote of the majority of the shares represented at such meeting, either in person or by proxy, but in the absence of a quorum, no other business may be transacted at such meeting. When any meeting of shareholders, whether annual or special, is adjourned to another time or place, notice need not be given of the adjourned meeting if the time and place thereof are announced at a meeting at which the adjournment is taken, unless a new record date for the adjourned meeting is fixed, or unless a new record date for the adjourned meeting is fixed, or unless the adjournment is for more than forty-five (45) days from the date set for the original meeting, in which case the board of directors shall set a new record date. Notice of any such adjourned meeting shall be given to each shareholder of record entitled to vote at the adjourned meeting in accordance with the provisions of paragraph 33 of these bylaws.

36. The transactions at any meeting of shareholders, whether annual or special, however called and noticed, and wherever held, shall be as valid as though had at a meeting duly held after regular call and notice, if a quorum be present either in person or by proxy, and if, either before or after the meeting, each person entitled to vote, not present in person or by proxy, signs a written waiver of notice or a consent to a holding of the meeting or any approval of the minutes thereof. All such waivers, consents, or approvals shall be filed with the corporate records of made a part of the minutes of the meeting.

37. A shareholder's attendance at a meeting shall constitute a waiver of notice of such meeting, except when the shareholder objects at the beginning of the meeting.

38. Any action which may be taken at a meeting of the shareholders may be taken without a meeting or notice of meeting if authorized by a consent in writing signed by all of the shareholders entitled to vote at a meeting for such purpose and filed with the Secretary of the corporation.

39. Unless otherwise provided by state law, any action which may be taken at any annual or special meeting of shareholders may be taken without a meeting and without prior notice if a consent in writing setting forth the action so taken shall be signed by the holders of outstanding shares having not less than the minimum number of votes that would be necessary to authorize or take such action at a meeting at which all shares entitled to vote thereon were present and voted.

40. Unless the consents of all shareholders entitled to vote have been solicited in writing, prompt notice shall be given of the taking of any other corporate action approved by shareholders without a meeting by less than unanimous written consent, to each of those shareholders entitled to vote who have not consented in writing.

41. Only persons in whose names shares entitled to vote stand on the stock records of the corporation on the day fixed by the board of directors for the determination of the shareholders of record shall be entitled to vote at any shareholders' meeting. The board of directors may fix a time as a record date for the determination of the shareholders entitled to notice of and to vote at any such meeting, or entitled to receive any such dividend or distribution or any allotment of rights or to exercise the rights in respect to any such change, conversion, or exchange of shares,

In such case only shareholders of record on the date so fixed shall be entitled to notice of and to vote at such meeting, or to receive such dividends, distribution, or allotment of rights or to exercise such rights, as the case may be, notwithstanding a transfer of any share on the books of the company after any record date fixed as aforesaid.

42. Every shareholder entitled to vote for directors or on any other matter shall have the right to do so either in person or by one or more agents authorized by a proxy validly executed by the shareholder. A proxy may be executed by written authorization signed, or by electronic transmission authorized, by the shareholder or the shareholder's attorney in fact, giving the proxy holder(s) the power to vote the shareholder's shares. A proxy shall be deemed signed if the shareholder's name or other authorization is placed on the proxy (whether by manual signature, typewriting, telegraphic or electronic transmission, or otherwise) by the shareholder or the shareholder's attorney in fact. A proxy may also be transmitted orally by telephone if submitted with information from which it may be determined that the proxy was authorized by the shareholder or the shareholder's attorney in fact. A validly executed proxy which does not state that it is irrevocable shall continue in full force and effect unless revoked by the person executing it, prior to the vote pursuant thereto, by a writing delivered to the corporation stating that the proxy is revoked or by a subsequent proxy executed by or attendance at the meeting and voting in person by the person executing the proxy; provided, however, that no such proxy shall be valid after the expiration of eleven (11) months from the date of such proxy, unless otherwise provided in the proxy.

43. The President, or in the absence of the President, any Vice President shall call the meeting of the shareholders to order and shall act as Chairman of the meeting. In the absence of the President and all the Vice Presidents, shareholders shall appoint a Chairman at such meeting. The Secretary of the corporation shall act as Secretary of all meetings of the shareholders, but in the absence of the Secretary at any meeting of the shareholders, the presiding officer shall appoint any person to act as such Secretary of the meeting.

Part D. Shares

44. Certificates for shares shall be of such form and device as the board of directors may designate and shall state the name of the record holder of the shares represented thereby; its number and date of issuance; the number of shares for which it is issued; a statement of the rights, privileges, preferences, and restrictions, if any; a statement as to the redemption or conversion, if any; a statement of liens or restrictions upon transfer or voting, if any; and if the shares be assessable or if assessments are collectible by personal action, a plain statement of such facts.

45. Upon surrender to the Secretary or transfer agent of the corporation of a certificate for shares duly endorsed or accompanied by proper evidence of succession, assignment, or authority to transfer, it shall be the duty of the corporation to issue a new certificate to the person entitled thereto, cancel the old certificate, and record the transaction on its books.

46. In order that the corporation may determine the shareholders entitled to notice of any meeting or to vote or entitled to receive payment of any dividend or other distribution or allotment of any rights or entitled to exercise any rights in respect of any lawful action, the board may fix in advance, a record date, which shall not be more than sixty (60) nor less than ten (10) days prior to the date of such meeting nor more than sixty (60) days prior to any other action. If no record date is fixed:

(a) The record date for determining shareholders entitled to notice of or to vote at a meeting of shareholders shall be at the close of the business on the business day next preceding the day on which notice is given or, if notice is waived, at close of business on the business day next preceding the day on which the meeting is held.

(b) The record date for determining shareholders entitled to give consent to corporate action in writing without a meeting, when no prior action by the board is necessary, shall be the day on which the first written consent is given.

(c) The record date for determining shareholders for any other purpose shall be the close of business on the day on which the board adopts the resolution relating thereto, or the sixtieth (60th) day prior to the date of such other action, whichever is later.

Part E. Miscellaneous Matters

47. The corporation may at its option, to the maximum extent permitted by law and by the articles, indemnify each of its agents against expenses, judgments, fines, settlements, and other amounts actually and reasonably incurred in connection with any proceeding arising by reason of the fact that such person is or was an agent of the corporation. For the purposes of this section, an "agent" of the corporation includes any person who is or was a director, officer, employee, or agent of another corporation, partnership, joint venture, trust, or other enterprise, or was a director, officer, employee, or agent of a corporation which was a predecessor corporation of the corporation or of any other enterprise at the request of such predecessor corporation.

48. The corporation shall keep at its principal executive office, or at the office of its transfer agent or registrar, if either be appointed, and as determined by resolution of the board of directors, a record of its shareholders and the number and class of shares held by each shareholder.

49. The corporation shall keep at its principal executive office, or if its principal executive office is not in this state, at its principal business office in this state, the original or a copy of the bylaws amended to date, which shall be open to inspection by the shareholders at all reasonable times during office hours.

50. The board of directors, except as in the bylaws otherwise provided, may authorize any officer or officers, agent or agents, to enter into any contract or execute any instrument in the name of and on behalf of the corporation, and such authority may be general or confined to specific instances; and, unless so authorized or ratified by the board of directors or within the agency power of any officer, no officer, agent, or employee shall have any power or authority to bind the corporation by any contract or engagement or to pledge its credit or to render it liable for any purpose or to any amount.

51. The Chairman of the Board, the President, or any Vice President, or any other person authorized by resolution of the board of directors or by any of the foregoing designated officers, is authorized to vote on behalf of the corporation any and all shares of any other corporation or corporations, foreign or domestic, standing in the name of the corporation. The authority herein granted to said officers to vote or represent on behalf of the corporation any and all shares held by the corporation in any other corporation or corporations may be exercised by any such officer in person or by any person authorized to do so by proxy duly elected by said officer.

52. These bylaws may be amended or repealed by the vote or written consent of holders of a majority of the outstanding shares entitled to vote; provided, however, that if the Articles of Incorporation of the corporation set forth the number of authorized directors of the corporation, the authorized number of directors may be changed only by an amendment of the Articles of Incorporation. Bylaws may be adopted, amended, or repealed by the board of directors.

CERTIFICATE

I, Michael Spadaccini, hereby certify that I am the Secretary of the initial meeting of (insert corporate name).

The foregoing bylaws, consisting of ____ pages, are a true and correct copy of the bylaws of the corporation.

IN WITNESS WHEREOF, I have hereunto set my hand and affixed the seal of the corporation this _____ day of __________, 2004.

____

Michael Spadaccini

181. Sample Minutes of Organizational Meeting of the Board of Directors

MINUTES OF FIRST MEETING OF OLDE CRAFT, INC. BOARD OF DIRECTORS

The first meeting of the board of directors was held at 123 Elm Street, San Francisco on the 27th day of December, 2003 at 4:00 o'clock p.m.

Present were: John Jones, John Smith, and John Miller, constituting a quorum of the board.

Also present was Michael Spadaccini, attorney to the corporation.

John Jones acted as Chairman of the meeting and John Miller acted as Secretary of the meeting.

The Articles of Incorporation of the corporation were filed in the office of the Secretary of State on July 31, 2003. A certified copy of the Articles of Incorporation has been inserted in the minute book of the corporation.

RESOLVED FURTHER: That John Jones, named as this corporation's (initial agent for service of process/resident agent/registered agent) in the Articles of Incorporation, is hereby confirmed in such capacity.

RESOLVED FURTHER: That the corporate seal in the form, words, and figures impressed upon the last page of these minutes be, and it hereby is, adopted as the seal of the corporation.

RESOLVED FURTHER: That the form of stock certificates present to the board be, and it hereby is, approved and adopted, and the Secretary of the corporation is directed to insert a specimen certificate in the minute book immediately following these minutes.

RESOLVED FURTHER: That 123 Elm Street, San Francisco, California, be, and the same hereby is, designated and fixed as the principal executive office for the transaction of the business of this corporation.

RESOLVED FURTHER: That the following persons were unanimously elected to the offices and at the annual salaries respectively set forth:

Title	**Name**	**Salary**
President/CEO	John Jones	0
CFO/Treasurer	John Smith	0
Secretary	John Miller	0

RESOLVED FURTHER: That the fiscal year of this corporation shall end on December 31 of each year.

RESOLVED FURTHER: That the officers of the corporation are authorized and directed to pay the expenses of its incorporation and organization, including effecting reimbursement to any persons who have advanced funds to the corporation for such purposes and payment of any amounts remaining owing to the corporation's attorney and accountant for services in connection therewith.

RESOLVED FURTHER: That all contracts and transactions entered into on behalf of and for the benefit of this corporation be, and they hereby are accepted, adopted, and ratified by this corporation.

RESOLVED FURTHER: That this corporation save, defend, indemnify, and hold harmless the persons who entered into said contracts and transactions on behalf and for the benefit of this corporation, from and against any liability or expense arising therefrom and thereunder.

RESOLVED FURTHER: That the officers of this corporation be, and they hereby are, authorized to sell and issue to the following persons the number of shares of capital stock of this corporation and for the consideration indicated opposite each name:

Name	Number of Shares	$ per Share	Type and Amount of Consideration
John Jones	100,000	$0.75	$75,000 in cash
John Smith	100,000	$0.75	$75,000 in property, specifically, the aggregate existing assets of the sole proprietorship known as Acme Iron Works, which includes, but is not limited to all tools, vehicles, good will, licenses, assets, bank accounts, cash, receivables.
John Miller	100,000	$0.75	$5,000 in past services, specifically, for services rendered to the corporation in connection with its organization. $70,000 in intangible assets, specifically, a 25-year license to use the trademark "Olde Craft" in connection with the sale of water, a copy of which license is attached.

RESOLVED FURTHER: That such shares shall be sold without the publication of any advertising or general solicitation.

RESOLVED FURTHER: That said shares shall be sold and issued only under exemption from both federal and state securities laws: the officers and directors of this corporation shall take such action as may be necessary or desirable to effect such exemption, and the corporation's shares shall be issued in accordance with the conditions thereof.

RESOLVED FURTHER: That each of the proposed issuees shall execute an investment representation with respect to the purchase of the securities of the corporation and set forth therein their respective preexisting personal or business relationship with one or more of the corporation's directors or officers or business or financial experience by reason of which they can reasonably by assumed to have the capacity to protect their own interests in connection with the transaction.

RESOLVED: That an election (will/will not) be made to secure Subchapter "S" status for the corporation, and that such elected be effectuated through all appropriate filings with the U.S. Internal Revenue Service.

DATE: ______________

____

John Jones, Meeting Chairman

____

John Miller, Meeting Secretary

182. Shareholder's Agreement

SHAREHOLDER'S AGREEMENT
BY AND AMONG THE SHAREHOLDERS
OF RETAIL FURNITURE COMPANY, INC.

THIS AGREEMENT BY AND AMONG SHAREHOLDERS is made and entered into as of 11/10/04 by and between RETAIL FURNITURE COMPANY, INC., a California Corporation (the "Company"), and Don Leland and Alexandra Leland, as Co-Trustees of the Don Leland and Alexandra Leland Family Trust, and David Kowalski (collectively the "Shareholders" and individually a "Shareholder").

RECITALS: This Agreement is made with reference to the following facts:

A. The Shareholders have formed the Company for the purpose of operating retail furniture stores.

B. The Company was incorporated as a California corporation on or about January 8, 1996. The Company has authorized a single class of stock, namely 100,000 shares of common stock.

C. The Shareholders wish to enter into this Agreement for the purpose of setting forth their respective rights and duties in connection with the formation of the Company and the financing, management, and operation of its business.

NOW, THEREFORE, it is agreed as follows:

1. Principal Office. The Company shall have its principal office at 631 Cedar St., Berkeley, California 94710.

2. Directors. The Company shall have a 3-person board of directors (the "Board") consisting of the following persons who shall serve initially until the next meeting of Shareholders is called to elect directors:

Donald Leland
Alexandra Leland
David Kowalski

At each successive annual meeting of shareholders, while this Agreement is in effect, the Shareholders agree to vote their shares in a manner that will ensure that the 3 directors named above shall continue in such capacity.

3. Officers. Initially and until changed by any regular or special meeting of the Board, the following persons shall be the duly constituted officers of the Company:

President: Donald Leland
CFO: David Kowalski
Secretary: Alexandra Leland

4. Stock. The Donald Leland and Alexandra Leland Family Trust is currently a holder of 7,500 shares of common stock (hereinafter "Shares") in the Company. David Kowalski is currently a holder of 833.33 Shares:

5. Repurchase by the Company. Ownership of the Shares shall be subject to certain repurchase rights. In the event of a termination of employment of any (i) Shareholder, or (ii) with respect to any shares held by a trust, all of the Principal Settlors of a trust, as defined below, by reason of the following "Repurchase Events": (i) death, (ii) total physical or mental disability for a period of 90 consecutive days, (iii) voluntary termination of employment, or (iv) involuntary termination of employment with or without cause, all Shares owned by such Shareholder or by trust shall be subject to repurchase, at the election of the Company, treating the Company as a going concern. For the purposes of this Agreement, no repurchase event shall operate against a trust unless all Principal Settlors meet the conditions of a repurchase event.

a. The "Repurchase Price" shall be determined as of the date of the event causing the transfer or repurchase of Shares (the "Effective Date"), and the Repurchase Price shall be determined as follows:

i. If the Effective date falls either on or between the dates of November 5, 2004 and November 5, 2004, the Repurchase Price of one Share of stock shall be $1,500,000.00 divided by the total number of Shares outstanding as of the Effective Date, plus 10% interest from the date of November 5, 2004.

ii. If the Effective date falls either on or after the date of November 6, 2004, the Repurchase Price shall be determined by the Company's CPA or by appraisal as described below.

b. If the Repurchase Price is to be determined by the Company's CPA or by appraisal, the computation shall be made as follows:

i. The Repurchase Price of the Shares shall be computed by the independent certified public accountant (CPA) regularly used by the Company or, if the Company has no CPA or if the CPA is unavailable, then by a qualified appraiser selected by the Company for this purpose. The Repurchase Price of one Share of the Company's stock shall be the sum of the Company's total Repurchase Price divided by the number of Shares then outstanding.

ii. The Repurchase Price of the Company shall be determined annually, and the Directors shall cause such an appraisal to be completed along with the Company's annual tax returns and provided to the shareholders in the form of a written appraisal report. The appraisal report shall value the Company as of the end of the last day of the Company's fiscal year. All Shareholders shall have 10 days from the receipt of the report to review the report and to raise any objections to the appraisal. Any objections to the appraisal shall be in writing and shall state the basis for the objection and shall be delivered to the CPA or appraiser and to all Shareholders. If no such objections are made, then the Shareholders are deemed to consent to the appraisal and shall be bound by it.

iii. The Repurchase Price stated in the appraisal report shall be deemed to be the value of the Company for one year from the date of the appraisal report.

iv. The CPA or appraiser shall complete the valuation and appraisal report using accounting practices in common usage, and may consider the following factors: (a) the value of comparable companies, if known, (b) any prior year's valuation, (c) the profits of the Company, (d) the face amount of any accounts payable, (e) the face amount of any accounts receivable, and (f) any other factors the CPA or appraiser deems appropriate.

c. In the event the Company repurchases Shares, the stock certificates representing the same shall forthwith be returned to the Company upon payment therefor by the Company.

d. For the purposes of this Agreement, the "Principal Settlor" of a trust shall be any individual who establishes a trust while a shareholder in the corporation either as record holder or by operation of community property, and who (i) transfers Shares in the corporation to such trust and (ii) maintains power of revocation over the Shares.

6. Manner of Payment for Repurchased Shares. In the event the Company elects to repurchase the restricted Shares (or if a Shareholder purchases Shares under the anti-deadlock provisions of Paragraph 13),

a. the Company (or Shareholder) shall be entitled to pay the Repurchase Price on the following terms : the Company (or purchasing Shareholder) shall pay 25% of the total Repurchase Price within 60 days of the Effective Date, and shall pay the remaining balance of the Repurchase Price in 24 successive equal monthly installments. Such installment payments shall be due on the first of the month that follows after the expiration of 60 days following the Effective Date, and shall continue on each successive first of the month until the balance of the Repurchase Price is paid. The installment payments shall also reflect 9% interest applied to the principal amount. There shall be no prepayment penalty.

7. Involuntary Termination of Employment. The employment of any employee who is also a Shareholder may be terminated only if a supermajority (defined as a 2/3 vote of all outstanding shares in the Company) agrees, and votes to terminate the employee.

8. Transfer of Shares. None of the Shares may be sold, transferred, or otherwise disposed of nor shall they be pledged or hypothecated by any Shareholder as long as the Company has the right hereunder to repurchase such

Shares. Notwithstanding such restrictions, however, so long as any Shareholder is the owner of the Shares or any portion of them, he/she shall be entitled to receive all dividends, if any, declared on the Shares.

9. Right of First Refusal. Neither any Shareholder who owns more than five percent (5%) of the outstanding Shares of the Company's common stock nor his/her heirs, personal representatives, successors, or assigns, shall have the right at any time to sell or transfer any portion of his or her Shares purchased hereunder unless:

a. Offer to Company. The selling Shareholder shall deliver a written notice to the Company, stating the price, terms, and conditions of the proposed sale or transfer, the Shares to be sold or transferred, and the identity of the proposed transferee ("Seller's Notice"). Within 10 days after receipt of the Seller's Notice, the Company shall have the right to purchase all or any portion of the Shares so offered at the Repurchase Price outlined above in Paragraph 5.

b. Offer to Other Shareholders. If the Company fails to purchase all of the Shares specified in the Seller's Notice, and if the Company has not then made an initial public offering of its common stock, the following procedure shall be followed with regard to any sale or transfer of Shares. The Company shall, at the expiration of 10 days after receipt of the Seller's Notice, notify each of the Shareholders of the total number of Shares not purchased by the Company, enclosing a copy of the Seller's Notice (the "Company's Notice"). Each of the Shareholders shall have 10 days after the mailing of the Company's Notice to notify the selling Shareholder in writing of his/her intention to purchase all or any specified portion of the available Shares at the Repurchase Price outlined above in Paragraph 5. Each Shareholder shall deliver to the selling Shareholder by mail or otherwise a written offer or offers to purchase all or any specified portion of the selling Shareholder's Shares remaining for sale ("Shares for Sale"). Each Shareholder shall be entitled to purchase the proportion of the Shares for Sale at the ratio that his or her Shares bear to the total Shares held by all Shareholders desiring to purchase Shares for Sale.

If the total Shares specified in the offers received within such period by the selling Shareholder exceed the Shares for Sale, each Shareholder desiring to purchase a percentage of the Shares for Sale in excess of his/her proportionate share shall be entitled to purchase the proportion of the Shares for Sale that remains undisposed of, at the ratio that his or her Shares bears to the total Shares held by all of the Shareholders desiring to purchase Shares in excess of those to which they are entitled under such prior apportionment. Such apportionment shall be made successively until all of the Shares for Sale shall have been allocated to purchasing Shareholders.

c. Transfer to Third Parties. If none or only a part of the Shares for Sale is bid for purchase by the other Shareholders, then the selling Shareholder may dispose of the remaining Shares for Sale to any person or persons but only within a period of 90 days from the date of the Seller's Notice. However, the selling Shareholder shall not sell or transfer any of the Shares for Sale at a lower price or on terms more favorable to the purchaser or transferee than those specified in the Seller's Notice. After the 90-day period, the procedure for first offering to the Company and other Shareholders shall again apply.

d. Transfer at Death. The first refusal rights granted above shall not apply to transfers by intestate succession or testamentary disposition on the Shareholder's death. However, the death of any Shareholder shall immediately trigger the repurchase provisions of paragraph 5.

10. Legends Imprinted on Certificates. By execution of this Agreement, the Shareholders indicate their agreement to the repurchase rights of the Company, the restrictions on resale, and the rights of first refusal. The Shareholders also acknowledge that neither the issuance nor the resale of the Shares has been registered or qualified under applicable federal or state securities laws.

The Shareholders agree that the following legends will be imprinted on each certificate representing Shares restricted from resale:

THE SECURITIES REPRESENTED BY THIS CERTIFICATE MAY NOT BE TRANSFERRED, SOLD, PLEDGED, HYPOTHECATED, OR OTHERWISE DISPOSED OF EXCEPT IN ACCORDANCE WITH AN AGREEMENT AMONG SHAREHOLDERS, A

COPY OF WHICH MAY BE OBTAINED FROM THE COMPANY.

The Shareholders agree that the following legends will be imprinted on all certificates representing Shares:

THE SHARES REPRESENTED BY THIS CERTIFICATE HAVE NOT BEEN REGISTERED UNDER THE SECURITIES ACT OF 1933 AND MAY BE TRANSFERRED ONLY IF THE COMPANY IS SATISFIED THAT NO VIOLATION OF SUCH ACT IS INVOLVED.

11. Term. This Agreement shall remain in effect until (i) the Company is merged into, or sells its assets to, or exchanges stock with, another corporation which has, after such merger, sale of assets, or exchange of stock, consolidated total assets of at least twenty million dollars ($20,000,000.00) and is qualified to be listed on NASDAQ, (ii) the Company effects a public offering of its securities, or (iii) the expiration of 10 years from the date of this Agreement, whichever occurs first.

12. Election for Tax Purposes. The Company shall elect to be taxed as a "small business corporation" under Subchapter S of the Internal Revenue Code. This determination shall continue until the Shareholders unanimously agree otherwise.

13. Termination upon 50/50 Deadlock. At any time that the Company shall have only two Shareholders, each owning the same number of Shares, either Shareholder may elect to terminate the relationship between the two Shareholders pursuant to the following provisions:

a. The terminating Shareholder shall notify the other Shareholder of the desire to terminate the relationship.

b. Within 10 days after such notice, the other Shareholder shall elect to either buy the other's Shares or sell his/her own Shares at the Repurchase Price, and shall notify the terminating Shareholder. Failure to give notice shall be irrevocably deemed to be an election by the other Shareholder to sell his or her Shares to the terminating Shareholder.

c. The transaction shall be consummated within 30 days of the election to purchase. If the purchasing Shareholder fails for any reason to consummate the sale, then the selling Shareholder may elect to purchase the purchasing Shareholder's Shares at 85% of the Repurchase Price, such transaction to be completed within 30 days following the failure to consummate the first transaction.

d. Once commenced, the procedures provided in this Section may not be terminated or revoked without the prior written consent of both Shareholders to such termination or revocation.

14. Entire Agreement. This Agreement embodies the entire agreement and understanding of the parties to this Agreement with respect to its subject matter and supersedes all prior agreements and understandings, whether written or oral, relating to such subject matter.

15. Governing Law. This Agreement shall be governed by and construed in accordance with the laws of the State of California.

16. Successors. Anything in the Agreement to the contrary, any transferee, successor, or assignee, whether voluntary, by operation of law, or otherwise, of the Shares of the Company shall be subject to and bound by the terms and conditions of this Agreement as fully as though such person were a signatory.

17. Severability. Any provision of this Agreement prohibited by or unlawful or unenforceable shall be stricken without affecting any other provision of this Agreement.

18. Any controversy or claim arising out of or relating to this Agreement, its terms, or the breach thereof, shall be settled by arbitration administered by the American Arbitration Association in accordance with its Commercial Arbitration Rules, and judgment on the award rendered by the arbitrator(s) may be entered in any court having jurisdiction thereof.

Date: ______________________________

____
Donald Leland

____
Alexandra Leland

____
David Kowalski

183. Share Transfer Ledger

Stock Certificate Number	Date of Original Issue	Stockholder Name	Number of Shares	Disposition of Shares (transferred or surrendered stock certificate)

184. Investment Representation Letter

July 31, 2004

To whom it may concern,

I am delivering this letter to Olde Craft, Inc. in connection with my purchase of 100,000 shares of Olde Craft, Inc. for a total sum of $75,000.00. I represent the following:

I am purchasing the shares in my own name and for my own account, for investment and not with an intent to sell or for sale in connection with any distribution of such stock; and no other person has any interest in or right with respect to the shares; nor have I agreed to give any person any such interest or right in the future.

I recognize that the shares have not been registered under the Federal Securities Act of 1933, as amended, or qualified under any state securities law, and that any sale or transfer of the shares is subject to restrictions imposed by federal and state law.

I also recognize that I cannot dispose of the shares absent registration and qualification or an available exemption from registration and qualification. I understand that no federal or state securities commission or other government body has approved of the fairness of the shares offered by the corporation and that the Commissioner has not and will not recommend or endorse the shares.

I have not seen or received any advertisement or general solicitation with respect to the sale of the shares.

I have a preexisting personal or business relationship with the Company or one or more of its officers, directors, or controlling persons and I am aware of its character and general financial and business circumstances.

I acknowledge that during the course of this transaction and before purchasing the shares I have been provided with financial and other written information about the Company. I have been given the opportunity by the Company to obtain any information and ask questions concerning the Company, the shares, and my investment that I felt necessary; and to the extent I availed myself of that opportunity, I have received satisfactory information and answers.

In reaching the decision to invest in the shares, I have carefully evaluated my financial resources and investment position and the risks associated with this investment, and I acknowledge that I am able to bear the economic risks of this investment.

____

John Miller

185. Appointment of Proxy for Annual or Special Shareholders' Meeting

APPOINTMENT OF PROXY FOR (ANNUAL/SPECIAL) MEETING

SuperCorp, Inc.

SHAREHOLDER: John Miller

NUMBER OF SHARES HELD: 100,000

I, the undersigned, as record holder of the shares of stock of SuperCorp, Inc. described above, revoke any previous proxies and appoint the person whose name appears just below this paragraph in the box to the right (**Note:** on a regular proxy form, this would appear) as my proxy to attend the (annual/special) shareholders' meeting on ________________ and any adjournment of that meeting.

THE BOARD STRONGLY RECOMMENDS THAT YOU RETURN THIS PROXY IF YOU DO NOT INTEND TO APPEAR PERSONALLY AT THE (ANNUAL/SPECIAL) SHAREHOLDERS' MEETING.

The person I want to appoint as my proxy is ________________

The proxy holder is entitled to cast a total number of votes equal to but not exceeding the number of shares which I would be entitled to cast if I were personally present.

I authorize my proxy holder to vote and otherwise represent me with regard to any business that may come before this meeting in the same manner and with the same effect as if I were personally present.

I may revoke this proxy at any time. This proxy will lapse three months after the date of its execution.

Please sign your name below and, if you are signing for a business entity, please state your title.

Date (*important*): ________________

____
Name

____
Title

ALL PROXIES MUST BE SIGNED. PLEASE SIGN EXACTLY AS YOUR NAME APPEARS ON YOUR STOCK CERTIFICATE. JOINT SHAREHOLDERS MUST EACH SIGN THIS PROXY. IF SIGNED BY AN ATTORNEY IN FACT, THE POWER OF ATTORNEY MUST BE ATTACHED.

IF YOU REQUIRE ASSISTANCE WITH THIS PROXY, PLEASE CONTACT THE CORPORATE SECRETARY, ____________________, AT 415-555-1212.

186. Long-Form Appointment of Proxy for Annual or Special Shareholders' Meeting

APPOINTMENT OF PROXY FOR (ANNUAL/SPECIAL) MEETING

SuperCorp, Inc.

SHAREHOLDER: John Miller

NUMBER OF SHARES HELD: 100,000

I, the undersigned, as record holder of the shares of stock of SuperCorp, Inc. described above, revoke any previous proxies and appoint the person whose name appears just below this paragraph in the box to the right (**Note:** on a regular proxy form, this would appear) as my proxy to attend the (annual/special) shareholders' meeting on ________________ and any adjournment of that meeting.

THE BOARD STRONGLY RECOMMENDS THAT YOU RETURN THIS PROXY IF YOU DO NOT INTEND TO APPEAR PERSONALLY AT THE (ANNUAL/SPECIAL) SHAREHOLDERS' MEETING.

The person I want to appoint as my proxy is __________________________

The proxy holder is entitled to cast a total number of votes equal to but not exceeding the number of shares which I would be entitled to cast if I were personally present.

The shares represented by this proxy shall be voted in the following manner:

ACTIONS PROPOSED TO BE TAKEN

1. Shareholder John Miller has proposed a shareholder vote to remove John Jones from the board of directors.

- ❑ I want my proxy to vote FOR this proposal.
- ❑ I want my proxy to vote AGAINST this proposal.
- ❑ I withhold my proxy with respect to this specific vote.

2. Shareholder John Miller has proposed a shareholder vote to elect to make the corporation a close corporation.

- ❑ I want my proxy to vote FOR this proposal.
- ❑ I want my proxy to vote AGAINST this proposal.
- ❑ I withhold my proxy with respect to this specific vote.

3. Shareholder John Miller has proposed, in the event that John Jones is removed from the board of directors, that he, John Miller, be elected to serve on the board of directors.

- ❑ I want my proxy to vote FOR this proposal.
- ❑ I want my proxy to vote AGAINST this proposal.
- ❑ I withhold my proxy with respect to this specific vote.

IF YOU DO NOT INDICATE HOW YOU DESIRE YOUR SHARES TO BE VOTED, THE PROXY HOLDER WILL HAVE COMPLETE DISCRETION IN VOTING THE SHARES ON ANY MATTER VOTED AT THE MEETING.

I may revoke this proxy at any time. This proxy will lapse three months after the date of its execution.

Please sign your name below and, if you are signing for a business entity, please state your title.

Date (*important*):____________________

____

Name

____

Title

ALL PROXIES MUST BE SIGNED. PLEASE SIGN EXACTLY AS YOUR NAME APPEARS ON YOUR STOCK CERTIFICATE. JOINT SHAREHOLDERS MUST EACH SIGN THIS PROXY. IF SIGNED BY AN ATTORNEY IN FACT, THE POWER OF ATTORNEY MUST BE ATTACHED.

IF YOU REQUIRE ASSISTANCE WITH THIS PROXY, PLEASE CONTACT THE CORPORATE SECRETARY: ____________________, AT 415-555-1212.

187. Call for Special Meeting of Shareholders

CALL FOR SPECIAL MEETING OF SHAREHOLDERS

TO: The Secretary of SuperCorp, Inc.

The party or parties whose name appears below, the holder(s) of shares entitled to cast not less than 10 percent of the votes of SuperCorp Inc., do hereby call a special meeting of the shareholders of said corporation to be held _______________ (date), at _______________ (time), for the purpose of considering and acting upon the following matters:

(Insert matters to be considered, such as "A proposal that John Jones be removed from the board of directors.")

You are directed to give notice of this special meeting, in the manner prescribed by the corporation's bylaws and by law, to all shareholders entitled to receive notice of the meeting.

Date ______________________

____

____

____

188. Notice of Special Meeting of Shareholders

NOTICE OF SPECIAL MEETING OF SHAREHOLDERS OF SUPERCORP, INC.

Pursuant to a call made by shareholders, notice is hereby given that a special meeting of the Shareholders of SuperCorp, Inc. be held on ______________ (date), at ______________ (time), at ____________________ (address), to consider and act on the following:

(insert matters to be considered, such as "A proposal that John Jones be removed from the board of directors.")

If you do not expect to be present at the meeting and wish your shares to be voted, you may complete the attached form of proxy and mail it in the enclosed addressed envelope.

Date ________________________

____

Corporate Secretary

189. Minutes of Annual or Special Meeting of Shareholders

MINUTES OF (ANNUAL/SPECIAL) MEETING OF SHAREHOLDERS OF SUPERCORP, INC.

The shareholders of SUPERCORP, INC., held a (special/annual) meeting on __________ (date), at ______________ (time), at ________________ (place).

The following shareholders were present at the meeting, in person or by proxy, representing shares as indicated:

John Jones, 100,000 shares
John Smith, 100,000 shares
John Miller, 75,000 shares

Also present were Michael Spadaccini, attorney to the corporation, and Lisa Jones, an employee of the corporation.

The president of the corporation called the meeting to order and announced that he would chair the meeting, that a quorum was present, and that the meeting was held pursuant to a written notice of meeting given to all shareholders of the corporation. A copy of this notice was ordered inserted in the minute book immediately preceding the minutes of this meeting.

The minutes of the previous meeting of shareholders were then read and approved. The minutes were then inserted into the minute book of the corporation.

The chairperson then announced that the election of directors was in order. The chairperson called the matter to a vote, noting that each shareholder had nominated himself (or herself) to serve. Directors were then elected to serve until the next annual meeting of stockholders and until their successors were duly elected and qualified, as follows:

John Jones
John Smith
John Miller

The chairperson then announced a proposal to change the corporation's fiscal year from December 31 to June 30. The chairperson advocated the change because he felt that the June 30 fiscal year would more closely reflect the seasonality of the corporation's sales. While John Smith and John Miller agreed with this point, they noted that the administrative work associated with the change would strain the organization, so they would not support the change. Thus, the matter was not brought to a vote. The chairperson noted that the board would bring the matter up at next year's meeting, and John Smith and John Miller agreed that was suitable.

The chairperson then announced a proposal for the company to obtain a credit line from a local bank. All the directors agreed that the company should pursue a credit line of up to $500,000 and that the credit line could be secured with the company's inventory. The chairperson noted that he had discussed the credit line with two banks, and both were interested in having the company apply. The chairperson then brought the matter to a vote, and the directors voted unanimously to pursue the credit line and to authorize the corporation to open the credit line.

There being no further business to come before the meeting, on motion duly made, seconded, and adopted, the meeting was adjourned.

I, the secretary of the corporation, attest that the foregoing minutes are a true and accurate description of the matters and votes brought before the corporation at the above-captioned meeting.

____

Corporate Secretary

190. Action by Written Consent of Shareholder(s)

ACTION BY WRITTEN CONSENT OF SHAREHOLDER(S) OF SUPERCORP, INC.

The undersigned shareholder(s) of SuperCorp, Inc., owning of record the number of shares entitled to vote as set forth, hereby consent(s) to the following corporate actions:

1. John Smith is hereby elected to serve on the board of directors and to occupy the vacancy left by the resignation of John Jones. He shall serve until the next annual meeting of shareholders.

2. The corporation hereby elects to be a close corporation.

3. The Articles of Incorporation shall be amended to include language sufficient to make the close corporation election under state law.

Date ______________________

____

John Smith

____

Number of Shares Owned

Date ______________________

____

John Miller

____

Number of Shares Owned

191. Call for Special Meeting of Directors

CALL FOR SPECIAL MEETING OF DIRECTORS

TO: The Secretary of SuperCorp, Inc.

The party whose name appears below, the (director/CEO/president), by this notice hereby calls a special meeting of directors, which shall be held on ____________(date), at ____________ (time), at ____________ (place), to consider and act on the following proposals and such other business as may properly come before the board.

1. Acceptance of resignation of John Jones as corporate secretary.

2. Appointment of John Miller to position of corporate secretary.

3. Consideration of acquisition of Newcorp, Inc. by Supercorp, Inc.

You are directed to give notice of this special meeting, in the manner prescribed by the corporation's bylaws and by law, to all shareholders entitled to receive notice of the meeting.

Date: ____________________

____
Name

____
Position (i.e., director, CEO, president)

192. Minutes of Annual Meeting of Directors

MINUTES OF ANNUAL MEETING OF THE DIRECTORS OF SUPERCORP, INC.

The directors of Supercorp, Inc. held an annual meeting on ______________ (date), at ______________ (time), at ______________ (place).

The following directors were present at the meeting:

John Jones
John Smith
John Miller

Also present were Michael Spadaccini, attorney to the corporation, and Lisa Jones.

The chairman called the meeting to order and announced that the meeting was held pursuant to the bylaws of the corporation and was held without notice.

It was then moved, seconded, and resolved to dispense with the reading of the minutes of the last meeting.

The directors considered the election of officers to serve until the next annual meeting of directors. The directors unanimously voted to elect the following persons to the corresponding positions:

John Jones, President and CEO
John Smith, Treasurer and CFO
John Miller, Corporate Secretary

There being no further business to come before the meeting, the meeting was duly adjourned.

____

Corporate Secretary

193. Minutes of Special Meeting of Directors

MINUTES OF SPECIAL MEETING OF THE DIRECTORS OF SUPERCORP, INC.

The directors of Supercorp, Inc. held a special meeting on ______________ (date), at ___________ (time), at _______________ (place).

The following directors were present at the meeting:

John Jones
John Smith
John Miller

Also present were Michael Spadaccini, attorney to the corporation, and Lisa Jones.

The chairman called the meeting to order and announced that the meeting was held pursuant to written waiver of notice and consent to the holding of the meeting. The waiver and consent was presented to the meeting and, on a motion duly made, seconded, and carried, was made a part of the records and ordered inserted in the minutes book immediately preceding the records of this meeting.

It was then moved, seconded, and resolved to dispense with the reading of the minutes of the last meeting.

The directors then considered the acceptance of the resignation of John Jones as corporate secretary. The directors, with John Jones abstaining from the vote, voted to accept the resignation of John Jones.

The directors then considered the appointment of John Miller to the position of corporate secretary. The directors, with John Miller abstaining from the vote, voted to appoint John Miller to the position of corporate secretary.

The directors next considered the acquisition of Newcorp, Inc. by Supercorp, Inc. The directors voted to execute an agreement of purchase of Newcorp, Inc.

There being no further business to come before the meeting, the meeting was duly adjourned.

____

Corporate Secretary

194. Action of Directors by Written Consent

ACTION OF DIRECTOR(S) BY WRITTEN CONSENT TO APPROVE STOCK OPTION PLAN AND TO ISSUE SHARES OF STOCK

The undersigned, the director(s) of Evolution Water Company, Inc., agree unanimously to the following:

RESOLVED, that the undersigned directors waive notice of a special meeting of directors pursuant to the corporation's bylaws and hereby agree that the following actions and resolutions be taken by this written consent.

RESOLVED, that the "Evolution Water Company Stock Option Plan" presented to the undersigned directors and attached to this written consent as an exhibit is hereby adopted by the corporation.

RESOLVED FURTHER: That the officers of this corporation be, and they hereby are, authorized to sell and issue to the following persons the number of shares of capital stock of this corporation and for the consideration indicated opposite each name:

NAME	NUMBER OF SHARES	$ PER SHARE	TYPE AND AMOUNT OF CONSIDERATION
John Jones	100,000	$0.75	$75,000 in cash

Date ______________

____
Scott Bess, Director

____
Brian Bess, Director

195. Written Consent of Directors Approving a Certificate of Amendment of Articles of Incorporation Changing Corporation's Name

ACTION OF DIRECTOR(S) BY WRITTEN CONSENT TO APPROVE AN AMENDMENT TO ARTICLES OF INCORPORATION CHANGING CORPORATE NAME

The undersigned, the director(s) of Plasticworld.com, Inc., a California corporation, agree unanimously to the following:

RESOLVED, that the undersigned directors waive notice of a special meeting of directors pursuant to the corporation's bylaws and hereby agree that the following actions and resolutions be taken by this written consent.

RESOLVED, that the Certificate of Amendment of Articles of Incorporation presented to the undersigned directors, specifically changing the name of the corporation to PlasticUniverse, Inc., be approved by the directors.

Date ______________________

____
Scott Bess, Director

____
Brian Bess, Director

196. Certificate of Amendment of Articles of Incorporation Changing Corporation's Name

CERTIFICATE OF AMENDMENT OF
ARTICLES OF INCORPORATION

The undersigned certify that:

1. They are the president and secretary, respectively, of PlasticWorld.com, Inc., corporation number 10134944.

2. Article I of the Articles of Incorporation of this corporation is hereby amended to read as follows:

The name of this Corporation is hereby changed to PlasticUnverse, Inc.

3. The foregoing Amendment of Articles of Incorporation has been duly approved by the board of directors.

4. The foregoing Amendment of Articles of Incorporation has been duly approved by the required vote of shareholders in accordance with state law. The total number of outstanding shares of the corporation is 10,000,000. The number of shares voting in favor of the amendment equaled or exceeded the vote required. The percentage vote required was more than 50%.

We further declare, under penalty of perjury under the laws of the State of California, that the matters set forth in this certificate are true and correct of our own knowledge.

Dated ____________________

____
Scott Bess, President

____
Brian Bess, Secretary

197. Certificate of Amendment of Articles of Incorporation Electing Close Corporation Status

CERTIFICATE OF AMENDMENT OF
ARTICLES OF INCORPORATION

The undersigned certify that:

1. They are the president and secretary, respectively, of Evolution Water Company, Inc., corporation number 1059964.

2. Article V of the Articles of Incorporation of this corporation is hereby added, and the Articles of Incorporation are hereby amended to read as follows:

All of this Corporation's issued shares of all classes shall be held of record by not more than 35 persons, and this Corporation is a close corporation.

3. The foregoing Amendment of Articles of Incorporation has been duly approved by the board of directors.

4. The foregoing Amendment of Articles of Incorporation has been duly approved by the required vote of shareholders. The total number of outstanding shares of the corporation is 98,333. The vote with respect to this amendment was unanimous.

We further declare, under penalty of perjury under the laws of the State of California, that the matters set forth in this certificate are true and correct of our own knowledge.

Dated ____________________

____
Donald Leland, President

____
Alexandra Leland, Secretary

Additional titles in *Entrepreneur's* Ultimate Series

- *Ultimate Book of Business Forms: 199 Forms You Can Customize!* by Michael Spadaccini
- *Ultimate Book of Franchises 2005: From the Franchise Experts at Entrepreneur Magazine* by Rieva Lesonsky and Maria Anton-Conley
- *Ultimate Book of Homebased Franchises* by Rieva Lesonsky and Maria Anton-Conley
- *Ultimate Book of Low Cost Franchises* by Rieva Lesonsky and Maria Anton-Conley
- *Ultimate Book of Restaurant and Food Service Franchises* by Rieva Lesonsky and Maria Anton-Conley
- *Ultimate Book on Forming Corporations, LLCs, Sole Proprietorships and Partnerships* by Michael Spadaccini
- *Ultimate Guide to Buying or Selling a Business: Trade Secrets That Will Save You Time and Money* by Ira Nottonson
- *Ultimate Guide to Forming an LLC in Any State: Everything You Need to Know* by Michael Spadaccini
- *Ultimate Guide to Incorporating in Any State: Everything You Need to Know* by Michael Spadaccini
- *Ultimate Guide to Workers' Compensation Insurance* by Edward Priz
- *Ultimate Homebased Business Handbook: How to Start, Run and Grow Your Own Profitable Business* by James Stephenson
- *Ultimate Small Business Advisor: All You Need to Know* by Andi Axman
- *Ultimate Small Business Marketing Guide: 1500 Great Marketing Tricks That Will Drive Your Business Through the Roof* by James Stephenson
- *Ultimate Start-Up Directory* by James Stephenson

The following pages contain the introduction from *Entrepreneur* magazine's *Ultimate Small Business Marketing Guide: 1500 Great Marketing Tricks That Will Drive Your Business Through the Roof* by James Stephenson. Available at all fine bookstores nationwide and online retailers.

ISBN: 1-932156-10-0 Price: $22.95

INTRODUCTION

Marketing, without question, is the single largest challenge facing small-business owners today. And to make matters worse, marketing success is always temporary. The minute you stop stoking the promotional boiler, the marketing train begins to stall. I wish there were a quick-fix solution that I could share with you or a magical marketing wand that you could wave to achieve instantaneous and permanent marketing success—but none exists.

However, for small-business owners who are prepared to roll up their sleeves and get to work to build and maintain a solid marketing foundation, I can offer you more than 1,500 great marketing tricks, tips, and ideas to help you achieve long-term marketing and business success.

Entrepreneur Magazine's Ultimate Small Business Marketing Guide has been specifically developed to help the millions of small-business owners across North America unlock the mysteries that surround marketing. This book will help you secure the big marketing opportunities and success you want and deserve. Each marketing trick, tip, and idea is presented in jargon-free terminology. This book is packed with information that is easy to understand and readily applied in a matter of minutes regardless of your marketing experience or skills. Successful marketing is a matter of dedication, hard work, research, planning, and a clear vision of what you want to achieve. The more than 1,500 marketing ideas and strategies presented in this book are time tested and proven to work. In fact, these are the same marketing strategies and ideas that top business and sales professionals use daily to win new business, devour the competition, and secure customers for life.

GETTING STARTED

My objective when creating a small-business marketing guide was to feature and explain hundreds of great marketing tricks and ideas representing a wide cross section of marketing and sales activities from public relations to direct marketing to retailing—marketing ideas the pros use. Some of these ideas and tricks will be familiar to you, many will be new. The data and information featured for each marketing trick, tip, or idea is brief and is meant to give a short synopsis of the underlying marketing concept and principle. In other words, the theme of this book is not to give a definitive and lengthy explanation of each marketing idea and activity featured, but rather a collection of great marketing ideas that can be used as a catalyst to get you thinking about ways these ideas and tricks can be applied and implemented with your own small business for success. I have had the pleasure and have been in the enviable position of working with top small-business owners and marketers for many years. The information featured in this book has been compiled from my own business and sales experience as well as from numerous conversations with a multitude of small-business owners and sales professionals.

HOW TO USE THIS BOOK

This book should not be taking a restful nap on a dusty shelf. On the contrary, this is a workbook. Use this book daily and keep it with you for those times when you have a few moments to spare and you are looking for great ways to increase revenues and profits. Invest in a highlighter pen and mark the information that is the most beneficial for your business. Let's face it though, no one has time to identify, test, and implement more than 1,500 marketing ideas; it's simply not feasible or cost effective. Therefore, you must take a bit of time to really dig in and locate a few marketing ideas that you believe will work for you—then put them to work. Use the book incrementally and set a target of testing or implementing perhaps one new marketing trick every week or month until you have built a powerful marketing arsenal.

WHAT YOU WILL DISCOVER INSIDE

All the marketing ideas in this book are indexed by marketing activities such as retailing, selling, advertising, networking, and so forth. However, do not read only select chapters, read the entire book. You will find sales ideas in the retailing chapter, networking ideas in the research chapter, and online marketing tricks in the advertising chapter. My point is this: As much as I tried to index and group information into specific chapters, it is not possible, simply due to the fact that successful marketing is a mixture of many marketing disciplines. The following is a bit of what you will discover inside:

- *Research and planning.* You will find great tricks that will assist you to research your markets, identify your customers, and plan for future business and marketing success.
- *Competition.* Learn the tricks the pros use to devour the competition whole before they even know what hit them.
- *Employees.* Inside are numerous tricks that will help you to increase employee productivity, enhance creativity, and become a strong leader and motivator.
- *Customer service.* Without customers, there is no business; with that in mind, extra attention was paid to present some really outstanding customer service ideas that will not only help you to serve your customers better, but secure their loyalty for a lifetime.
- *Home office.* Small-business owners and professionals working from a homebased location will find the ideas featured in the home office chapter to be particularly helpful and insightful.
- *Technology and communications.* Though not categorized in a separate chapter, you will discover throughout the book lots of great cutting-edge ideas for the use of technology in marketing as well as fantastic communications tricks that will help you convey your marketing message with perfect clarity.
- *Advertising and direct marketing.* Managing and making the best use of your precious marketing capital means your advertising, direct-marketing, and telemarketing efforts must be perfectly aimed at your target audience.
- *Public relations.* Discover tricks that will help you grab the attention of the press, secure free and valuable media attention, and develop a public-relations strategy that will produce results year in and year out. PR is not just for the big boys anymore.
- *Networking and prospecting.* Inside you will find powerful ways to network your present contacts for more business. You will also learn how to source new contacts for networking and prospecting purposes. If you don't know what the headcount rule is, you soon will.
- *Presentations and closing.* Closing is the natural progression of the sales presentation and in these chapters you will discover how this is accomplished and much, much more. And did I mention that you will learn the negotiation tricks that top sales pros use to ensure they never leave money on the table?
- *Creative selling.* Often the best and most profitable selling strategies are the simplest ones,

and that is what the creative selling chapter will reveal: easy, straightforward, and truly profitable creative selling strategies.

- *Retailing*. A chapter packed to the rafters with knockout retail marketing tricks that will set your cash register on fire.
- *Service providers*. A bonus chapter for service providers packed with great marketing ideas.
- *Web site and online marketing*. Simple tricks that will help you optimize your Web site for the flood of new traffic your site will get after you implement a few of the clever tricks and tips in this chapter.
- *Trade shows and seminars*. In this section you will find ideas to help you tap into the multibillion dollar marketing machines that are trade show and seminar marketing. You will find super-helpful planning checklists that will ensure your next exhibition event is a raging success.

CHECKLISTS

Throughout this guide you will find numerous helpful checklists that can be utilized as they are featured. Alternately, you can customize each checklist and create one that is relevant to your business, industry, products, services, or marketing objectives. Likewise, you will find many examples, such as a sample press release, to help explain the marketing trick that is being featured. You can also use these examples or samples as a template and from there customize to suit your business and objectives.

ICON SYSTEM

As you read through the *Ultimate Small Business Marketing Guide* you will notice a series of icons accompanying each great marketing tip and trick featured. These icons represent additional condensed information such as the approximate cost to implement the idea, whether the marketing trick is a do-it-yourself project or if you should call in a professional to help out. And, an icon that will let you know at a glance if there are legal issues that must be considered in terms of the marketing idea or activity. Additionally, you will find numerous handy online and publication resources. The purpose of the icon system is to give you, the reader, additional need-to-know information at a glance. Information that can assist in helping you decide on marketing ideas, tricks, and strategies that might be right to be put into action for your small business.

$ *Cost to Implement*

All of the great marketing tips, tricks, and ideas featured in this book include an approximate financial investment needed to implement the marketing idea or activity. This is generalized information and should only be used as a yardstick to determine the approximate costs associated with the specific marketing trick, idea, or activity. Occasionally the dollar sign icon will be followed by a plus sign (+); this simply means that the cost to implement the idea greatly varies, but will be greater then the lowest cost indicated. Always keep in mind that successful entrepreneurs carefully research and plan every aspect of marketing, including what each new marketing idea will cost to activate.

$	Less than $1,000
$$	$1,000–$10,000
$$$	$10,000–$25,000
$$$$	Greater than $25,000

Do-It-Yourself

By their very nature, entrepreneurs are resourceful hands-on types of individuals accustomed to rolling up their sleeves and getting to work, building or providing innovative solutions. When you see the hammer-and-nails icon featured in the book, this means that the marketing trick or idea featured is one that you can tackle yourself without having to call in the professionals. You might still have to conduct a little research and be prepared to learn by trial and error, but most readers will already be accustomed to doing that. Occasionally you will see that the do-it-yourself and a call-in-the-professionals icons are featured together. This simply means that the marketing trick or idea might be a do-it-yourself project for the more experienced marketers, or that calling in the professionals should also be considered. But fear not, the vast majority of marketing tricks and ideas featured in this book are included because they can be successfully implemented or carried out by any small-business owners regardless of marketing experience.

Call in the Professionals

When you see the telephone icon featured in the book alongside a marketing trick you might just want to stop and call in the professionals for help and guidance. Sometimes all the best intentions, hard work, and effort cannot replace experience and special education in terms of accomplishing certain marketing tasks and activities. And, with that said, I have tried to take the guesswork out of what should be considered a do-it-yourself marketing activity and one that would be best left to the professionals to tackle. As mentioned previously, occasionally you will see the do-it-yourself and the call-in-the-professionals icons featured together on the same marketing idea. Every small-business owner's marketing experience and specialty will vary—while one person may find a particular marketing activity easy to carry out, another may want to seek assistance from an outside professional.

Legal Issues

The scale-of-justice symbol indicates that there might be one or a combination of permits, licenses, liability insurance, certificates, or training required to employ the marketing trick, idea, or strategy that is featured. Remember that it the responsibility of all small-business owners to carefully research any marketing activity prior to implementing or testing the effectiveness of the idea for their businesses. You must make sure that what you are doing is legal within the community in which you conduct business.

Web Resource

Located throughout this book you will find numerous handy Web resources that are indicated by a mouse icon. The purpose of the Web resources is not to promote or endorse any one company, product, service, individual, Web site, or organization, but to give you an additional research tool in terms of learning more about a particular marketing trick or idea featured. For instance, you might be interested in finding a source for printable advertising specialties such as pens, calendars, coffee mugs, and memo pads, and you may be able to find a source for these items online. In a nutshell, the numerous Web resources throughout this book are fantastic research tools that enable you to quickly explore and compile further data and information about a particular marketing idea, activity, or strategy that you would like to learn more about.

Book Resources

Located at the end of each chapter is a suggested additional reading list, the purpose of which is not to promote or endorse any one author, book title, or publisher. The book resources are there to give you a research tool in terms of finding additional information and advice about specific marketing activities and strategies. Likewise, the suggested reading list is not meant to inspire you to run out and spend hundreds of dollars on new books, though investments made into products that can assist you to become a better business operator and marketer are without question wise business and personal investments. However, once again do not feel compelled to purchase these titles, if you come across one that interests you, start your search at the local library and take it for a marketing test drive first, so to speak.

◆ ◆ ◆

Entrepreneur Magazine's Ultimate Small Business Marketing Guide is the most authoritative and comprehensive marketing book available. This book gives you the ability to identify numerous great marketing ideas that will work for your small business. Harness the power of this book and put it to work for you starting today.